Ronald Reagan
A Political Biography

Ronald Reagan
A Political Biography

Revised, Updated and Expanded Edition

by
LEE EDWARDS

Foreword by
WILLIAM F. BUCKLEY, JR.

NORDLAND PUBLISHING INTERNATIONAL, INC. (WAA)
P.O. Box 31609
Houston, Texas 77035

A catalog of other works published by Nordland, including books about contemporary issues, literature, and scholarly works, is available by writing to Nordland Publishing International, Inc., P.O. Box 25388, Houston, Texas, 77005.

Library of Congress Catalog Card Number 80-83789
ISBN 0-913124-47-8

Printed in the United States of America

To Willard and Leila Edwards, who opened up the world of politics for me.

Contents

Acknowledgments

My thanks to *Human Events,* where parts of this book appeared in abbreviated form. And to Anne and Elizabeth Edwards for their research assistance, as well as to Robert Moffit, to Dr. Richard S. Haugh and Paul Kachur.

As I said in the first edition, this is not an authorized biography. Ronald Reagan will see this book at the same time that everyone else does—when it is published.

About the Author

Lee Edwards is president of Lee Edwards and Associates, Inc., a Washington-based public affairs firm. Since the company's founding in 1965, his clients have included leading US corporations and trade associations, members of Congress and political candidates. He currently serves as a consultant to the National Right to Work Committee, Young Americans for Freedom, and the Lincoln Institute for Research and Education.

A former reporter for the *Washington Times-Herald* and *Broadcasting* magazine, Mr. Edwards has written several books including *You Can Make The Difference*, a grass roots political handbook written in collaboration with his wife, Anne, and *Reagan: A Political Biography*.

Founding editor of *The New Guard, Conservative Digest* and *The Right Report*, Mr. Edwards has written "World Outlook" and "The Right Side," foreign affairs columns appearing in over 150 newspapers from coast to coast.

Mr. Edwards was former Secretary of the Committee of One Million and is now secretary of the American Council for World Freedom, a public policy research institution contributing to public understanding of international affairs.

Mr. Edwards was born in Chicago, Illinois on December 1, 1932. He attended public schools in Silver Spring, Md. and then Bullis Prep. He graduated from Duke University in 1954 with a BA in English. After serving in the US Army for two years (the last 18 months in West Germany), he attended the Sorbonne in Paris, graduating with a *certificat* in 1957, lived in Europe and traveled extensively to other continents including Latin America, Asia and Africa.

Mr. Edwards and his wife Anne have two daughters, Elizabeth and Catherine, and live in Bethesda, Maryland.

Foreword
by
WILLIAM F. BUCKLEY, JR.

I was delighted to be asked to write this introduction about a politician for whom I have so much admiration and by a writer for whom I have such affection.

I met Ronald Reagan about 20 years ago. He was to introduce me at a lecture that night at Beverly Hills. He arrived at the school auditorium to find consternation. The house was full and the crowd impatient, but the microphone was dead; the student who was to have shown up at the control room above the balcony to turn on the current hadn't.

Reagan quickly took over. He instructed an assistant to call the principal and see if he could get a key. He then bounded onto the stage and shouted as loud as he could to make himself heard. In a very few minutes the audience was greatly enjoying itself. Then word came to him: no answer at the principal's telephone.

Reagan went offstage and looked out the window. There was a ledge, a foot wide, two stories above the street level, running along the side of the window back to the locked control room. He climbed out on the ledge and sidestepped carefully, arms stretched out to help him balance, until he had gone the long way to the window, which he broken open with his elbow, lifting it open from the inside and jumping into the darkness. In a moment, the lights were on, the amplifying knobs turned up, the speaker introduced.

During those days he was busy delivering his own speech. *The* speech, it came to be called—probably the most frequently uttered since William Jennings Bryan's on the golden crucifixion. All over the land, to hundreds of audiences, a deft and rollicking indictment of overweening government.

And then the speech became the most galvanizing fund raiser

in political history. He televised it during the Goldwater campaign in 1964 for a statewide showing in California. "And then," Reagan recalls, "an hour before it was scheduled to go on, word came from Goldwater's headquarters to hold it—the boys at HQ had heard it rumored that it was 'too extreme.' I remember I went to the nearest pay booth, just by a gas station, and called Goldwater.

"There were only minutes to go. Luckily he was on the ground. I reached him in Arizona. 'Barry,' I said, 'I don't have time to tell you everything that's in the speech, but you can take it from me, buddy, there isn't a kooky line in it.' Goldwater said: 'I'll take your word for it,' and I called the studio in the nick of time."

If Goldwater hadn't been at the other end of the telephone, Reagan would not have become governor. Because the speech was an incomparable success, statewide and subsequently nationwide. (It is said to have elicited almost $5 million in dollar-bill contributions.) It was on account of that speech that the Reagan-for-governor talk began.

I saw him during a long evening a few weeks after Goldwater's defeat, when the Reagan movement was just beginning to stir. We talked about the national calamity for the conservative movement and how it bore on his own situation. He was then quite positive that the Republican Party of California would not want him, especially not in the aftermath of so definitive a loss. But, he said, he wasn't going to say anything Shermanesque.

He talked about the problems of California. The discussion was in generalities, very different from a second conversation a year later, in December, 1965, on the eve of the year when he would run. The change was striking. He knew a great deal about the specific problems of California. But he had grown, too, in other ways. I remember being especially impressed when, looking out over the city from the elevation of Pacific Palisades, he remarked: "You know, it's probable that the cost of eliminating the smog is a cost the people who want the smog to be eliminated are not, when it comes to it, willing to pay."

Still later, on a half-dozen occasions, I noticed the ongoing improvement in his personal style, particularly in his handling of the press. In Omaha, after a press conference before his speech to the Young Republicans, the *New York Times* correspondent impulsively blurted out to a young correspondent he hardly knew: "I've never seen anything like it. I've been covering them since Truman. There isn't anybody who can touch Reagan."

It's something people are going to have to get used to. "To

those unfamiliar with Reagan's big-league savvy,'' *Newsweek,*
pained, dutifully pointed out after observing Ronald Reagan and
Bobby Kennedy in a joint appearance answering student questions
on Vietnam, ''The ease with which (Reagan) fielded questions about
Vietnam may come as a revelation. . . . Political rookie Reagan
left old campaigner Kennedy blinking when the session ended.''

It was December 1966, and Richard Nixon was in the room.
Who, someone asked, would the Republican Party consider eligible
in 1968? Nixon gave the usual names—and added Ronald Reagan's
name. I objected. It strikes me, I said, as inconceivable. ''Why?''
Nixon asked. ''Suppose he makes a very good record as Governor
of California.'' Because, I said, people won't get used to the notion
of a former actor being President. People are very stuffy about
presidential candidates. Remember what Raymond Moley said when
someone asked him how to account for Kefauver's beating Adlai
Stevenson in the Minnesota primary in 1956: ''Did *you* ever tell a
joke in Minneapolis?''

And then—I added, carried away by my conviction—how does
one go about being a good governor in an age when the major moves
are, after all, up to the federal government?

It is the federal government that will decide how much inflation
there is going to be, how far the monopoly labor unions can go,
whether there will be praying in the schools, where the main high-
ways will come from and where they will go, how the water flowing
in from nature is to be allocated, how large Social Security payments
will be. Are there interstices within which, nowadays, a governor
can move, sufficiently to keep himself in focus and establish his
special competence?

Reagan clearly thinks so. Always there is *some* room. ''To
live,'' Whittaker Chambers wrote, ''is to maneuver. The choices
of maneuver are now visibly narrow. (But) a conservatism that
cannot find room in its folds for the actualities is a conservatism
that is not a political force, or even a twitch: it has become a literary
whimsy. Those who remain in the world, if they will not surrender
on its terms, must maneuver within its terms.''

The knowledge of that is what causes the very liberal to call
Reagan a hypocrite. Brings the very conservative to consider him
an imposter. Brings George Wallace to call him a lightweight. They
say his accomplishments are few, that he is only rhetoric. But the
rhetoric is the principal thing. It precedes all action. All thoughtful
action. Reagan's rhetoric is that of someone who is profoundly

committed *mutatis mutandis,* to the ancient ways. His perspectives are essentially undoubting.

Ronald Reagan's acceptance speech at the Republican convention in Detroit was classified by CBS observer Jeff Greenfield as proof that he is the principal rhetorician in American politics. It was lucid, galvanizing, transparently genuine; and its force was enhanced by the awful congruity of the rhetoric and the current crisis.

It was an awesome performance by a man born to unite—and to govern.

In the following pages, you will learn from a writer who has made Ronald Reagan his special study for many years, all about a citizen politician whose special talents are precisely, I believe, what our nation now urgently needs.

Prologue

The tall, handsome, tanned man in the dark blue suit and muted tie looked at the silent delegates in the crowded convention hall and beyond them to the millions of television viewers in their homes and talked quietly about his vision of America—what she was, what she is and what she can be.

Simply, but eloquently, he summoned them to "a community of shared values"—family, work, neighborhood, peace and freedom—that transcended party lines and philosophical labels. His first promise was to promote equal rights for women. He committed himself to social security and the preservation of the "safety net" beneath the needy. He asserted that he would "pursue any reasonable avenue that holds forth the promise of lessening tensions and furthering the prospects of peace." He quoted Thomas Paine and Abraham Lincoln and Franklin D. Roosevelt.

It was the evening of July 17, 1980, and Ronald Reagan gratefully accepted the Republican Party's nomination for President of the United States.

He touched the deep concern of every American when he warned that big government "is never more dangerous than when our desire to have it help us blinds us to its great power to harm us. . . . High taxes, we are told, are somehow good for us, as if, when government spends our money, it isn't inflationary, but when we spend it, it is. . . .

"We must have the clarity of vision to see the difference between what is essential and what is merely desirable; and then the courage to bring our Government back under control."

He assured those listening and watching that creating new jobs was vital: "It's time to put America back to work. . . . For those without skills, we'll find a way to help them get skills. For those without job opportunities, we'll stimulate new opportunities, particularly in the inner cities where they live."

He spoke directly to the disadvantaged in America, promising: "We have to move ahead, but we're not going to leave anyone behind. I ask you to trust that American spirit which knows no ethnic, religious, social, political or economic boundaries; the spirit that burned with zeal in the hearts of millions of immigrants from every corner of the earth who came here in search of freedom."

He stressed that while America needed a more vigorous foreign policy, it would operate within a framework of peace through strength. "We're not a warlike people. Quite the opposite. . . . We resort to force infrequently, and with great reluctance—and only after we've determined that it is absolutely necessary."

But, he cautioned, "neither can we be naive or foolish. Four times in my lifetime America has gone to war, bleeding the lives of its young men into the sands of beachheads, the fields of Europe and the jungles and rice paddies of Asia. We know only too well that war comes not when the forces of freedom are strong, but when they are weak. It is then that tyrants are tempted."

As he neared the end of his prepared remarks, he hesitated, his eyes glistening, and then he said: "I'll confess that I've been a little afraid to suggest what I'm going to suggest. I'm more afraid not to." He paused. "Can we begin our crusade joined together in a moment of silent prayer?"

He bowed his head and the only sound that could be heard in Joe Louis Arena was the hum of the air conditioning. After fifteen spell-binding seconds, Ronald Reagan lifted his head, his eyes still misty with tears, and almost whispered: "God bless America."

The convention hall erupted into a tumultuous demonstration that lasted for over thirty minutes. Iowa Governor Robert Ray, who had fought Reagan throughout the primaries, said: "He touched the soul of America."

PART ONE

THE ACTOR

Chapter One

A Little Country Town

Tampico, Illinois, is 86 miles from Chicago and 788 miles from the Nation's Capital. It's a cozy little town of barely a thousand inhabitants hiding in the heart of the fertile Midwest. It has a handsome park with a Civil War monument in its center, a railroad track on which trains used to chug and puff, and white clapboard houses with wide green lawns.

There on February 6, 1911, Ronald Wilson Reagan was born. Ron was the younger of two boys, John Neil ("Moon") Reagan having been born over two years earlier, also in Tampico, on September 16, 1908. There were to be no other children. As the grand new baby cried out lustily, his father remarked: "For such a little bit of a fat Dutchman, he makes a hell of a lot of noise, doesn't he?"*

It was a typically boisterous remark by the new father, John Edward Reagan (pronounced Raygun). Jack Reagan was born in Bennett, Iowa, on July 13, 1883, and was orphaned at the age of three. He was reared by a succession of aunts and uncles, finally settling while still a youngster in Fulton, Illinois. There he met pretty Nelle Clyde Wilson. A native of Fulton, Nelle was born on July 24, 1883. The two children grew up together in the small Illinois town and were married there in 1906.

They made quite a contrast. Jack, standing almost six feet, was tall, muscular, of swarthy complexion with thick, wavy, brown hair. Nelle was small and slender with light brown hair and blue eyes. He was outspoken, quick-tempered, a natural raconteur. She was gentle and soft-spoken. He was Catholic, an indifferent churchgoer;

---

*"Dutch" still is Ronald Reagan's family nickname.

she was Protestant and deeply religious. He was too fond of alcohol, she was a teetotaler.

The Reagans were Democrats. Jack was staunch in his views. Nelle, in her older son's words, "just went along." Ron and Neil followed their father and also counted themselves Democrats, although Neil became a Republican after voting for Franklin Delano Roosevelt in 1932.

A fierce individualist, Jack Reagan believed literally, according to his sons, that all men were created equal. Ron recalls that when the film *The Birth of a Nation* came to town, "my brother and I were the only kids not to see it." Explained their father, "It deals with the Ku Klux Klan against the colored folks, and I'm damned if anyone in this family will go see it."

Jack tried to enlist in the armed forces during World War I, but was rejected because he was married and had two children.

He was never a financial success. He never owned his own home and he never made more than $55 a week at any time in his life. Comments his younger son: "Our family didn't exactly come from the wrong side of the tracks, but we were certainly always within sound of the train whistles." Both sons went to work when barely in their teens.

Jack Reagan was "in" shoes, working variously as a shoe clerk, the manager of a shoe department and part-owner of a shoe store. His younger son remembers that he "loved shoes" and "even studied a correspondence course about how to sell more sabots, and spent hours analyzing the bones of the foot." But Jack loved the bottle too, like many an Irishman before him,* and this weakness coupled with frequent bad investments kept him an also-ran in business—although he was always welcome wherever he went because of his rib-tickling, story-telling ability. Jack never completed grade school. Nelle did but went no further. However, both were avid readers and their home was always filled with books. Mrs. Reagan, in fact, arranged regular readings of plays and stories for the various ladies societies in Tampico and the other Illinois towns in which the Reagans lived. Nelle and Jack frequently played the leads.

By the time Ron was nine, he had lived in a number of small Illinois towns west of Chicago as well as the Windy City itself for a brief period: Tampico, Galesburg, Monmouth, Tampico again,

---

* "My mother, bless her soul," says Reagan, "told my brother and me from the time we were little to understand this was a sickness and we weren't to hold it as a grudge, no matter what hardship it brought."

and at last Dixon, where the Reagans put down roots until Ron was past twenty-one. Frequently, Neil Reagan recalls, "The Reagan family really didn't know where the next buck was coming from, but Nelle always had the right outlook on life and was sure that, 'Before the next payment was due, God would find a way.' "

In a letter to this writer, Neil Reagan described the Dixon, Illinois, of 1920:

"At that time Dixon was a town of about 10,000, built on gently rolling northern Illinois hills. The Rock River cut through the heart of town with one bridge across the river in those days. There was a large Borden Milk plant, a wire screen factory, a J. I. Case Plow Company factory and a Portland Cement plant in the town. It was a bustling town, progressive, and the county seat of Lee County.

"The courthouse stood in the middle of a square across the street from the Nachusa Tavern, which still stands and is still operated as a hotel. Its claim to fame, as well as being a fine hotel, is that on occasion Abraham Lincoln, General Grant and celebrities of that era enjoyed its hospitality. We, as youngsters, always held it sort of in awe."

There was also the Family Theatre, a public library and North High School, for which Ron passionately desired to play football. The game attracted him because of its physical challenge and because his extremely poor eyesight would not be a handicap. Baseball was impossible—he couldn't see a pitch until it was practically at the end of his bat. Contact lenses, which Reagan wears today, were not available in those days but in football, in the line, you only had to see a few feet in all directions.

When Dutch entered North High School he was only five-foot-three and weighed 108 pounds, a size more suitable for manager than player. But he persisted and in the middle of his junior year he became and stayed a regular at right guard. He also read just about everything he could find in the library, including Horatio Alger. He had the lead in several high school plays and in the opinion of a friendly observer, his brother, "was very good." Ron capped his high school career by being elected president of the student body in his senior year.

Comments a fellow student, football player and actor, R. A. McNichol: "Dutch was a very capable, loyal and personable individual with strong convictions—and a determination to accomplish that in which he believes."

According to Bernard J. Frazer, who taught social science at North High School and had many talks with young Reagan: "He happens to be an example of that rare individual who carried into adulthood most of the dreams and enthusiasm for life that he had in youth. Perhaps he was more idealistic; perhaps more fortunate in his experiences and the influences which shaped them, than most youngsters. For example, his very unusual mother had that rare ability to make the ideal and fine seem quite practical to others.''

Frazer remembers that his young pupil ''was a natural leader in school activities . . . endowed with a curious, keen and retentive mind.''

He was an instinctive crusader. ''In high school,'' says the former teacher, ''he, as do many young people, bled for humanity and deplored the world's materialism, its selfishness and inability to cooperate. However, even then he seemed to feel that, if they so desired, men could shape their own destiny. To him, as a teen-ager, the idea of the State taking over, or even attempting to control the individual's choices was very distasteful.''

In the summers Dutch worked. When he was fourteen he was a construction worker at thirty-five cents an hour on a ten-hour day, six-day week. His speciality: digging foundations in heavy clay and soil. In the summer of 1925 he made $200 but did not spend it. In his own words, ''I knew it was for something else—college.''

The next summer, at fifteen, he got a job he was to keep for seven summers—lifeguard at Lowell Park, a recreation area on the Rock River. His salary was $15 a week. During his stay at Lowell Park (named after the poet, James Russell Lowell), Reagan estimates that he saved seventy-seven people. ''The only money I ever got,'' he recalls, ''was ten dollars for diving for an old man's upper plate that he lost going down our slide.''

Ron was saving for one particular school: Eureka College, lo-cated some seventy miles south of Dixon and twenty miles from Peoria, Illinois. College was *not* the normal next step for a high school graduate in the late 1920's. In fact, less than 10 percent of the graduating seniors then went on to a college or university. (The figure in 1978 was 60 percent.) Furthermore, the economy was beginning to show the stresses and strains which were to erupt so tragically on Black Tuesday, October 29, 1929.

Although it had a modest tuition and other expenses, Eureka still cost $900 a year—a considerable sum for a family like the Reagans with their uneven income. Also, in those days, there was widespread feeling that college demanded four years that would be better occupied earning a living.

One Reagan brother agreed—at least for a while. ''My brother

Neil," remembers Ronald Reagan, "thought college was a waste of time; also an impossibility, if you had to do it on your own."

Not so Ron, who selected Eureka College for a number of reasons: (1) it was small, less than 250 students; (2) it was coeducational, about half boys and half girls; (3) it had a good football team; (4) it was run by the Christian Church, of which Ronald Reagan is a member today; and (5) the most important factor of all for the seventeen-year-old young man, his high school sweetheart, Margaret Cleaver, had announced her intention to attend Eureka.

However, despite the summer savings he had so carefully accumulated, Ron still did not have enough money for the $180 tuition, plus room and board. Using his ability to persuade others, which would later impress political observers, the young student argued his case. Eureka official considered the applicant's athletic ability, the earnings from his summer jobs, his obvious eagerness to attend their school. They offered him a scholarship for half his tuition and a job for his board. He would have to pay for his room and any luxuries out of his savings. It wasn't a free ride, but it was all the aid Ron needed.

In the fall of 1928, he entered Eureka College with pride to equal any freshman Ivy Leaguer—and determination to meet the challenge and justify the faith of the school dons.

Chapter Two

Down the Old Ox Road

During his four years at Eureka, Ron Reagan played a lot of football, joined a fraternity, fell in and out of love, read several hundred books, won an acting award in a national play contest, was elected student body president and participated in his first strike. Through it all, money continued to be so serious a problem that he almost didn't return to school after his freshman year.

The young student was now six-foot-one and weiged 175 pounds. He had thick brown hair, blue eyes and a ready smile. He quickly pledged Tau Kappa Epsilon, one of the more prestigious national fraternities on campus. He became a reporter for the school paper, *The Pegasus*. Within a few weeks of arrival, he was tabbed as a sure Big Man on Campus. It was almost natural, therefore, that he should be picked as the freshman representative on the strike committee.

The campus strike followed in the wake of a decision by Eureka President Burt Wilson to cut the curriculum. The cut was part of a proposed economy program designed to save Eureka, whose normal sources of financial support were being dried up by the impending Depression. The plan, in Reagan's words, called for such drastic academic reductions "that many juniors and seniors would have been cut off without the courses needed for graduation in their chosen majors. Needless to say, the faculty would have been decimated and Eureka would have lost its high academic standing."

The student body, with the approval of "almost every professor on campus," submitted a counter-plan to the president, who rejected it. The students then presented a petition, signed by 143 of the 220 students, including Reagan, to the college's board of trustees demanding the resignation of President Wilson. Meeting this challenge head on, Wilson announced that he had submitted his own resignation. Friendly faculty members and other sources, however, revealed that the trustees intended to reject the resignation, give Wilson a vote of confidence and discipline the student body.

The Eureka students also made plans. It was near midnight the following week, November 27, 1928, when the trustees emerged from their conference with the president. To their great surprise, they were greeted by a student committee, including freshman Ron Reagan, who wanted to know their decision. Informed that the trustees had indeed rejected Wilson's resignation, the students gave a prearranged signal. The "old college bell started tolling," calling the student body and faculty to the chapel. There, freshman Ron Reagan delivered a ringing, dramatic speech.

"When I came to actually presenting the motion," Reagan remembers, "there was no need for parliamentary procedure; they came to their feet with a roar—even the faculty members present voted by acclamation. It was heady wine."

After Thanksgiving, the students put their simple plan into effect: no attendance at classes until their demands were met. Few attended any classes. (Two students who did were President Wilson's two daughters.) Professors went to their classrooms and marked all absentees present. To pass the time, the strike committee sponsored a dance every afternoon but always ended it at four o'clock—for basketball practice.

Studies, however, were not neglected. The strike committee established study hours and enforced them; it even made up assignments which were scrupulously carried out. In Reagan's words, "ours was no riotous burning in effigy but a serious, well-planned program, engineered from the ground up by students but with the full support and approval of almost every professor on the campus."

News of the strike spread quickly. Reporters converged on Eureka and the strike committee set up a "regular press headquarters" to service the gentlemen of the Fourth Estate. To counteract the administration, which was flooding the campus with mimeographed statements, a faculty-student panel was formed to issue regular bulletins.

After one week of suffering these slings and arrows, President Wilson again offered his resignation. The trustees, by a seven-to-five vote, accepted it. Meetings were held between the trustees, students and faculty. An amicable understanding was arrived at. The strike was called off, the faculty agreed to withhold any salary demands for "an indefinite period," and Eureka returned to normalcy.

Despite the excitement and rewards of his first year, Ron Reagan returned home that summer wondering whether Eureka was for him. By fall, he had decided not to return to college but to take a job as a surveyor's assistant. He had decided he couldn't afford Eureka even with the scholarship and the job. More importantly in the mind of the young athelete, he believed the football coach, Ralph McKinzie, was "against" him and would *never* let him play. Ron bid a sorrowful farewell to his sweetheart, Margaret, who was returning to Eureka. But with the dawn came a torrent of rain and no surveying for the day. The young man rode back to Eureka with his girl for a visit, saw the football coach and the inviting new football uniforms, found a job washing dishes in the girls' dormitory, was told by the college that it would defer half of his tuition until after graduation and decided to stay at Eureka after all.

In his autobiography, *Where's the Rest of Me?*,* published in 1965, Reagan waxes lyrical about the next three years:

"Oh, it was a small town, a small school, with small doings. It was in a poor time without money, without ceremony, with pleasant thoughts of the past to balance fears of the uncertain future. . . . Those were the nights when we spent all of twenty cents on a date: two big cherry phosphates at the drug counter (with the big colored jars of water lighted up) and a walk home. Or when we danced in somebody's house or in the fraternity living rooms under the dimmest of lights, while the chaperones—always old Eureka grads who had met each other this way themselves—took a turn around outside or just dozed. Or when we devoured homemade cake and repressed heartburnings of a different sort as we strolled under the campus elms. And there was the wonderful thing of inviting older people who knew some jokes and the ways of the world and how to talk to us without condescending; scrambling eggs before an open fire and talking about Hoover and his calm statements on prosperity; whipping up the hot chocolate and shaking our heads over this upstart Franklin D. Roosevelt, who was beginning to criticize from New York."

Through with sulking, Ron decided he was going to show Coach McKinzie how wrong he had been about his playing. By the third Saturday he was starting at right guard and for three seasons "av-

* *Where's the Rest of Me?* by Ronald Reagan with Richard G. Hubler, Duell, Sloan & Pearce.

eraged all but two minutes of every game." In the spring, he went out for the swimming team and eventually wound up as captain. He also tried out for track and won his letter in that sport as well.

It was easy to keep in training because Eureka took its religion seriously. Bible courses were required and daily chapel was mandatory during the week. Smoking was not allowed on campus and in Neil Reagan's words, "the thought of having a drink was unheard of." The training took: Ronald Reagan never has smoked and takes only an occasional drink.

In between sports and classes, Ron joined the campus dramatic society and enrolled in the dramatics course under Miss Ellen Marie Johnson, who saw talent in the tall, handsome young man with the resonant, baritone voice. The high point of his collegiate dramatic career came in his junior year when Miss Johnson entered Eureka in the annual one-act play contest sponsored by Northwestern University. Only twelve colleges and universities were invited to present their plays out of hundreds of applicants from across the country. Eureka, which had chosen Edna St. Vincent Millay's fantasy, *Aria da Capo,* was one of the twelve and the *only* school without a drama department to be so honored.

Writes Reagan: "Ours was really a homegrown effort, with Grecian costumes copied from our history books and sewed together by coeds in the various sororities. Quarterback Bud Cole and I played the Greek shepherd boys who carry the anti-war plot. My high spot was a death scene wherein I was strangled by Bud. No actor can ask for more. Dying is the way to live in the theater."

To almost everyone's amazement, especially the actors in *Aria da Capo,* Eureka finished second, and Ron Reagan was one of six actors who received awards for their dramatic excellence. After the contest, the head of Northwestern's drama department asked Ron if he had ever considered the stage as a career. Some fertile seeds had been planted.

There was politics too. Ron was elected president of his fraternity. Tau Kappa Epsilon. For three years, he served as president of the Booster Club, the student organization which coordinated the annual homecoming weekend with its football game, alumni banquet, dance and other entertainments. He was also the principal basketball cheerleader, three years the school's top swimmer, one year its swimming coach and two years the feature editor of the year book. Finally, as a rising senior he was elected president of Eureka's student body.

Football coach McKinzie has said: "Dutch was not an outstand-

ing football player, but he was a good plugger, dedicated, put out
a lot, had a lot of spirit and desire. He got some scholarship help,
but mostly worked his way through school by waiting on tables,
washing windows and raking lawns. He was ambitious and determined. Nobody was paying the bills for him.''

Ernest E. Higdon, who taught Reagan at Eureka, has said: ''He's
one of the finest men I've ever known. I don't agree with his politics;
I'm a Democrat. But if I had lived in California I'd have voted for
him, because I know him and what he stands for.''

More gratifying than all these honors, perhaps, was the decision
by his brother Neil to enrol at Eureka. In the Reagan tradition, Neil
got a job working in the coeds' kitchen and a scholarship to play
football. Ron did not discover until years later why his brother
decided to quit the cement plant in Dixon and go to school:

''Working in a grimy atmosphere of limestone dust, Moon (a
nickname since high school) was teamed with an elderly immigrant
who could barely manage our language. This oddly assorted pair
became friends and exchanged information as men will about their
families and backgrounds. The old man constantly queried Moon
as to why he wasn't in college as I was. Then one day very quietly
he presented Moon with the alternative to college. 'Look at
me—we'll alvays vork together, chust you and me, and someday
you'll be chust like me—isn't that nize?' (The old man) never
mentioned it again—he didn't have to.''*

On sun-bright June day in 1932, Ronald Wilson Reagan was
graduated from Eureka College with a degree in economics and
sociology. He had earned his letter in football, track and swimming.
He had served as student body president. He had played the lead
in several dramatic plays and had won an acting award in a national
competition. The campus was agreed that Ron Reagan was bound
to succeed—but where? He was twenty-one years old and broke.
An old friend of the family asked him: ''What do you think you'd
like to do?''

Ron had a ready answer: ''Show business.''

---

* When Lou Cannon of the *Washington Post* asked Reagan in 1980 to name the single-
most important influence in his life, the presidential candidate replied, unsurprisingly, ''The
Depression.'' It was, after all, the Depression which cost his father a partnership in a Dixon
shoe store he had opened with borrowed money. It sent his mother to work in a dress shop
for $14 a week. Reagan once sent $50 home to his mother without his father's knowing so
the family could continue to shop at the grocery store.

Chapter Three

The Voice of the Chicago Cubs

"The problem," recalls Reagan, "was how to go about it. Broadway and Hollywood were as inaccessible as outer space." He decided to try his luck closer to home in a phase of show business where his fine voice would be an asset—radio. Specifically, he aspired to be a sports announcer.

Neil Reagan remembers well his brother's determination to succeed: "While still in college he decided that he would be a sports announcer on radio, drove us nuts in the fraternity as he walked around broadcasting imaginary football games play by play and never lost sight of this goal until he landed the job at WOC in Davenport, Iowa."

At the end of summer, Ron hitchhiked to Chicago, the center of American radio in the thirties. He had no contacts, no letters of introduction, and no experience. For several days, he walked the hard pavements of Chicago, visiting the outlets of the major networks as well as large and small independent stations, like WGN. He got nowhere, except at NBC he was told that the program director interviews "on Thursdays." On Thursday, Ron timidly explained to the girl at the reception desk why he was there. A lady appeared from the inner sanctum and, seated on a couch in the reception room, listened to the young man's story.

Her reaction and advice were to the point: You have no experience. This is the "big time." Try to get a job with one of the smaller stations "in the sticks" and then come back and see me.

As so often in his life, Ron took the good advice and hitchhiked a hundred thirty miles back to Dixon, unfortunately traveling the last thirty miles with a man who had been hunting skunks. That night over supper, Jack Reagan listened to his son's experiences and then offered him the family Oldsmobile to visit radio stations in the general neighborhood.

The following Monday, Ron made his first call at Station WOC, located in Davenport, Iowa, seventy-five miles away. He asked to see the program director, who turned out to be a veteran of vaudeville, born in Scotland, named Peter MacArthur.

"Where the hell have ye been?" MacArthur roared in his Highland burr. "Don't ye ever listen to the radio?"

It seemed that for one month WOC had been advertising for a staff announcer and had hired one out of ninety-five applicants only the week before.

Young Reagan's temper flared and he abruptly left, crying out behind him: "How in hell does a guy ever get to be a sports announcer if he can't get inside a station?"

Reagan was standing at the elevator when he heard a great thumping and loud talking down the hallway. A can rapped him on the shin. It was MacArthur, who, crippled by arthritis, used two canes to move about.

"Do ye perhaps know football?" asked the program director, scowling.

The would-be announcer replied that he had played the game for eight years, and before he could say anything else, he was led into a vacant studio and told to describe a football game "and make me see it."

More than a little bewildered, Reagan looked at the heavy blue velvet covering the walls and then at the microphone. The red lights flashed "on" and Ron began describing, from memory, the fourth quarter of a game played between Western State University and Eureka College the previous fall. Twenty minutes later, wringing wet from tension and determination, he wound up his "broadcast" with the traditional, "we return you now to our main studio."

MacArthur entered the studio, chuckling and growling at the same time. "You did great! Now, Luke, we have a sponsor for four University of Iowa games. Ye be here a week from Saturday and I'll give ye five dollars and bus fare. If ye do all right on that one, ye'll do the other three."

Ronald Reagan had convinced a thirty-year veteran in the business that he could handle the job—no mean feat for a twenty-one-year old who had never stood before a microphone before.

The following Saturday after the University of Iowa game, MacArthur told the rookie announcer without any hyperbole, "Ye'll do the rest of the games.'' He was even given a raise: $10 a game plus bus fare.

At the end of the season, Ron returned to Dixon to wait for the call he fervently hoped would come. Finally, it did, a few days after New Year's Day, 1933. An announcer had left WOC and MacArthur offered Ron $100 a month as a staff announcer.

''My bag,'' Reagan says, ''and you can keep that singular—was packed, and I moved to Davenport. I was hired. I would be fired, I would be rehired, but I was out in the world at last.''

At home, Jack Reagan went to work for the federal government (Franklin Delano Roosevelt had been elected, and as a long-loyal Democrat, Jack was rewarded). The senior Reagan distributed food-stuffs as well as government scrip which the poor and needy used at the grocery. Dixon was hard hit: the cement plant for which ''Moon'' had worked closed down, adding one thousand more to the already long list of unemployed.

Jack spent much of this time finding and assigning jobs for the unemployed. He worked days and nights on a schedule of rotating jobs so that every man would have at least a couple of days work at a stretch.

But then welfare workers arrived from back East with files and furniture to begin institutionalizing the process. ''Wheels,'' remarks Ronald Reagan, ''were turning in Washington and government was busy at the job it does best—growing.'' The day inevitably came when Jack offered a week's work to a group of men, who replied, ''Jack, we can't take it.'' They explained that the last time they took jobs the welfare office had cut off their relief. When they stopped working, several days later, they had to reopen their ''case'' at the welfare office and submit to new interviews, applications and cards. ''The process took three weeks,'' recalls Reagan, ''and in the meantime their families went hungry—all because they'd done a few days' honest work.''

Shortly thereafter, Jack Reagan was appointed local adminis-trator of the Works Progress Administration (WPA). Under his direction, there were no boondoggles in Dixon and he constantly came up with ingenious projects for the able-bodied men of Dixon. Once he even figured out a way to use the old streetcar rails, torn from the main street, as structural steel in a hangar at the new airport.

And all the while he battled the ''welfare band,'' who used every pretext, including physical unfitness, to resist ''releasing their charges to WPA.''

It was Ronald Reagan's first close look at the ways of the federal government and it made a lasting impression.

At Station WOC, Ron was having problems. To this day, he is not good at reading a manuscript.* He tried to read the commercials they gave him, but without much success. His voice was stiff and wooden. He knew it and so did the sponsors. Before long he was told he would be replaced as a staff announcer but would be "kept in mind" for sports events.

His replacement arrived and Ron was directed to break him in. But when the new man learned the circumstances of his predecessor's dismissal, he demanded a contract. WOC's management refused and Ron was asked to stay on "for the time being." Reagan vowed to show the station he could be an announcer, commercials and all. The challenge was just what he needed. With his adrenaline flowing freely, he read every piece of copy they handed him like an old pro and very soon there was no more talk of a replacement.

Reagan rose swiftly to the top of his profession, becoming one of the best-known sports announcers in the Midwest. His rise was boosted considerably when WOC merged with its sister station, WHO, to become WHO Des Moines, NBC's key station in the Corn Belt. WHO built a 50 kilowatt transmitter, one of only twelve such rigs in the country. Ron's salary went to $75 a week—plus bonuses and fees for "touring the banquet circuit, writing a guest column, and hiring out to handle public-address system chores at events we weren't broadcasting."

One of the other announcers at WHO was Ed Reimers, the long-time man with the cupped hands for Allstate Insurance ("You're in good hands with Allstate"). Reimers describes Reagan as "a great sports announcer . . . a good actor . . . certainly one of the better presidents the Screen Actors Guild has ever had. . . . If he's half as good a governor as he was a sportscaster he'll be great. . . . I'm proud to know him. I'd be proud to know him even if he wasn't governor."

Former Congressman H. R. Gross of Iowa, who became nationally famous for his scrutiny of the fine print in the federal budget, was also on WHO's staff in the 1930's as a newscaster. He remembers "Dutch" as an "outstanding sports announcer—he was actually sports editor of the station—and very popular in the state of Iowa. I always thought he had very strong political possibili-

---

* He rarely uses a prepared text, preferring to speak from 3 × 5 index cards which he has personally researched and written.

ties. . . . He was conscientious, he had ability, he was honest and decent. What else can you say about a man?''

Reagan estimates that during this period he broadcast forty-five college football games from every ''major press box in the Midwest,'' covered more than six hundred major league baseball games by telegraph, and handled swimming meets and track meets as well. He interviewed famous sports personalities, including Doc Kearns, former manager of Jack Dempsey, Ed ''Strangler'' Lewis, and Max Baer. He also remembers meeting the English actor and Hollywood star, Leslie Howard, at a fund-raising event for victims of an Ohio River flood.

One night he even interviewed the famous evangelist, Aimee Semple McPherson. Unfamiliar with her work, Ron let Mrs. McPherson do most of the talking, which she did beautifully until she suddenly said ''good night'' with four minutes to go on the program. Not knowing enough about the evangelist to fill the remaining time himself, Ron made a circular motion with his hand, the signal for the playing of a phonograph record.

''A sleepy engineer in the control room,'' he recounts, ''reached out, pulled a record off a stack, put it on the turntable, and nodded to go ahead. In my most dulcet tones, I said, 'Ladies and gentlemen, we conclude this broadcast by the noted evangelist, Aimee Semple McPherson, with a brief interlude of transcribed music.' I expected nothing less than the 'Ave Maria.' The Mills Brothers started singing 'Minnie the Moocher's Wedding Day.' ''

One Friday night, Reagan invented a new program which became ''a steppingstone for someone else's career.'' Given a half hour to play records, Reagan presented nothing but college sons and filled in the gaps with the next day's schedule of football games plus predictions of the winners. On a subsequent Friday night, his brother, Neil, who had graduated from Eureka, was seated in the studio. Neil began shaking his head in disagreement about some of his brother's predictions. Ron switched on the mike and the two brothers debated back and forth for a half hour about the games, promising the audience at the conclusion that they would report who had the best percentage the following Friday.

The joint appearance led, Reagan tells, ''to a fifteen-dollar-a-week job for Moon, doing the football scoreboard on Saturday nights because I was still out of town on my football broadcasts. That job led Moon to an announcing job at the reinstituted WOC in Davenport, to program directing, network producing, and to Los An-

geles as vice president of an advertising agency.''*   While in Des
Moines, Ron fulfilled one of his basic loves—riding—by applying
for a commission in the US Cavalry Reserves. The opportunity to
ride wonderful mounts and receive expert training in horsemanship
was irresistible to Reagan, who says, ''I think the Irish are one of
the lost tribes of the Arabs.'' He avoided a physical examination
for years because of his poor eyesight and then bluffed his way
through the exam to become a second lieutenant on June 18, 1937.**

During one bitter cold Iowa winter, Reagan decided that he
would be a much better voice of the Chicago Cubs if he accompanied
the team on its spring training trip to Catalina Island, only fifty
miles across the water from warm, sun-drenched Los Angeles. He
told the station that the trip would provide him with ''color and
atmosphere'' for the coming season. To his delight, they agreed and
he took his first trip west of Kansas City.

He made the annual trip to Catalina Island until the spring of
1937, when a growing restlessness and dissatisfaction gripped him.
Sports announcing had become too confining. One night, while in
Los Angeles, he visited an alumna of WHO, Joy Hodges, who was
singing at the Biltmore Bowl. Over dinner, Reagan told Joy about
the Des Moines theater manager who had suggested a screen test
for him, the performers on the WHO program who had been hired
for a Hollywood film, and the fact that he had picked sports announcing five years before as a path to acting. What did *she* think?

''Take off your glasses,'' was her first remark. Then she set up
an appointment with a Hollywood agent, William Meiklejohn, who
''will be honest with you.'' But, ''for heaven's sake,'' she persisted,
''don't see him with those glasses on!''

Reagan remembers this as a very funny line for ''without the
glasses I couldn't see him at all—but the important thing was, he'd
see me.''

The next morning Meiklejohn listened to Reagan outline his
acting experience, his salary needs and his high hopes. The young
announcer concluded: ''Should I go back to Des Moines and forget
this, or what do I do?''

The agent picked up the telephone, dialed Warner Brothers and
asked for Max Arnow, the casting director. ''Max,'' said Meikle-

---

* Neil Reagan was national vice president in charge of radio and television programming
for the giant agency, McCann-Erickson. He is now retired.

**Reagan wore glasses most of the time then, uses contact lenses today and Benjamin
Franklin half-glasses over them for very heavy reading.

john without any preliminaries, "I have another Robert Taylor in my office."

Arnow's booming reply was quite audible: "God made only one Robert Taylor!"

Nevertheless, Arnow invited them over and after sizing up Reagan's shoulders and listening to his voice, scheduled a screen test the following Tuesday—a scene from Philip Barry's play, *Holiday*.

Reagan did the scene, after the make-up man had tried vainly to do something with his crewcut. When it was over, he was informed that it would be several days before Jack Warner could see the film and of course he would stand by. To which the young midwesterner replied, "No, I will be on the train tomorrow—me and the Cubs are going home."

On the train, he wondered whether he "had blown the whole thing" but reflected that at least he had a good story to tell. As Reagan has since written, "I had done, through ignorance, the smartest thing it was possible to do. Hollywood just *loves* people who don't need Hollywood."

Before he was back in Des Moines one day, a telegram arrived: "Warners offer contract seven years, one year's option, starting at $200 a week. What shall I do? Meiklejohn."

Reagan sent an immediate reply: "Sign before they change their minds." And then he yelled a yell of joy and delight as only a smalltown boy from Illinois can who is going to Hollywood to be a movie star. He was twenty-six.

Chapter Four

"Where's the Rest of Me?"

Warner Brothers liked Ronald Reagan very much. During his first eleven months, he appeared in eight pictures—an unusually heavy schedule for an unknown actor who had never appeared on Broadway or been inside a film studio. Most young contract players wait months before getting a part. But not Reagan, who was immediately given the lead in a sixty-one-minute film called *Love Is On the Air*. It was a "B" picture, as were most of the pictures in which he would appear for several years. The young actor didn't mind: "All I knew was I was starring in my first movie, and that seemed to make a great deal of sense."

During that first year, he learned how to keep his head still in close-ups; to watch for the chalk marks on the floor which marked your position for that scene; to review in the evening the "rushes" of that day's filming; and how to make love, which was just about the most difficult challenge of all.

"I discovered," he remembers, 'that a kiss is only beautiful to the two people engaged in doing it. If you really kiss the girl, it shoves her fact out of shape. . . . This was not my only fault. My head was casting a shadow by getting in the path of her key light; my collar was pulled out of shape by the position of my arm; all in all, I had to draw back and start over with the realization that work is work, fun is fun, and kissing was more fun at the high school picnic."

He also lost forever, at least publicly, the nickname of Dutch, an appellation which caused unrestrained shudders in Warner's publicity department.

Picture followed on picture: *Submarine D-1* and *Hollywood Hotel* (in 1937); *Swing Your Lady, Sergeant Murphy, Accidents Will*

Happen, Girls on Probation, Boy Meets Girl, Cowboy From Brooklyn, Brother Rat and *Going Places* (in 1938), and many others. In his own words, Ronald Reagan became "the Errol Flynn of the B's. I was as brave as Errol, but in a low-budget fashion." The films usually took three weeks to make. They were rewrites and remakes of movies which were good enough for one more variation on an old familiar theme. Today, such "B" films make up much of television's nightly fare. Like Flynn, Reagan did many of his own stunts—fighting, jumping, diving and the like. He was encouraged to do so; it enabled the director to cut his schedule in half by shooting over the villain's shoulder on Ron's face for most of the fight.

Reagan made friends quickly and easily: established stars like Pat O'Brien, Dick Powell, Jimmy Cagney, Humphrey Bogart, Frank McHugh and others took to the keen-witted young man who worked so hard at his trade.

He was given a good part in what turned out to be a highly successful film and a solid money maker: *Brother Rat*, the story of three cadets at Virginia Military Institute. The other stars were Eddie Albert, who had the lead in the Broadway version, Wayne Morris and Jane Wyman, who became Reagan's romantic interest off camera and ultimately his wife in 1940. They were married in Wee Kirk O'Heather Chapel in Glendale, California, on January 26. A daughter, Maureen Elizabeth, was born in 1941. In 1945, they adopted a boy, Michael. They were divorced on June 28, 1948, after eight years of marriage.

Miss Wyman had been married once before to manufacturer Myron Futterman, and was divorced from Futterman in December 1938. Reagan has never talked publicly about his divorce from Jane Wyman. During the divorce proceedings in 1948, Miss Wyman stated that she did not share her husband's intense interest in politics and the Screen Actors Guild. In answer to a question put by Judge Thurmond Clarke, she explained she had nothing against the Guild but that "most of their discussions were far above me."

In his autobiography, Reagan wrote: "The problem hurt our children most. . . . There is no easy way to break up a home, and I don't think there is any way to ease the bewildered pain of children at such times." Maureen, married and divorced twice, is at thirty-nine an ardent feminist. Although she disagrees firmly with her father over ERA, Maureen has campaigned enthusiastically and effectively for him as governor and presidential candidate. Michael, at 35, is a successful businessman in gasohol. He and his attractive wife, Colleen, have one child, Cameron.

With the release of *Brother Rat,* Ronald Reagan was assured of steady employment if not yet stardom, and brought his mother and father to Hollywood. Although Jack Reagan's heart condition severely limited what he could do, his actor son put him in charge of handling his fan mail. The responsibility satisfied his father's desire to feel useful and the son's concern lest the job be too taxing. Until his death in 1941, Jack Reagan continued to help his son.

Everybody has a special picture which he thinks should be made. For Ronald Reagan, it was the story of Knute Rockne, the legendary football coach at Notre Dame. As he explains, "I had no intention of playing Rockne. I had always seen Pat O'Brien as the logical star in the title role. I had something else in mind for myself—a fellow named George Gipp."

Reagan lobbied all over Hollywood, asking everyone how you went about transforming an idea into a picture. One day he picked up a copy of *Variety,* the motion picture trade paper, to read that Warner Brothers was going to do the life story of Knute Rockne, with Pat O'Brien in the starring role!

He immediately called on a director and good friend, Brynie Foy, who told him, grinning all the while, "You talk too much." Reagan quickly explained that all he was interested in was the part of George Gipp. Foy replied: "Well, you'd better do something because they've already tested ten fellows for the part." Ron made an appointment to see Robert Fellows, the film's producer.

But Fellows declined to believe that Ronald Reagan could play the part and kept repeating over and over again: "Gipp was the greatest player in the country." Protests by the broad-shouldered actor that he had played football for eight years and had even won a football scholarship to college had no effect.

Then, Reagan remembered the advice of a friend: "You have to realize these fellows only believe what they see on film." He abruptly left the producer's office for his home where he uncovered several photographs from his football days at Eureka College. Within minutes he was back at the studio, and invading the producer's sanctum once again, "slapped the pictures down on his desk. . . . I was smart enough to keep my mouth shut and let the photographs talk."

Fellows asked if he could keep the photographs. Reagan replied simply, "Sure," and drove home slowly. He had been in his house barely fifteen minutes when the telephone rang. He was to test for the part of George Gipp at eight o'clock the next morning.

He got the part, which although it occupied only one reel of the picture, was "a nearly perfect part from an actor's standpoint. A great entrance, an action middle, and a death scene to finish up." *Knute Rockne, All American* was sneak-previewed in Pasadena in the early fall of 1940. The next morning, before he was even out of bed, Warner Brothers telephoned Reagan to tell him he had been cast as the second lead in an Errol Flynn picture, *Santa Fe Trail.* "A new door had been opened," he recalls. "Suddenly there were people on the lot greeting me who hadn't previously acknowledged my existence."

That morning at the studio Reagan watched a wardrobe man rush into the fitting room. "Without a word, he gathered the completed uniforms (of the actor who had initially been cast) in one arm, threw them in a corner, and hung the new ones in their place. It occurred to me then that it would be just as easy someday to throw my clothes in the corner and hang some other actor's in their place."

But such black possibilities were then exceedingly unlikely in the mind of Ronald Reagan.

The parts and the pictures got better and better: *The Badman,* with Wallace Beery and Lionel Barrymore; *International Squadron,* in which he played the lead, and finally in 1941, *King's Row,* which made Ronald Reagan a Hollywood star, and paradoxically, made him begin to wonder whether that was all he wanted to be.

Reagan played the part of Drake McHugh, a happy-go-lucky ladies' man in a small town who had spent most of a rather large inheritance. His key scene came when he awakened in his own bed to realize that his two legs had been amputated following an accident in a railroad yard. His line was: "Where's the rest of me?"

He has written: "A whole actor would find such a scene difficult; giving it the necessary dramatic impact as half an actor was murderous. I felt I had neither the experience nor the talent to fake it. I simply had to find out how it really felt, short of actual amputation."

He rehearsed the scene for days. He delivered the line a hundred different ways. He talked to disabled people "trying to brew in myself the caldron of emotions a man must feel who wakes up one sunny morning to find half of himself gone." Despite all his rehearsal and research, he still felt he had not penetrated the heart of the scene.

The morning of the shooting, uncertain of how to read the line, Reagan walked over to the set in his nightshirt. There he found that the prop men had cut a hole in the mattress of the bed and put a supporting box underneath. On an overwhelming impulse, he climbed into the rig and spent almost an hour there, staring at the smooth bottom of the bed where his legs should have been.

"Gradually," he remembers, "the affair began to terrify me. In some weird way, I felt something terrible had happened to my body." The director, Sam Wood, quietly gave the word, "Action!" and there was the sharp *clack* of the wooden clapper board which signals the beginning of every scene. Reagan looked down at the flat surface of the bed, tried to reach for his legs and then called out the question which had been haunting him for weeks: "Where's the rest of me?"

The question continued to haunt Ronald Reagan for years—until he finally and ultimately answered it in 1966 when he ran for the office of Governor of California.

In his autobiography, written in 1963, many months before he decided to run for public office and while he still thought of himself as an actor, Reagan revealed why he finally found himself in politics:

"If he is only an actor, I feel, he is much like I was in *King's Row,* only half a man—no matter how great his talents. I regard acting with the greatest affection; it has made my life for me. But I realize it tends to become an island of exaggerated importance. During my career on the screen, I have commanded excellent salaries, some admiration, fan mail, and a reputation—and my world contracted into not much more than a sound stage, my home, and occasional nights on the town. The circle of my friends closed in. The demands of my work—sometimes as much as fourteen hours a day—cut me off even from my brother Neil, who lived within half a mile of my apartment.

"I began to feel like a shut-in invalid, nursed by publicity. I have always liked space, the feeling of freedom, a broad range of friends, and variety (not excluding the publication). Now I had become a semi-automaton 'creating' a character another had written, doing what still another person told me to do on the set. Seeing the rushes, I could barely believe the colored shadow on the screen was myself.

"Possibly this was the reason I decided to find the rest of me. I loved three things: drama, politics, and sports, and I'm not sure they always come in that order. In all three of them I came out of the monastery of movies into the world. . . ."

On December 7, 1941, the Japanese bombed Pearl Harbor and the world was never again the same for millions of young Americans, including Ronald Reagan.

Chapter Five

Fort Roach

King's Row had not yet been released and Ronald Reagan had been collecting his new "star" salary of $3,500 a week for less than three months when an envelope stamped, "Immediate Action Active Duty," arrived.

The war interrupted a career which had left "B" pictures far behind. In the 1940-41 season, Ronald Reagan was chosen in the movie exhibitors' poll, "Stars of Tomorrow," as one of five new players most likely to emerge as stars. At Warner Brothers, Reagan surged into second place in studio fan mail, according to an article in the Los Angeles *Times* dated December 2, 1941. The thirty-year-old actor ranked second only to Errol Flynn, replacing James Cagney as runner-up.

When he took his physical examination, the doctors demanded to know how he had passed the eye test years before. "If we sent you overseas, you'd shoot a general," one exclaimed. "Yes, and you'd miss him," replied another. Reagan confessed that he had tricked the examining officer years before. He was inducted but his papers were stamped, "No combat duty."

His first assignment (he was inducted April 14, 1942) was Fort Mason, San Francisco, as a liaison officer loading convoys. Although he tried to stick to the business of cargo and shipping dates, Lieutenant Reagan found himself constantly called upon to perform various show business "duties." First there was an interview with a San Francisco movie columnist, followed by bond rallies and charity benefits. *King's Row* came to the post theater and the young officer was introduced and asked to say a few words. Lieutenant Reagan was next called to Hollywood to appear at a giant rally of film stars launching the brand new USO (United Service Organizations).

The Monday following the rally, Fort Mason's commanding general called in the young officer to have a little chat about military priorities in a war. Reagan, who had been bothered by the flood of requests, quickly expressed *his* dissatisfaction as well and asked permission to refer all future invitations to the general's office which could then assign him as it saw fit. The general, who had been ready to lay down a heavy barrage, decided to hold his fire and before the meeting was over had promised Reagan his office would do what he had suggested. It was a small but significant incident. Reagan had met and overcome a difficult situation by being honest and himself. It is his invariable practice to this day.

A short while later, Lieutenant Reagan was transferred from the Army to the Air Force and from Fort Mason to a special "base" outside Los Angeles. The Air Force was starting a motion picture unit and needed men experienced in filmmaking.

Colonel Philip Booker, Reagan's commanding officer at Fort Mason, overrode his young subordinate's doubts with the comment: "To tell you the truth, whether you're willing or not, you're going—because in thirty-four years, this is the first time I've ever seen the Army make sense. This is putting a square peg in a square hole."

And so the "square" lieutenant returned to Hollywood. The unit soon located at the Hal Roach Studios, which quickly became known as "Fort Roach," and in more satirical circles, "Fort Wacky."

It was an unusual military installation, beyond doubt, but "from a motion picture standpoint," argues Reagan, "it added up to about two hundred million dollars worth of talent on the hoof. We would turn out training films and documentaries, and conduct a training school for combat camera crews. . . . I have yet to go out on a personal appearance without having at least several TV or news photographers tell me, after a press conference, they learned their trade in our combat camera school."

Fort Roach numbered 1,300 men and officers. Reagan was appointed base adjutant, that is, administrative officer. He was promoted to captain but asked that his promotion to major be canceled. "Who was I," he asks, "to be a major for serving in California without ever hearing a shot fired in anger?"

Reagan is proud of the job performed by the men at Fort Roach, explaining that "the military has need of many things, in wartime

especially, so there will always be a need for specialized posts. . . .
None has ever been more successful in fulfilling its mission than
was our wacky Hollywood stepchild. One of our thirty-minute training films cut the training period for aerial gunners by six weeks.''

They also worked on two important classified projects. The first
concerned the destruction of the Nazi V-2 rocket launching sites at
Peenemünde, Germany. The rockets were not only damaging the
civilian morale in England but would have affected the Normandy
invasion if they had continued to operate at full efficiency. Details
of their location and construction were obtained. Exact replicas of
the sites were built in Florida and experimental bombings were
carried out to discover how best to destroy the rocket installations.
Reagan's camera crews at Fort Roach filmed the raids.

"Day after day," remembers Reagan, "we sat in a projection
room in Culver City and saw fantastic slow-motion films of huge
bombs bouncing off these concrete buildings as if they were pebbles,
until one day we saw on-screen, armor-piercing bombs dropped
from low altitudes, going through the huge concrete walls as if
through cheese. Those films were flown directly to the Eighth Air
Force, and the launch sites were knocked out in time to postpone
the V-2 launchings long enough for D-Day to take place on
schedule.''

More spectacular and important was the project which dealt with
the front thousands of miles away in the Pacific. As American
airplanes began to hit closer and closer to Japan, film experts at Fort
Roach concluded that bomber crews could reduce their losses and
improve their efficiency if they knew exactly where they were going
before they arrived there.

On their own, without any orders from the Pentagon, the special
effects men at Fort Wacky built a complete miniature of Tokyo. It
filled a sound stage. They erected a crane and camera mount above
the model city and photographed it, creating the on-screen effect
of movies taken from an airplane flying at various heights and
speeds.

A group of distinguished generals were invited to a "sneak
preview" at the studios. Real scenes taken by planes flying over
Tokyo were mixed in with scenes of the model. The generals were
informed of the melange and challenged to tell which were which.
Although several had flown over Tokyo they could not. "Skepticism
turned to enthusiasm," says Reagan and before long the sound stage
was put under twenty-four-hour guard and all but qualified personnel
were denied admission.

Additional models of other Japanese cities were constructed. The special effects men became so proficient that they could show a bomb run as seen through the bombsight and even portray what the target would look like in darkness or bad weather.

Reagan was the narrator of the bombing runs, the briefing officer if you will, and would describe the entire flight from the first sighting of the island target to the command, "Bombs away!" "We kept these simulated bomb runs so authentic," he recalls, "that following each raid, recon planes would fly their film from Saipan direct to us so that we could burn out portions of our target scene and put in the scars of the bombing. Our film then would always look exactly the way the target would appear to the crews going in on the next run."

Reagan argues that "only an outfit like ours could have accomplished this task. Here was the true magic of motion picture making. . . ."

As the war drew to a close, Captain Reagan experienced his first direct contact with civilian bureaucracy, which resulted in "the first crack in my staunch liberalism."

Because of his classified status, Fort Roach did not have civilian employees until the last year and a half of the war. But one day two Civil Service representatives appeared to inform the base's adjutant (Ronald Reagan) that civilians were on their way. Two weeks later, 250 civilians arrived.

Fort Roach's military personnel section—responsible for 1,300 men—was half the size of the personnel office that maintained the files of the 250 civilians. "Their rules and regulations," Reagan says, "filled shelves from floor to ceiling, around virtually four walls of a barrack-sized building."

In his autobiography, Reagan tells the story of an officer-writer who came storming into his office one day, declaring he had to have a new secretary. The one assigned him by civilian personnel couldn't spell "cat"! When informed of the officer's request, the civilian personnel director calmly replied that there was no problem. She would simply draw up the papers and the officer would "sign the charges."

When the suspicious officer asked her to explain what she meant, the personnel director said that there would have to be a trial during which the officer would take "the stand in (his secretary's) presence and establish her incompetence."

Repelled by such procedure the officer refused to sign a complaint. Captain Reagan, by now familiar with Civil Service, inquired if there wasn't possibly any other way of solving the officer's problem.

As he suspected, the personnel director was ready with the perfect bureaucratic solution: she would transfer a qualified secretary to the officer and move the girl who couldn't spell "cat" to another office and a *better* job, thereby pleasing everyone and upsetting no one.

"So," Reagan has written, "the incompetent wound up with a promotion and a raise in pay. No one in the administrative hierarchy of Civil Service will ever interfere with this upgrading process because his own pay and rating are based on the number of employees beneath him and grades of those employees.

"It's a built-in process for empire building."

And it was to become a favorite theme of Ronald Reagan in the years ahead.

Chapter Six

Strikes, Communists, and a Loaded Gun

Serious strikes had begun in Hollywood even before the war's end as unions fought for jurisdiction of a $5 billion a year industry. Between 1945 and 1947, there were half a dozen major strikes in Hollywood, costing movie makers approximately $150 million. About 8,000 workers, it is estimated, lost 9 million man hours and some $28 million in wages.

The bitter struggle was created to a great extent by communist attempts to seize control of one of the most important media in the nation. Their role was not obvious, or even admitted, by many in Hollywood, including Ronald Reagan. At this time, Reagan was admittedly naive about Communism. "I thought," he says, "the nearest Communists were fighting in Stalingrad." He also admits that he was a "near hopeless hemophilic liberal."

Following in his father's political footsteps, he had voted for Roosevelt all through the 1930's and 1940's. His army experience with civilian bureaucracy shook him but he still voted for Harry Truman in 1948, heading the Labor League of Hollywood Voters for him.

In fact, when he was discharged from the army at the end of 1945, his sympathies were unreservedly liberal, and his ambitions universal: "I would work with the tools I had: my thoughts, my speaking abilities, my reputation as an actor. I would try to bring about the regeneration of the world I believed should have automatically appeared" after World War II. He joined every organization he could find "that would guarantee to save the world."

51

(Among them were the United World Federalists and, later, Americans for Democratic Action.)

For over a year, he made speeches denouncing fascism to enthusiastic applause. Then one night, at the suggestion of a minister, he added a new last paragraph also denouncing communism. The audience sat sullen and silent and quite abruptly Reagan realized that the people he had been talking to were curiously one-minded.

He cut back drastically on his speaking engagements, especially for the American Veterans Committee, and started intense personal research on current affairs. He began to appreciate the very real menace of communism as he devoted more time to the Screen Actors Guild (SAG), of which he was a director, and its efforts to settle the still continuing jurisdictional strike.

Reagan had been appointed a member of the SAG board in 1941. For all of his adult life he has been a union man, saying in 1966, for example, "I . . . continue to be a strong believer in the rights of unions, as well as in the rights of individuals. I think we have the right as free men to refuse to work for just grievances: the strike is an inalienable weapon of any citizen."

SAG's efforts became all-important as violence increased. Autos were overturned. Clubs, chains, bottles, bricks and two-by-four planks were used in scuffles between the warring unions. Homes of members were bombed and individuals were mugged.

Unable to look on passively any longer, SAG volunteered as a mediator and came close to finding a solution on several occasions. But each time its efforts failed, often at the very last moment. The reason why they failed was later revealed by congressional committees.

Both the House Committee on Un-American Activities of the US Congress and the Senate Fact-Finding Committee on Un-American Activities of the California Legislature traced the strike to communists. In 1959, the California committee reported:

"The Communist Party working in Hollywood wanted control over everything that moved on wheels. . . . They soon moved Communist units into those unions having jurisdiction over carpenters, painters, musicians, grips and electricians. To control these trade unions was to control the motion picture industry."

The strike, which was finally settled when responsible union leaders endorsed the position of the old-line International Alliance of Theatrical Stage Employees, had a profound effect on Ronald Reagan. He says, "I owe it to that period that I managed to sort out a lot of items in my personal life. From being an active (although unconscious) partisan in what now and then turned out to be communist causes, I little by little became . . . awakened.''

One man in particular who helped awaken him was film star George Murphy, a close friend and a former president of the Screen Actors Guild and US Senator from California. Reminiscing in a room off the Senate floor in Washington, D. C., in 1967, Senator Murphy told me:

''In those days I was interested in the activities and programs of the communists to a greater degree than most of the fellows. I tried to explain to Ron but he thought I was trying to convince him he ought to be a Republican. Because of his involvement with labor he had automatically become involved with the Democratic party.

''Then later on he discovered what I had been trying to tell him and like all people who discover the faults of something they believe in very strongly, he swung around hard and became an active Republican—just as I did. You see, I had been a Democrat originally in 1939.''

That Ronald Reagan evolved into a hard-hitting, effective anti-communist was confirmed in 1951 in testimony before the House Committee on Un-American Activities when actor Sterling Hayden confessed his involvement in the communist plot. Testifying on communist maneuvers to capture Hollywood, Hayden was asked what stopped them. His answer: We ''ran into the Board of Directors of the SAG and particularly into Ronald Reagan, who was a one-man battalion.''

The prize which the communists sought was worth more than all the booty sought by Kubla Khan. As Reagan pointed out years later, the communists wanted the motion picture industry as a ''world-wide propaganda base. In those days before television and massive foreign film production, American films dominated 95 percent of the world's movie screens. We had a weekly audience of about 500,000,000 souls.''

But the communists were stopped by liberals turned anti-communists like Ronald Reagan. One of his first experiences with communists was their infiltration of the Hollywood branch of the American Veterans Committee, of which he was a national board member. Reagan worked hard for the AVC until one day he was told to report in full Air Corps uniform to picket a studio. He investigated the order and discovered that the action had been taken by a vote of 73 members out of a total of 1,300.

Reagan called headquarters to warn that if the picket was held as an official action of AVC membership, he would take full-page advertisements in the local newspapers denouncing it. In less than an hour the picket line was canceled. Shortly thereafter, in 1947, he resigned from the Hollywood chapter of the American Veterans Committee. "It had become," he wrote, "a hotbed of communists in Hollywood, according to activities which were reported on by the California Senate Fact-Finding Committee on Un-American Activities. . . . Its reputation suffered so much that it had to be taken over in its entirety and cleansed by the national organization."

Another group which invited Ronald Reagan in 1946 to serve on its board was the Hollywood Independent Citizens Committee of Arts, Sciences and Professions (HICCASP), an ostensibly respectable and responsible organization. But when he attended his first board meeting, Reagan noted to his surprise the presence of several people with far-left and worse records.

The meeting proceeded smoothly until one board member rose to state that he was concerned as were several others about the persistent rumor that HICCASP was a communist-front organization. He suggested the board clear the air by issuing a statement repudiating communism.

Reagan enthusiastically supported the suggestion, only to be bombarded with such epithets as "capitalist scum," "enemy of the proletariat," and "fascist."

Those in favor of the anti-communist statement met later that evening at the apartment of Olivia de Havilland. There Reagan was told that the whole thing had been staged to smoke out the "others." Reagan looked at Olivia: "I thought you were one," he said. Miss de Havilland murmured back: "I thought *you* were one."

They set to work drafting a statement, with Reagan writing the first draft on the back of an envelope. The final version ended: "We reaffirm our belief in free enterprise and the democratic system and repudiate communism." When this statement was submitted for a vote to the members of a special HICCASP executive committee, it received one favorable ballot, that of Olivia de Havilland.

Reagan resigned from the board by telegram that night, as did others. Shortly thereafter, HICCASP folded.

As a result of this and other anti-communist activity, Reagan began receiving threats against his life. One night, on location, he was called to a phone where an unidentified voice told him: "There's a group being formed to deal with you. They're going to fix you so you won't ever act again."

The next day, at the insistence of friends and associates, Warner Brothers Studios arranged for the police to issue Reagan a license to carry a gun. He wore a loaded .32 Smith & Wesson revolver in a shoulder holster for months.

What convinced him to keep wearing it was the story told him that "They" were scoffing at such precautions: "This is all cooked up nonsense," they were reported as saying. "If we had wanted to throw acid in Reagan's face, we would have done it, not talked about it."

As the actor wrote: "No one had mentioned acid-throwing—up to that revealing moment."

During this turbulent period, Ronald Reagan was elected president of the fifteen-thousand-member Screen Actors Guild, succeeding Robert Montgomery. He was elected president a total of six times—more than any more prexy. He also served on SAG's board of directors for sixteen years. He received many awards for his union activities, including a certificate from the American Newspaper Guild (CIO) in 1952, praising him for "spearheading the fight against communism in Hollywood." He was also cited by the AFL Auto Workers Union.

Under his leadership, the SAG purged its ranks of actors who were not cleared of communist charges. SAG later adopted as official policy the condemnation of all members "who have been named as past or present Communist Party members and in appearing before the House Committee on Un-American Activities refused to state whether they are or ever have been members of the Party."

The Guild also declared that any applicant for membership must sign the following statement: "I am not now and will not become a member of the Communist Party or of any other organization that seeks to overthrow the government of the United States by force and violence."

In summing up these long months of struggle against the communists, Reagan has written: "We fought on the issues and proved that if you keep the people informed on those issues, they won't make a mistake."

He has always had great confidence in the people and great mistrust of any attempts to control or manage them. In May 1947, he said:

"Our highest aim should be the cultivation of freedom of the individual, for therein lies the highest dignity of man. Tyranny is tyranny and—whether it comes from the Right, Left or Center—it is evil. I suspect the Extreme Right and the Extreme Left of political ideologies, though seeming to branch off in opposite directions, curve to a common meeting point.

"I believe the only logical way to save our country from both extremes is to remove conditions that supply fuel for the totalitarian fire."

Reagan's administrative ability was recognized again in 1949 when he was elected chairman of the Motion Picture Industry Council, which represents 35,000 members of nine major acting, labor and management groups, and is the film capital's most prestigious organization. He served for ten years on the Council's board of directors.

His duties as SAG president were many and demanding. Following settlement of the strike in 1947, he was called to Washington, D.C. to appear before the House Committee on Un-American Activities. There he testified about communist infiltration of Hollywood and reiterated his faith in democracy, saying:

"I would hesitate, or not like, to see any political party outlawed on the basis of ideology. We have spent 170 years in this country on the basis that democracy is strong enough to stand up and fight against the inroads of any ideology. However, if it is proven that an organization is an agent of a power, a foreign power or in any way not a legitimate political party, and I think the government is capable of proving that, if the proof is there, then that is another matter."

Ronald Reagan was and is a man who is steadfastly against giving *any* government, federal, state or local, too much power, whatever the reason. In his testimony before the House Committee on Un-American Activities, he said that he detested and abhorred communism and its "fifth column" tactics, but added, "At the same time I never as a citizen want to see our country become urged, by either fear or resentment of this group, that we ever compromise with any of our democratic principles through that fear or resentment."

One of those principles is the right of dissent, which he exercised in 1959 by refusing to attend a party given by 20th Century Fox for visiting Soviet Premier Nikita Khrushchev.

As SAG President, he also testified in Los Angeles before a special subcommittee of the House Committee on Education and Labor. The two-year film strike consumed hundreds of hours of Ronald Reagan's time, as did normal negotiations about wages and working conditions of SAG members. He concedes that his long association with the Screen Actors Guild hurt his movie career, but he has a typical explanation:

"I think I became too identified with the serious side of Hollywood's off-screen life—there were too many people who saw me only as a committee member. Would I do it again? Yes—this has been the best of all possible lives for me and I think you have to do something to pay your way in life."

Taft Schreiber, his agent for thirty years and former vice-president of the giant entertainment company, MCA, corroborates Reagan's deep-rooted belief in public service. "(He) was not at a point in his life when he needed the Union activities to make personal progress—he had a substantial contract, had achieved stability and permanence for himself in the industry, and it was rare that anyone as young and as involved in screen work would give of himself to the extent required, for it meant negotiating, and giving many extra curricular hours to this responsibility that only the most dedicated would choose to undertake."

Unfortunately for his career, he did so well as SAG head that his fellow actors elected him again and again as their president. *Life* magazine commented: "Reagan was an extremely capable labor leader and the guild's esteem for him is evidenced by the fact that he was recalled to the union presidency in a 1959 emergency, to lead a successful strike against the studios over the issue of TV residual pay for actors."

That same year, 1959, he testified in Washington on behalf of the Screen Actors Guild in favor of tax-cut legislation. After criticizing the theory of progressive taxation, he took the opportunity, as he usually did, to describe the American dream, waxing so eloquent that Rep. John Byrnes of Wisconsin was moved to comment:

"May I make a comment that I think Mr. Reagan ought to run for Congress because we need more of his philosophy and persuasiveness here in Congress."

In Reagan's own mind, the most important dividend of his union presidency was a meeting in 1951 with a lovely twenty-seven-year-old actress named Nancy Davis. He met Nancy, the daughter of a famed Chicago neurosurgeon, Loyal Davis, after director Mervyn Le Roy had asked the SAG president to help a young MGM actress. It seemed that the young lady's name kept appearing on communist front rosters and she was receiving notices about pro-communist meetings she had no intention of attending. After a quick check which revealed that the young lady was a very vocal anti-communist, Reagan decided to reassure the young actress in person—over an early dinner. The small (five-foot-four) girl with the wide brown eyes so intrigued the union head that the evening did not end until 3:30 a.m.

Nancy was a graduate of Girls Latin School in Chicago and Smith College and came by her interest in acting familially—her mother appeared on Broadway as Edith Luckett. She came to Hollywood, after some summer stock with such stars as Zasu Pitts, "because acting offered a different way of life. I didn't want to go back to Chicago and lead the life of a sub-deb."

Nancy's father is past president of such organizations as the American Surgical Association, the American College of Surgeons and the Society of Neurological Surgeons. A well-known and articulate conservative, Dr. Davis has edited a number of medical journals and textbooks. He was largely responsible for his daughter's anti-communism, which matched so well the viewpoint of the SAG president.

Recalls Nancy, "Ronnie made me aware of all that was going on. That was one of the first things that impressed me and attracted me to him. He had so many other interests beside the film business. I can't remember him talking about his last picture. He had such a fund of knowledge—he could talk about horses, wine, books, politics. He's the best story-teller I ever heard."

Ron and Nancy dated for over a year before it finally dawned on him (at a SAG meeting) that they ought to get married—which they did on March 4, 1952, at the Little Brown Church in the Valley in North Hollywood, with William Holden as best man, and Mrs. Holden as the matron of honor. Nancy stopped acting (she had appeared in eight films), explaining that "if you try to make two careers work, one of them has to suffer. Maybe some women can do it, but not me." They have two children, Patricia Ann (Patti), born in 1953, and Ronald Prescott (Skipper), born in 1958.

For a number of reasons, good pictures now came less frequently. Reagan was so busy with SAG business that producers now typecast him as an off-screen rather than on-screen personality.

Second, the public no longer depended exclusively on movies for its entertainment: television was beginning to cast its flickering shadow across the nation and on Hollywood.

Third, in Reagan's words, "my Air Corps chores had exposed me to the Monday morning conversation of a lot of Civil Service stenographers, average age eighteen, and they weren't 'oohing and aahing' over Robert Taylor, Jimmy Stewart, or Tyrone Power, let alone me. Their age group was about sixty percent of the movie audience and they had come to ticket-buying age while all of us were off-screen. They had a new set of heroes."

Finally, there were a couple of serious illnesses which interrupted a film career already in shadow because of intense Screen Actors Guild activity. One night, for example, Ronald Reagan went to a premiere at the Carthay Circle Theater, but before the evening was out he was in Cedars of Lebanon Hospital with a brand of virus pneumonia, on which miracle drugs had no effect. Reagan was desperately sick for weeks and remembers one night when he almost decided to stop breathing. An anonymous nurse persuaded him to take more more breath and then another and "she was so nice and persistent that I let her have her way."

Reagan's agent then negotiated a new contract with Warner's which gave the actor the right to do outside prictures: he was now freelance. Universal Pictures immediately signed him up for five pictures in five years, the first one a crime film with top actress Ida Lupino. On the Sunday before the first day's shooting, June 19, 1949, Reagan played as usual in a baseball game benefiting the City of Hope Hospital. "Before the end of the first inning, I was lying just off first base with a comminuted multiple fracture of my right thigh." He was in traction for two months, and underwent a year of therapy before his leg would support him and his knee recovered about 85 percent of its normal resiliency.

With bills piling up and on his own as a freelance actor, Ronald Reagan had two choices: take whatever came along to get ahead financially or wait for the right part in the right picture. The Reagans decided to ride out the rough weather. For fourteen months, he turned down every script offered him for the simplest of all reasons: they were terrible. He also told MCA, which was now handling him, that both Broadway and a television series were on the "won't do" list. Reagan was opposed to a TV series because, in his opinion, the actors in it were forever afterward identified with those roles.

MCA suggested a nightclub act in Las Vegas, and Reagan reluctantly agreed. He appeared at The Last Frontier "for a wonderfully successful two weeks, with a sellout every night and offers from the Waldorf in New York and top clubs from Miami to Chicago." But the Reagans decided that two weeks were enough and went home to ride and raise horses, and cattle too, on their 370 acre ranch in the Malibu Hills. The ranch, purchased in 1952, was named Yearling Row.*

And then, at last, came the "part" which was to give him a brand new career in a new medium—and complete his political transformation from liberal Democrat to conservative Republican.

---

* In later years, political opponents would make fun of his acting ability, but critics were usually complimentary. For example, *Newsweek* called his portrayal of a wartime serviceman in *Voice of the Turtle* "sensitive." And the renowned Bosley Crowther of the *New York Times* said Reagan's performance in *John Loves Mary* had "dignity."

Chapter Seven

A Rendezvous with Destiny

General Electric was looking for a new television program, something that would last. Revue Productions, a subsidiary of MCA, thought it had the answer: a weekly dramatic series featuring top Hollywood stars with Ronald Reagan as the host and lead in half a dozen plays each year. What made the proposal so unusual and attractive was that off-screen Reagan would make personal appearances at GE's plants and in selected communities as part of the company's Employee and Community Relations Program. Was Reagan interested? He certainly was. So was General Electric.

In the fall of 1954, *GE Theater* began an eight-year run "with more 'firsts' to its credit than anything on television before or since," boasts its host. Among them were (a) the first series to emanate from both New York and Hollywood, and (b) the first series to alternate between live and filmed shows. For seven of the eight years, *GE Theater* ranked first in a prime spot—nine o'clock Sunday night.

"Our secret wasn't any secret at all," says Reagan; "we tried for variety and quality in our stories, and we cast with the best we could get—particularly from the world of motion pictures. In our eight years we starred half a hundred Academy Award winners—many made their first, and some their only, television appearance on our show."

GE Theater made Ronald Reagan a star in the most important medium in the nation. It brought him financial security with an annual salary of $120,000, which finally reached $165,000 when he became part-owner of the series. And it put him on the road for GE from coast to coast, talking to people in thirty-one different states. Reagan has estimated that in those eight years he visited all

135 GE plants and personally met every one of its 250,000 employees. "Two of the eight years were spent traveling, and with speeches sometimes running at fourteen a day, I was on my feet in front of a 'mike' for about 250,000 minutes."

He got to know these employees, ordinary everyday citizens like most of us, and he is fond of remarking that too many political leaders "have underestimated them." He is convinced, reflecting this conviction today, that "they want the truth. . . . They are concerned, not with security as some would have us believe, but with their very firm personal liberties."

He worked hard. At one plant he autographed ten thousand photographs in two days. At another, he stood in a receiving line and shook two thousand hands. At a plant in Louisville, Ky., he walked miles of assembly line twice, once for the day shift and a second time for the night shift. He recalls punningly: "No barnstorming politician ever met the people on quite such a common footing."

The community relations part of his job started more slowly but in a few months he was talking to dozens of civic and educational organizations about Hollywood, the *real* Hollywood. The most dramatic section of his remarks dealt with the attempted takeover of the film industry by the communists. Reagan was dumbfounded to discover how "completely uninformed the average audience was concerning internal Communism and how it operated." He determined to educate them, and in the process, his speeches began to concentrate more and more on communism *and* collectivism. "The Hollywood portion of the talk shortened and disappeared," he admits. "The warning words of what could happen changed to concrete examples of what has already happened, and I learned very early to document those examples."

That "I" comes naturally. In an age of omnipresent speech writers, Ronald Reagan researches and writes many of his own speeches. He is particularly proud of two awards he has received: Freedoms Foundation Awards in 1960 and 1962 for "outstanding achievement in bringing about a better understanding of the American way of life."

His addresses during the 1950's and early 1960's were carefully nonpartisan. He emphasized that the problem of centralized power in Washington cut across political lines and that government could grow so large that it usurped the policy-making functions of *all* parties.

From the very first, he was well received. Speaking invitations poured into General Electric offices. When *GE Theater* went off the air in 1962, speaking tours had to be canceled as far ahead as 1966. Reagan modestly explains the overwhelming reception:

"I think the real reason had to do with a change that was taking place all over America. People wanted to talk about and hear about encroaching government control, and hopefully they wanted suggestions as to what they themselves could do to turn the tide."

They also wanted to hear someone who spoke with so much conviction and urgency about what was happening to them and their country.

Earl Dunkel, the General Electric representative who first accompanied Reagan on his travels, remembers that the actor had "an almost mystical ability to achieve an empathy with almost any audience." Now a Washington public relations consultant, Dunkel says that Reagan was able to talk on *any* subject, for example education, and persuade a group of educators that he must have had his training in that area. And "in those days he spoke totally off the cuff—not even note cards."

He was unusually thoughtful about others, recalls Dunkel, who tells this story:

"In Erie, Pa., one night we came back to the hotel so dog-tired all we wanted was to go right to bed. But there was a young girl who had been sitting in the lobby for four hours, waiting. She wanted to be an actress. She had all the posturings of the would-be actress. Ronnie was a hero from out of the screen-play magazines and she wanted to know what to do. And this man, dog-tired as he was, recognizing that this little girl was going just the wrong route sat down in that lobby with her for an hour and a half, explaining what to do if she were really serious. His advice was to do things right there in Erie, Pa.—get on radio, get on television, get in the little theater—pointing out that if she could win an audience in Erie, she could win an audience anywhere."

He was far less vain than a celebrity has a right to be, insists Dunkel, who remembers that when they arrived at the usual two-bedroom hotel suite he and Reagan would flip a coin, with the winner getting the big room and the loser the small one.

George Dalen succeeded Earl Dunkel and was to accompany Reagan around the country, north, south, east and west, for nearly seven years. He too remembers the actor's non-prima donna behavior:

"We boarded a pullman* late one night to head back to New York from Rhode Island. We were somewhat disconcerted on awakening to find that we were still in the yards at Providence. A driving snow storm had stalled the trains. . . .

"Since this was a night train, there was naturally, no food service aboard. We had with us a box of jellybeans which Reagan regularly carried on these jaunts and a couple bags of popcorn we had picked up in the station the night before. The porter on the train had a thermos of coffee.

"As we discussed our mutual plight, the three of us sat down in the porter's quarters and shared jellybeans, popcorn and the porter's coffee which was sufficient to sustain us to New York. Here again, it was not a question of making a gesture—it was just the natural and human thing to do, so he did it."

That he liked people can be seen from this listing of the varied groups he would meet on a "typical" day: "a press conference breakfast; G.E. employees ranging from secretarial, management, shop workers, and professional engineers and technical people; G.E. distributors and dealers; city fathers; women's clubs' administrative associations; plus others, as well as speaking to Chamber of Commerce, Kiwanis, Rotary, school groups, et cetera."

Dalen makes the telling point that while Reagan attracted attention as a Hollywood star, he *retained* people's interest because he was "so articulate and well-informed."

Sometimes, however, he ran into opposition. In 1959, he was scheduled to speak at a Los Angeles convention when a GE officer informed him that a federal government official had protested to the company about Reagan's proposed speech. He planned to use the Tennessee Valley Authority (TVA) as an example of how government programs can expand beyond their original purpose. It was suggested, Reagan recounts, that he be fired and pointed references were made to the millions of dollars worth of business that GE did with the federal government every year.

Reagan asked how Ralph Cordiner, GE's president, had reacted. Cordiner, he was told, had said that GE "would not tell any individual what he could not say," and that Cordiner would handle the matter personally.

The government official was incredulous, but GE stood firm.

---

* Reagan grounded himself after World War II, and thereafter traveled exclusively by train or car until 1965 when he again began to fly, explaining, "I think I have to be willing to do whatever the job (of governor) requires, particularly in the line of travel."

However, Reagan began to wonder whether he had "carte blanche" to say whatever he wanted—and jeopardize so much business for his sponsor. Reagan decided to call Cordiner in New York. The GE chairman stated that he was sorry that Reagan had learned about the affair, that "it's my problem and I've taken it on." Reagan responded by saying that he wouldn't want to think GE might have to fire several thousand men because of what he said. Cordiner did not pick up the hint. Finally, Reagan realized it was up to him:

"Mr. Cordiner," he asked, "what would you say if I said I could make my speech just as effectively without mentioning TVA?"

After a long pause, the reply came: "Well, it would make my job easier."

Reagan recounts: "Dropping TVA from the speech was no problem. You can reach out blindfolded and grab a hundred examples of overgrown government. The whole attempt only served to illustrate how it is if we are to save freedom."

It also served to illustrate that big business is not always ready to abandon principle for a piece of the federal pork barrel.

One of our nation's outstanding businessmen, Ralph Cordiner has tremendous respect for Reagan and his ability to establish rapport with either large or small audiences. "I think," he told this writer, "the listening and viewing audience is impressed with his sincerity, his thoughtfulness and his forthrightness." The former chief executive of General Electric is also struck by Reagan's unusual habit, for so busy a man, of personally studying a subject. "Ronald Reagan is a student," he says, "and does not appear before an audience, write a speech, deliver a paper or even have a discussion with a very small group unless he has researched and reviewed the subject before the group for consideration." The actor, he emphasizes, was a "unanimous" choice as host of the *GE Theater* and as "a spokesman, not for the Company, but for what he personally thought were the important issues and some of the basic truths that many of us knew during boyhood or an earlier period, and which apparently were presently being forgotten or ignored."

Ronald Reagan was involved in other incidents that revealed the changing times and his changing personality. One night, he was scheduled to speak in St. Paul, Minnesota, at an assembly at Central High School. But when he arrived he was greeted by the news that the Teachers Federation had passed a resolution the night before demanding that Ronald Reagan not be allowed to address the students because he was a "controversial personality." (This was sev-

eral years after the end of the alleged Reign of Terror carried out
by Sen. Joseph McCarthy of Wisconsin.)

That morning Reagan stepped out onto the stage of the high
school auditorium not knowing how the students would react. He
needn't have worried. They gave him a five-minute standing ovation. "They damn well didn't want someone telling them," Reagan
says, "whom they could or couldn't listen to."

The next night in Minneapolis, just across the river, where
Reagan was the banquet speaker, a St. Paul teacher asked to say
a few words to the audience. He proceeded to make a public apology
on behalf of the St. Paul teachers for the anti-Reagan resolution.
Reagan later learned from a reporter that only a handful of teachers
out of a membership of 1,200 had attended the meeting at which
the resolution was passed.

Reagan's early experience as a labor negotiator and battler
against the communists now stood him in good stead. As he became
more and more determined and more and more effective, the attacks
increased in ferocity.

At last, he received the inevitable decoration of every effective
conservative and/or anti-communist: an attack by Drew Pearson.
Early one morning, in his California home, Reagan was awakened
by a Pearson assistant and asked about his views on Medicare. As
he says: "Somehow my answers must not have weathered the trip
from Los Angeles by phone to Washington, and through Pearson's
typewriter, because they came out turned around in a vitriolic attack
against me and the American Medical Association. It made it easier
to understand why three United States Presidents of both parties had
publicly questioned his tactics."

For seven years, Sunday night at nine belonged to the General
Electric's dramatic series. But in television, even the top-rated
shows eventually lose favor and the *GE Theater* at last met its match
in the eighth year—a cowboy spectacular called *Bonanza*. It wasn't
a real contest: "Our half-hour, black and white, was up against an
hour color program with four permanent stars, plus a weekly guest
star, all wrapped up in a budget several millions of dollars greater
than ours."

Another factor in GE's decision to cancel the show was the
activities of the host and their company representative. Ronald Reagan was no longer just a Hollywood and television star. His activities had become increasingly political. In 1960, he campaigned
openly for Richard Nixon's presidential candidacy. "I literally traveled," he recalls, "the same kind of campaign route the candidate

himself traveled—all over the country." It was not a halfhearted commitment: Reagan made over two-hundred speeches for Nixon as a Democrat.*

In 1962, when Nixon ran for Governor of California, Reagan again took to the hustings, this time as a Republican. He says, "I didn't want to become a professional Democrat for Republican candidates and I registered as a Republican in January, 1962." Later that year, he served as honorary campaign chairman for Loyd Wright, a staunch conservative and distinguished lawyer, in the Republican primary against incumbent Sen. Thomas Kuchel, an equally undiluted liberal. Kuchel, who won handily, repaid Reagan in kind in 1966 by supporting the actor's opponent, George Christopher, in the GOP gubernatorial primary.

Another candidate the actor "campaigned" for in 1962 was Rep. John Rousselot, then a prominent member of the John Birch Society, who had been elected to Congress in 1960. Reagan critics have tried to magnify this political coupling out of all proportion. Here are the facts: On August 30 Reagan traveled to Pasadena to speak at a $50-a-plate fund raising affair for Rousselot. That was the total extent of his campaigning for the Congressman except as Reagan says, "I urged in my talks the voting of a solid ticket. If you send the general, you send the troops with him."

He did not abandon acting by any means. In 1964, he signed up as host and occasional star of the television series, *Death Valley Days,* beginning its thirteenth season. He appeared in Ernest Hemingway's *The Killers* (the last, as it turned out, of his fifty-five feature films). Despite his forays into politics in 1960 and 1962, Ronald Reagan seemed to be settling into the comfortable routine of a successful Hollywood and television star in middle age. He and Nancy and the two children were happy in their handsome, $100,000 home in the Los Angeles suburb of Pacific Palisades overlooking the Pacific Ocean. On weekends and often during the week, they would retreat to their ranch, Yearling Row, where Reagan would

* Ten years before, he supported Congresswoman Helen Gahagan Douglas when she ran against then Congressman Richard Nixon for the US Senate from California. Although he has been described as having campaigned actively for Mrs. Douglas, Reagan told me, "I don't actually recall ever doing anything particularly for her as an individual. But as a Democrat I supported the ticket from top to bottom." In answer to a detailed letter of mine, Mrs. Douglas simply replied, "Ronald Reagan supported my campaign for the Senate in 1950. At that time, he was a Democrat." The 1950 campaign was to be the last one in which he supported the Democratic ticket *in toto.* In 1952, Reagan backed Dwight Eisenhower for President.

ride his favorite mount, a dapple gray named Nancy D.* There were cookouts in dungarees with old friends like the Robert Taylors. As they always had, the Reagans shunned the restaurant-night club-premiere life of Hollywood.

However, Ronald Reagan continued to speak across the country and he continued to discover that what he said received perceptibly more partisan reactions.

"It's a curious thing," he wrote in his autobiography in 1965; "I talked on this theme of big government during six years of the Eisenhower administration and was accepted as presenting a non-partisan viewpoint. The same speech delivered *after* Jan. 20, 1961, brought down thunders of wrath on my mind, the charge that my speech was a partisan political attack, an expression of right wing extremism. My erstwhile associates in organized labor at the top level of the AFL-CIO assail me as a 'strident voice of the right wing lunatic fringe.' Sadly I have come to realize that a great many so-called liberals aren't liberal—they will defend to the death your right to agree with them."

He concluded what a large number of political philosophers have come to admit, "the labels somehow have got pasted on the wrong people.

"The conservatives believe the collective responsibility of the qualified men in a community should decide its course. The liberals believe in remote and massive strong-arming from afar, usually Washington, D.C. The conservatives believe in the unique powers of the individual and his personal opinions. The liberals lean increasingly toward bureaucracy, operation by computer minds and forced fiat, the submergence of man in statistics. . . .

"It is a fascinating phenomenon of our times. One of change, certainly; perhaps degeneracy. Our weaknesses have overnight become strengths."

Many public figures, including Sen. Barry Goldwater of Arizona, were making the same analysis and sounding the same warning but few equaled Reagan's ability to simplify and dramatize the philosophical change taking place. It seemed obvious to many people, and a growing number of politicians, that the actor's real place was not Hollywood, but Sacramento or Washington, D.C. This was not a new thought: Democrats had attempted to persuade Ronald

---

* In 1966, a few days before Election Day, he sold the ranch to 20th Century Fox for a reported $2 million, retaining the right to use the ranch until the film studio formally moved there.

Reagan to run for Congress in the late forties—against Congressman Donald Jackson, a member, of all things, of the House Committee on Un-American Activities. Reagan rejected the Democratic offer. He was approached in 1962 to run for either the Republican gubernatorial or senatorial nomination, but turned both down, campaigning strenuously for Nixon. In 1964, he was again approached by Republicans, this time about the senatorial nomination. He again declined and his old friend, George Murphy, was tapped to run against Pierre Salinger, beating the former press secretary to John F. Kennedy in a major upset. So it might have continued for years, with his conscience gnawing at him but he not knowing exactly how to still it. But then, in the fall of 1964, he made The Speech.

Ronald Reagan and Barry Goldwater had been good friends for many years (the Reagan family vacationed every year in Phoenix—Goldwater's home town) and when Goldwater was nominated for President it was the most natural of appointments for Reagan to become co-chairman of California Citizens for Goldwater-Miller. Once again, as he had done for Nixon, he hit the "sawdust trail," made speeches, attended fund-raising events and impressed the voters of California. A late October telecast revealed nationally what a lot of Californians already knew: Ronald Reagan was a natural politician.

The broadcast came late in the campaign, on Tuesday evening, October 27, only one week before Election Day. Senator Goldwater's campaign manager, Denison Kitchel, and the Senator's single most important backroom advisor, William Baroody, had read the script of the proposed telecast and were against it. It was too "emotional" and "un-scholarly," they agreed. And it referred to social security in such a negative way that it was certain, they insisted, to stir up public fears once again about Barry Goldwater's views on social security. Here is the passage that so concerned Baroody and the others:

"Now are we so lacking in business sense that we cannot put this (Social Security) program on a sound actuarial basis, so that those who do depend on it won't come to the cupboard and find it bare, and at the same time can't we introduce voluntary features so that those who can make better provisions for themselves are allowed to do so? Incidentally, we might also allow participants in Social Security to name their own beneficiaries, which they cannot do in the present program. These are not insurmountable problems."

Dangerous and negative, concluded Baroody and the others. But they were in a dilemma. They had bought a half-hour of prime television time and they had to fill it with *something*. Someone suggested a rerun of a program called "Brunch with Barry," which featured the Senator and a half-dozen ladies talking about the high prices and the war in Vietnam. "Brunch with Barry" had been well received when it was first viewed and was effective enough in a low-key way. But it was scarcely the blockbuster of a program urgently needed in the fading days of a national campaign.

A call came in from California, less than three hours before show-time. The chairman of the Goldwater TV Committee stated politely but firmly that Baroody and Kitchel had better okay the Reagan telecast—or find the money for their program. The TV Committee would *not* release funds for any other show. Faced with this ultimatum, Baroody reluctantly granted permission for showing the television program which was to make political history.

The next morning, a flood of telegrams, letters and telephone calls hit the Republican National Committee, lauding the Reagan show and asking for a repeat. The program was shown again nationally the following Saturday night and was telecast hundres of times by state, county and local Goldwater committees.

"A Time for Choosing," as it was called, shifted tens of thousands of votes. It raised over $600,000 for the national campaign through a brief plea for funds which ended the program. It was called the "one bright spot in a dismal campaign" by *Time*. Authors David Broder and Stephen Hess called the speech "the most successful national political debut since William Jennings Bryan electrified the 1896 Democratic convention. . . ." And, it made Ronald Reagan a national political "star" overnight.*

The Speech embodies all of Reagan's very best qualities. It is filled with facts and specifics. It has humor. It takes firm stands based on principles. It is dramatic, poetic, and profoundly moving. Reagan delivered it superbly, not simply because he is a trained speaker and actor, but because he believed it, and had believed it for many years. It was not a script he was handed to study and memorize a few days before the broadcast. It was the product of his own thinking and research, it was the essence of his philosophy which had crystallized and matured years before and which now received its first national exposure.

America had come, he said, to "a time for choosing" between free enterprise and big government—between individual liberty and "the ant heap of totalitarianism." The results were electric and its

---

* Nelle Reagan was not there to share her son's triumph, having died in 1962.

concluding sentences were prophetic, especially for the man who uttered them:

"You and I have a rendezvous with destiny. We can preserve for our children this the last best hope of man on earth or we can sentence them to take the first step into a thousand years of darkness. If we fail, at least let our children and our children's children say of us we justified our brief moment here. We did all that could be done."

PART TWO

THE CANDIDATE

Chapter Eight

The *Only* Candidate

In late February of 1965 a group of influential leaders in the California Republican Party called on Ronald Reagan. Among them were A. C. (Cy) Rubel, former head of Union Oil Company; Henry Salvatori, chairman of the Western Geophysical Company of America, and Holmes Tuttle, one of the biggest auto distributors in Los Angeles. All were conservatives, all had raised millions of dollars for the GOP, and all were tired of losing elections. They came right to the point:

"Ron," they said, in essence, "we think you are the only candidate around whom the party can rally in the 1966 gubernatorial race. We think you can win and we are willing to underwrite your 'campaigning' for the rest of the year. Travel around the state, find out for yourself whether you are acceptable to the party and if you are, *run*."

At first Reagan said flatly, "No." Then at their insistence, he agreed to think it over. He was very skeptical. He had never seriously considered running for public office. He had turned down similar offers in 1962 and 1964. He knew that the nomination contest and the general election afterwards would demand more of him than anything he had ever done before. After all, he had always campaigned for someone else—never himself. But so many people now insisted that *he* run. The preceding November, Frank Jordan, California's Secretary of State and the only Republican to hold statewide office, had publicly declared, "I would certainly like to see Reagan run for governor." The actor himself had admitted in the same month that the mail reaction to his national telecast for Barry Goldwater had exceeded anything else in his career. It was causing him, he added, to give some "second thoughts" to his political future.

Finally, after many talks with his wife Nancy, and ensuing sleepless nights, he told the group that he would run *provided* that he became convinced that the party would unite behind him. Political considerations were not his sole motivation. He also decided to run through that sense of duty which has always motivated him. He was determined not to be the cause of any intraparty squabbles such as had seriously weakened the party in 1958, 1962 and 1964. He also knew that a Republican can only win in California, with its three-to-two Democratic registration, with a united Republican Party behind him. As he later explained, "I happen to feel very strongly that we have reached a period in which the philosophical differences between the two parties are so great that it is high time that more people from the rank and file of the citizenry involve themselves, so that we can have govenment *of and by,* as well as for the people."

Why did these prominent Republicans think so highly of Reagan? Because in many ways, he was an ideal candidate for the giant, golden state of California.

(1) He had unquestioned charm and voter appeal, to men as well as women. As *Los Angeles* magazine stated: "He is one of those rare men whom other men can stomach even while large groups of women are adoring him."

(2) He lived in Los Angeles in the more populous southern half of the state. Nearly 40 percent of the electorate resides in the greater Los Angeles area.

(3) He was assured of substantial financial backing, an absolute necessity in a state of then over 19 million people and a coastline that stretches 840 miles.

(4) He would have organizational muscle: the same dedicated people who worked so hard for Barry Goldwater in California in 1964 could be depended upon to turn out for Reagan.

(5) As a former Democrat, he cut across party lines in a state where party loyalty had never been strong. Starting with Gov. Hiram Johnson back in 1911, statewide candidates invariably ran on their records and personalities.

(6) He was a master of television, the medium which is so important in the far-flung reaches of California.

(7) He had a name already known by millions of people through his movies and television series. (According to polls, he began the campaign with a 97 percent identity factor.)

(8) For all the Hollywood glow, Reagan was an earnest, intelligent man who projected these qualities in person or on the screen.

And George Murphy's senatorial victory in 1964 showed that

the "mere actor" charge was not very effective with California voters.

Finally, those who had studied his career knew that he was blessed with that elusive quality ever present in winners—luck. In college, radio, Hollywood, business, television and politics, he was usually in the right place at the right time with the right answer.

The answer which he developed in the coming months for a badly divided Republican Party was: Let's work and win together. Let's stop pinning labels on each other, and start pinning back the ears of the opposition. It was just the right balm for California Republicans still aching and smarting from the deep wounds of the Goldwater versus Rockefeller presidential primary in 1964, the Dick Nixon versus Joseph Shell gubernatorial primary in 1962 and the William Knowland-Goodwin Knight-George Christopher debacle in 1958.

After three straight major defeats the party wanted a winner, and the small group of Republicans who came calling on Reagan in early 1965 aimed to oblige. They demonstrated their seriousness by enabling Reagan to hire the best political campaign firm in the state, Spencer-Roberts and Haffner of Los Angeles and San Francisco, to help Reagan. The signing up of this firm was most important—politically and psychologically.

Formed in 1960, Spencer-Roberts had compiled an impressive record of forty-one victories out of forty-eight major political races. Among its clients had been Rep. John Rousselot (1960), Sen. Thomas Kuchel (1962), Representatives Del Clawson and Don Clausen (1962), Nelson Rockefeller (the 1964 presidential primary) and several Los Angeles County Council candidates. They were hired to run Sen. Thomas Kuchel's reelection campaign in 1968, but liberal Kuchel lost to conservative Max Rafferty in the GOP primary.

Spencer-Robers did not handle Democrats but did service a wide variety of Republicans—excepting what they call "kooks." All Republicans were agreed that the firm was the number one political management outfit in California. (Barry Goldwater sought its expertise for the 1964 California primary but made a firm offer too late—a Rockefeller man was there first with a blank check.) Stu Spencer and Bill Roberts, then in their early forties, were indefatigable men who thrived on eighteen-hour days.

Reagan insisted to Rubel, Salvatori and Tuttle that he wanted the best professional help available. Spencer and Roberts met the actor for the very first time in April 1965, at a Hollywood restaurant. A second meeting took place at Reagan's home in Pacific Palisades, with partner Fred Haffner of San Francisco participating. Most of the questions were asked by the three political pros. At a third meeting, held again at the prospective candidate's home in early May, Reagan asked most of the questions. Finally, there was nothing more to ask. The four men looked at each other and with smiles all around made a commitment to "go all the way if things went right."

Bill Roberts, who functioned as campaign director throughout 1965 and 1966, told me that Ronald Reagan "in all sincerity approached this thing with the idea he could help the Party and unify the Party. We thought so too. We also thought he could win."

With the skilled Spencer-Roberts team in his corner and solid financial backing, Ronald Reagan began traveling in the spring of 1965—packing houses and setting attendance records wherever he went. His charm, his articulateness and his candor captivated audiences from San Diego to Redding.

In June, 1965, a blue-chip citizens committee was formed, called "Friends of Ronald Reagan," to demonstrate widespread party support for his impending candidacy. Its leadership included many of the top Republicans, liberal and conservative, in the state. Among them were:

(1) Cy Rubel, a delegate to the 1964 GOP National Convention, finance chairman for Joseph Shell in 1962 and a member of the Murphy for Senator Finance Committee in 1964.

(2) David Chow, an importer-exporter, who headed Chinese-American committees for Nixon in 1952, Goodwin Knight in 1954, and Kuchel in 1962.

(3) Philip Davis, attorney, co-chairman in 1964 of California Citizens for Goldwater-Miller.

(4) Dr. Nolan Frizzelle, optometrist, 1964 president of the California Republican Assembly, one of the two important political organizations in the state which operates outside the regular party.

(5) Bruce Reagan (no relation), business executive, a founder of the United Republicans of California, the other statewide political organization outside the GOP.

(6) Walter Knott, one of the top conservatives and fund raisers in California.

(7) Henry Salvatori, one of the GOP's chief financial supporters and a strong Nixon and Goldwater backer.

(8) Mrs. Norman Taurog, civic and social leader, a Rockefeller delegate in 1964.

(9) Jack L. Warner, film executive and a prominent Kuchel supporter.*

Friends of Ronald Reagan went to work lining up other prominent Republicans of every philosophical bent—and raising money as well. By late summer of 1965 a GOP consensus was beginning to coalesce that Ronald Reagan ought to be the man to run against Gov. Edmund (Pat) Brown.

The actor surprised a lot of people by displaying more than a passing knowledge of state issues. It was no accident. Spencer and Roberts closeted him with experts on every imaginable California subject, from redwoods to water to taxes to agriculture. Many of them were academicians (especially from UCLA—University of California at Los Angeles) who gave both sides of a problem and recommended books and pamphlets for additional study. Comments Roberts: "Reagan has an extremely retentive mind and is a voracious reader."

By September, Ronald Reagan had pretty much made up his mind to run for the nomination, expressing his growing confidence by publicly saying:

"My initial explorations and conversations lead me to feel that I can obtain the necessary support within my party as well as gain the support of hundreds of thousands of disenchanted Democrats so necessary for a Republican victory."

Democrats had much about which to be disenchanted and discouraged. No matter where they looked, they were confronted with most unpleasant statistics.

Taxes were up. Per capita state taxes since 1959 (Brown's first year in office) had increased from $117.58 to $157.36. Brown estimated that more than $250 million in new taxes would be needed in 1966.

State spending was up. Brown had proposed a budget of $4.5 billion—the highest state budget ever recorded in US history (until Reagan's first budget). During Brown's tenure in office, California population increased 27 percent while the state budget increased 87 percent.

Crime was up, California's crime rate rising 12 percent in 1965. With 9 percent of the nation's population, California accounted for 17 percent of the crime.

---

* Warner's enlistment took much of the bite out of the oft-quoted story of what he was reported to have said when told that Reagan might run for governor. "No," said Warner. "Jimmy Stewart for governor. Ronald Reagan for best friend."

Prices were up. Pollution and traffic were up. Welfare costs had increased 73 percent during Brown's administration.

The Berkeley demonstrations and the Watts riots had stained California's reputation from coast to coast.

Gov. Brown, though clearly not responsible for *all* California's problems, had to assume responsibility for them as chief executive—and accept the voters' displeasure as well.

Issues were one side of the frayed Brown image. The other side was the man himself. When asked what he thought of Brown, the average Californian would usually reply, "Well, I like him—but he's kind of indecisive (or bumbling) (or erratic) (or slow) (or naive)."

Democratic leaders could read the writing on the wall as well as anyone but they were stymied. Brown announced he was going to run for a third four-year term. He had the patronage and the organizational leverage as governor. Furthermore, President Johnson had quietly indicated that Brown was his man and he wanted no fuss and no primary challenge. LBJ was not to get his wish because of the feisty, maverick Democratic Mayor of Los Angeles, Sam Yorty.

However, it wasn't all smooth riding for the Reagan bandwagon. In August, a director of the California Republican Assembly declared that Ronald Reagan had boasted that the public relations director of the John Birch Society would endorse him for governor or attach him, whichever would do the most good. If true, the charge would have been damaging in two ways: first, it would have suggested that Reagan was on intimate terms with a top Birch official, lending credence to the claim that he was a "captive" of the extremists; and second, it would have revealed Reagan as a slick political operator and opportunist, rather than the citizen candidate he asserted himself to be.

The CRA director was Mrs. Jane Alexander, who turned out to be a supporter of Joseph Shell for the gubernatorial nomination and, by her own admission, "no fan" of Reagan's. Furthermore, Rousselot had called political manager Bill Roberts months before and had merely offered to "talk up" Reagan in private conversations. Finally, Reagan explained that he had made the reference to Rousselot in a humorous vein but apparently some people had taken him all too seriously.*

The Rousselot offer of support was to be a minor irritant to Reagan for the rest of 1965 and throughout 1966. It was one of the major reasons for his statement on the John Birch Society which he released at the annual meeting of the Republican State Central Committee in San Francisco in late September.

By this time, the only Republican who had publicly declared his candidacy for the gubernatorial nomination was Laughlin Waters, a Los Angeles attorney and a former US attorney for Southern California. He was not a significant candidate.

Other possible candidates were former Governor Goodwin Knight, almost 70; conservative Joseph Shell; and the most serious challenger of them all, George Christopher, San Francisco's mayor from 1956 to 1964.**

Christopher was a bona fide liberal who had served as Northern California chairman of Rockefeller's unsuccessful primary drive in 1964. In 1958, he was beaten in the Republican primary for the US Senate nomination by then Governor Knight. In 1962, he was defeated for lieutenant governor by Glenn Anderson although he did come closer to winning than Richard Nixon. Christopher, in the words of one reporter, "looks and talks like a losing television wrestler."

At the September State Central Committee meeting, Christopher held a news conference which underscored the reporter's description. One sample of his malaprop prose:

"We (Republicans) have straddled the fence with both ears to the ground at the same time too long."

Christopher denounced John Birchers—implying that Reagan was their candidate—and the next moment claimed Reagan was once a member of three communist-front organizations.

Asked to identify the three communist fronts, Christopher said: "They're in his book." (An apparent reference to Reagan's autobiography, *Where's the Rest of Me?)* Pressed further about his

* That fall, on October 16, Mrs. Alexander was ousted as a director-at-large of the California Republican Assembly by a vote of 27-9. She was removed on charges that she had embarrassed the CRA by a "breach of confidence" that "brought discredit" on Ronald Reagan.

** Senator Thomas Kuchel, who led every other Republican against Pat Brown in the polls, took himself irrevocably out of the governor's race in mid-September.

charge, Christopher said he didn't have the names of the three organizations "at my fingertips."

The news conference broke up with reporters shaking their heads and Christopher supporters concealing their despair as best as they could.

At this same meeting, on September 24, 1965, Reagan released a one-page statement about the John Birch Society, which became one of his most widely distributed pieces of campaign literature. It deserves to be quoted in its entirety:

"Many words have been spoken and written about the John Birch Society as an issue, particularly with regard to the stance and attitude of the Republican Party, even though the Society claims it is non-partisan and that its membership is almost equally divided between Democrats and Republicans. In recent months my name has been repeatedly injected into articles and discussions concerning the John Birch Society and its membership.

"I have never been and I am not now a member of the John Birch Society, nor do I have any intention of every becoming a member. I have never sought Birch Society support, nor do I have any intention of doing so should I become a candidate for public office.

"In my opinion those persons who are members of the John Birch Society have a decision to make concerning the reckless and imprudent statements of their leader, Mr. Welch.

"In all fairness to the members of this Society, I believe this statement would be incomplete if I failed to point out that despite the heavy criticism of the Society by many citizens, Mr. J. Edgar Hoover, Director of the FBI, is on record as stating that the FBI has not investigated the Birch Society because it only investigates subversive organizations. Furthermore, the California Senate Sub-Committee in its 1963 report found the 'Birch Society to be a Right, anti-communist, fundamentalist organization . . . neither secret nor fascist, nor have we found the great majority of its members in California to be mentally unstable, crackpots, or hysterical about the threat of Communist subversion.' The report, however, was highly critical of the Society's domination by its founder, Robert Welch, and of his book, *The Politician,* published several years before the Society was formed. I wish at this time to reaffirm my criticism of Mr. Welch and restate that I am in great disagreement with much of what he says. In my opinion, his charges against former President Eisenhower are utterly reprehensible.

"The 1965 California Senate report does not disavow any of the

1963 findings, but is more critical of the Society mainly because of 'inexcusable actions of a minority of irresponsible members and evidence of anti-Semitism in that minority.' According to this report, the Society has grown tremendously since 1963 and has attracted a 'lunatic fringe of emotionally unstable people.' Again, however, the Committee points out they are not representative of the Society's official policy. In my opinion, the Society has a responsibility to maintain vigilance to see that this element does not use the Society for witch-hunting, anti-semitism or any other un-American activity.

"For the record, I would like also to state that I am opposed in principle to seeking support of any blocks or groups because in principle to do so implies a willingness to make promises in return for such support. It would be my intention, if I seek public office, to seek the support of individuals by persuading them to accept my philosophy, not by my accepting theirs. I would campaign on such important issues as the bureaucratic growth of our State Government, the excessive taxation that is already slowing California's economic growth and reducing job opportunities, and the increasing crime rate that makes our cities' streets a place of danger after dark."

Reagan made it clear: he would not seek support of the society (which does not endorse political candidates anyway); he described Robert Welch as "reckless and imprudent," and he quoted two California legislative reports which criticized the society but did not make any blanket condemnation of the society. It was to be his firm stand throughout the campaign. As he was to say again and again:

"If anyone chooses to vote for me, they are buying my views, I am not buying theirs."

Still another statement at the meeting, this one by a non-candidate, was to play a major role, not only in the nomination race but in the general election as well. Dr. Gaylord Parkinson, chairman of the California Republican Party, issued a statement to the news media entitled, "Parkinson's Eleventh Commandment." It began:

"I want to tell you how the Republicans are going to conduct themselves in this campaign. . . . That day has passed when we can permit ourselves to air differences we have in the press or on television. To attack another Republican leader in the public media, that Republican will suffer severe reverses. . . .

"The reverses I refer to involve what might be called a revulsion of that candidate across the board. His ratings will drop drastically in the public opinion polls, his workers will wither away, his financial resources will dry up and he will be rejected at the polls."

Parkinson said he was offering his Eleventh Commandment to all who would become Republican candidates in 1966:

"Thou shall not speak ill of any Republican."

Parkinson, while not detailing how he would enforce it, warned that "if henceforth and until November, 1966, any Republican candidate or leader in California deliberately speaks out against the party or against a fellow Republican that activity will endanger his very position of leadership, his candidacy, and most important, the good of the party."

A number of reporters smiled cynically at Parkinson's ploy, remembering the divisive battles of 1958, 1962 and 1964. What they apparently did not realize was that the very memories of those self-destructive campaigns would make the Eleventh Commandment almost irresistible. Beyond dispute, Parkinson's Commandment was to help cement the GOP for the next fifteen months, and to make it virtually impossible for candidates like George Christopher to attack without cause the smiling frontrunner, Ronald Reagan. The State Central Committee unanimously endorsed the Eleventh Commandment. Reagan was delighted. He knew he needed a united GOP behind him to win the general election.

Chapter Nine

Hat in the Ring

In the wake of the State Central Committee meeting, at which the efforts of George Christopher and Goodwin Knight upset even their most partisan supporters, anti-Reagan forces within the GOP began casting about frantically for a candidate. The certain black aftermath of a Reagan victory was described for them by Sen. Kuchel who urged Republicans to keep a "fanatical neo-Fascist political cult" from taking over the party. The gentle Senator named no names, of course.

In this emotional atmosphere, still another name was suggested: Robert T. Monagan, Republican leader of the State Assembly. At forty-five, Monagan had established himself in the legislature as an excellent legislator and was looked on with favor by almost all of the liberals and many conservatives as well. But, and it was a big but, Monagan came from a small town in Northern California, the less populous half of the state; he was not well known to the general public; he had no organizaton and no visible money. Monagan supporters pushed his name hard for several weeks, and did succeed in getting the Republican legislator mentioned in the state and national press. Columnists Rowland Evans and Robert Novak described Monagan as "highly respected" in the California legislature. But that was just about all. Monagan's candidacy, at best a slim possibility, disappeared completely when George Christopher formally announced on October 26, 1965, that he was running for the Republican nomination.

Speaking in ten cities on a whirlwind schedule, the former mayor of San Francisco declared that he had the administrative and executive experience to be governor unlike some others he could name—like Ronald Reagan. He pointed to the polls which showed

85

he was running 4.9 percent better than Reagan against Pat Brown. He did not mention that the same polls showed him running 10 percent *behind* Reagan among Republican voters. Eight months later, on the eve of the June primary, Christopher was seventeen points behind Reagan among Republicans.

Some comic relief was injected on November 15 when William P. Patric, a thirty-five-year-old cosmetics manufacturer who had never before run for public office, announced his candidacy for the Republican nomination for Governor of California. Patrick was outwardly serious about his intentions and asserted he had $1.5 million to spend on his campaign. He termed himself a progressive Republican with views more like Sen. Kuchel "than anyone else in California politics." If he had been a serious candidate, his entry would have hurt liberal Christopher. But Patrick was never a factor although he did obtain considerable publicity for himself and his cosmetics firm.

Three weeks later, at the first annual convention of the California Republican League, a brand-new liberally oriented volunteer organization, candidate Laughlin Waters got off several blasts at Reagan, who also attended the meeting. In his formal remarks, although he refrained from using names, Waters declared: "We cannot afford to put up a candidate who is a political switch-hitter, or a tyro, or who appeals only to a minority even in our own party."

That just about covered all bases: (1) "political switch-hitter" obviously referred to Reagan's past as a liberal Democrat; (2) "tyro" referred to Reagan's non-experience in public office; and (3) "appeals only to a minority" meant, in Waters' opinion, that Reagan's brand of conservatism was very limited in its appeal.

Waters really warmed up during a panel discussion. When Reagan told a questioner that he was "not at this time" a candidate for governor, Waters accused the actor of "political dishonesty," asserting that he had told a group in October that "he had passed the point of no return in his candidacy."

The former US attorney for Southern California also repeated the old story, attributed to Reagan, that John Rousselot, the public relations director of the John Birch Society, had offered to support or oppose Reagan, "whichever was deemed to be better."

As he was to do throughout 1966, Reagan kept his cool. He explained that he had made the remark about Rousselot "facetiously" and reiterated that he was not soliciting the support of the John Birch Society, was not a member and had "no intention of soliciting their support."

As for the nomination, he stated that while it had to be assumed his answer on a formal declaration of candidacy would be yes, "I've also said, of course, you keep one foot back in case the sky starts to fall."

It didn't and on January 4, 1966, after traveling ten thousand miles and making 150 speeches, Ronald Reagan announced his candidacy for the Republican nomination for governor in a superbly staged television appearance, news conference and public reception. The thirty-minute television program was carried on sixteen stations throughout the state—a first in California politics for a gubernatorial candidate. A top Reagan advisor told me they used this technique to prevent any Goldwaterizing of the candidate. The heavy use of television was to be a consistent pattern for the rest of the year: put Ronald Reagan directly before the people and let *them* make up their own minds, without benefit of interpretation by anyone, as to whether he would make a good governor.

The timing of the announcement was carefully planned. A preview of the TV program for the news media was followed by a regular news conference which ended at 5 p.m. The program was aired at 6 p.m., meaning that the public had an unobstructed viewing of Reagan.

In his television talk, the candidate, speaking without notes, stressed such bread and butter issues as property taxes (too high), relief (too many "freeloaders"), rising crime, and too high unemployment. Among his proposed solutions were a tax moratorium on homes owned by elderly citizens, an improved business climate, laws permitting "local ordinances that will restore to the police the flexibility and power in making arrests," and higher pay for state legislators.

As he had for many years, he emphasized the dangerous growth of big government, asking: "Can we possibly believe that anyone can manage our lives better than we can manage them ourselves?"

Reagan intended to base his campaign on the belief that the majority's answer would be "no"—if the people could be convinced that a governor *would* let them govern themselves whenever and wherever possible.

The candidate's presentation over television was described by the *New York Times* as "highly effective—so effective in fact, that he stood a solid chance of winning not only the nomination but also the office."

Equally impressive was his performance before two hundred reporters (the largest turnout ever for a purely state political event) at the news conference that followed the preview of his TV talk. They threw everything they could think of at Reagan and he caught every one, with a smile. The candidate answered questions from the stage of a ballroom at the Statler Hilton in downtown Los Angeles. The stage was flanked by six-foot photographs of him and his name was spelled out in glittering silver letters that ran some twenty feet across the wall behind him. Nancy Reagan, in a red, fur-trimmed dress, was by his side.

Almost the first question was about the John Birch Society—would he oppose their support?

"It is my understanding," Reagan replied, "that the Birch Society does not support either candidates or political parties and has stated that its membership is roughly, even divided between the two parties."

How would he describe his relations with John Rousselot, the society's director of public relations?

"Well, I haven't seen him for quite some time. The last time really that I was with him was when he was a Republican Congressman and it was friendly."

Had he ever had any discussion with John Birch officials about his candidacy?

"Never."

Did he believe there were members of the Birch Society in the Republican Party?

"I have issued a statement.* It is available here as to how I feel. I am not going to submit a loyalty oath or test to anybody who decides he wants to vote for me. I don't know how I could do it. If anybody decides he wants to vote for me, he has bought my philosophy; I haven't bought his."

Did he believe there was a place in the Republican Party for Birch Society members?

"I think there is a place in any political party for anyone who feels he can conscientiously support the aims and the goals of that party."

More substantive questions were asked. What about Watts; what could be done about the situation there?

"I think one idea, pattern to be extended and followed is the very fine example that has been set by the Los Angeles Chamber of Commerce which has already enlisted the aid of more than 100

* See above, chapter 8.

industries and expects to expand that (and) has already found jobs for more than a thousand. . . .

"I think an expansion of this is what I referred to in my statement, an expansion of that idea of improving the business climate and seeking out what inducements you could think of, or incentives, to improve the business climate, including the possibilities of tax incentives. . . . I think basically with a great many of these problems, their solution lies in more jobs for people."

What about his lack of political background?

"As I have stated, I am not a politician in the sense of every having held public office. My administrative and executive experience has been what I outlined briefly in my statement—business experience. But I just happen to have a deep-seated belief that it is high time that some of the people from the rank-and-file citizenry should involve themselves in government so that it will be a government of and by, as well as for, the people. And feeling that way, I think I can qualify as a citizen-politician and I don't believe that the country was created by men who were politicians."

What about his past as a Democrat; why and when did he become disenchanted?

"My disenchantment was a growing thing. I wasn't as smart as Al Smith; I didn't do it that early. I have often said that I think that there was as much the Democratic Party leaving me, or the leadership of that party leaving me, as my leaving the party."

Was there any real difference between the Republican approach to problems and the Democratic approach such as the Great Society?

"Yes . . . . I again think I voiced it in my statement that I don't believe the pattern that has been laid down by the present Great Society can at the same time include a free society. And I think what we must have in America is the opportunity for all who are willing to accept opportunity; and, at the same time, compassion and care for all those who, through no fault of their own, are unable to accept it.

"You know the Jewish book, the Talmud, has several steps for helping people: the least desirable, the last resort, is the handout, the dole; the most desirable and the most effective is to help people to help themselves and that, I think, probably typifies the Republican approach."

Was he a right-wing Republican?

"No, and I don't believe any more in hyphenating Republicans than I do in hyphenating Americans, I don't think the labels mean anything any more, and I think if people will listen to my specific

views in the months ahead on issues and where I stand, there won't
be any need for such labels.''

How would his campaign appeal to Democrats as well as Republicans?

"Again, I think the problems that face California cross party
lines. I think that the solutions *must* cross party lines and I don't
know of anyone who knows any better on the Republican side how
Democrats think than I do. I was one for most of my life, and I
believe that there are millions of fine, patriotic and sincere Democrats who are as concerned as anyone about fiscal irresponsibility,
excessive taxation, the growth of government—and I expect to appeal to them.''

Would he accept the challenge from George Christopher to have
a television debate?

"I'm not in favor and I don't believe in Republican debating
Republican in public. I think we have had too much of that already.
My contest is with the present administration in Sacramento and I
intend to keep it that way.''

Would he debate Gov. Brown?

"There is a long way until you get to that. There's a primary
contest in between. Then I have a hunch that I'll be debating him
quite actively in the months ahead. But I don't know. Maybe Mr.
Salinger would advise him not to.''*

Did he really feel that he could bring about the changes he
thought were so necessary in only four years as governor?

"Let me say that anyone would be naive as far as this is, to
think that suddenly you could wave a wand and make a great change.
I think what has to happen is you first dig in your heels and slow
down the toboggan and hope you can bring it to a stop and then
you start trying to push it back up the hill. I would think your aim
would be, and mine certainly would be, to start pushing it back up
the hill as fast as I could. But in the meantime, I'd first be trying
to slow it down.''

What was the one issue above all others in the campaign?

"To retire Pat Brown.''

The reporters roared with laughter, but Pat Brown didn't. He
immediately issued a twelve-page statement which, the governor
claimed, refuted Reagan's criticisms of him and his administration.
It received scant attention. In truth, the Democrats were very wor-

* Pierre Salinger was decisively bested by George Murphy in a series of TV debates in
1964.

ried. The State Democratic Chairman, Robert L. Coate, declared that Reagan was "an extremely strong candidate. We fear him." Reagan's Republican opponents were no less concerned.

Sniffed George Christopher about the TV talk: "It was a well-rehearsed production." But he wondered how Reagan would handle such "real-life" problems as crime or tax reform that were outside his world of "make-believe."

Laughlin Waters huffed: "I'm all for on-the-job training but not at the gubernatorial level." He added that Reagan's announcement would give the California GOP an opportunity to decide whether it chooses "to attempt again positions which were overwhelmingly rejected nationally and in California during the last election or whether it will return to the moderate and winning position."

Reagan's response to his fellow Republicans was simple and effective: "I will have no word of criticism for any Republican."

The definitive word about his kick-off news conference was written by Carl Greenburg, political editor of the Los Angeles *Times,* and one of the most objective of all California political analysts:

"If Ronald Reagan is the complete political nincompoop his opponents claim, they certainly went to a lot of trouble paying attention to him when he announced his candidacy for the Republican gubernatorial nomination.

"He was drenched in vitriol and sprayed with verbal napalm. . . .

"Whether I agreed with everything Reagan had to say is unimportant, but to this observer his handling of questions at the press conference that followed his announcement indicated Reagan is no novice or babe-in-the-woods."

Chapter Ten

On the Hustings

The polls showed that the people liked the actor turned candidate. The State Poll, sponsored by the Los Angeles *Times,* gave Ronald Reagan 41.2 percent of the Republican vote; George Christopher 27.8 percent, and former Governor Goodwin J. Knight 9.6 percent. However, in a sampling of both parties Reagan ranked over Pat Brown by only 46.8 percent to 42.4 percent, while George Christopher was far ahead of the Democratic governor, 50.3 percent to 35.2 percent. "Goody" Knight also topped Brown by 45.3 to 40.1. The message was clear: Republicans preferred Reagan by a wide margin but the general public wasn't quite sure just what kind of a governor he would make. The brand new candidate set out to convince the people of California that he would do very well indeed.

Campaigning was neither strange nor new to Ronald Reagan. He had campaigned extensively for two presidential candidates and one gubernatorial candidate. In 1953, he campaigned vigorously for Mayor Fletcher Bowron of Los Angeles in a hard fought reelection contest. Nine years later he was honorary campaign chairman for Loyd Wright in his try for the GOP nomination for US Senator.

In his eight years with the *General Electric Theater,* he had traveled tens of thousands of miles back and forth across the United States visiting with and listening to people. Reagan liked to talk, he liked to get up on a platform, he liked the challenge of the question and answer period which follows many speeches. He also happened to believe that the kind of government he proposed was urgently needed. His campaign for better, more responsive, less costly and more creative government swept away many of the public's hesitations and doubts in the next ten months.

He worked hard. He had to. California is not only the largest state in population but the third largest in area, with 156,573 square miles. It has fifty-eight counties, ranging from tiny Alpine with only four hundred inhabitants to gigantic, sprawling Los Angeles with over seven million people.

California is a state of contrasts and extremes. Its highest point is Mount Whitney, 14,495 feet high. Its lowest point is Death Valley, 282 feet below sea level, the lowest in the nation. It is the nation's leading state in farm marketing income and second only to New York in manufacturing. It ranks first in chickens and turkeys, third in sheep, fifth in cattle. It grows more fruit than you can shake a bowl at. Its vineyards are a major industry in themselves, and produce wines which are as good as anything found in France outside the great Bordeaux and Burgundy growths.

California has Disneyland, Knott's Berry Farm, Balboa Park, Sea World, the San Diego Zoo, three major league baseball teams, four major league football teams, Hollywood, Lake Tahoe, San Simeon, Monterey, the Golden Gate Bridge, and more automobiles than any other state.

California has 182 institutions of higher learning—84 privately owned colleges and universities, 18 state colleges and the famous University of California with its nine-campus complex.

It has sun, sand, surf and snow. It gave birth to the topless dancer, the topless waitress and the topless political worker.*

It had in 1966 a restless, non-party oriented, TV-minded electorate of 8 million men and women who liked to confound the pollsters, and often did. It was for their attention and their votes that the candidates vied.

Throughout January and February, Ronald Reagan toured up and down the state in a bus, concentrating his attention and his attacks on Gov. Brown and his administration in Sacramento.

He pledged a "moral crusade" to end the "arrogance" of the Brown administration in Sacramento. He spoke of the need for "common sense government." Increasingly he referred to what he called the "creative society,"** which would call upon the talents and abilities of individual citizens, outside as well as inside government, to solve the social and economic problems of California.

---

* In July, 1964, at the GOP National Convention, a young lady in short shorts and a tight blouse selected the partisan-packed lobby of the Mark Hopkins Hotel, headquarters for Barry Goldwater and William Scranton, to remove her blouse and reveal a well-developed unfettered torso while television cameras whirred and whirled.

** A phrase suggested by Rev. W. S. McBirnie, pastor of the United Community Church of Glendale and news analyst on a conservative radio program, "Voice of Americanism."

His favorite target was Pat Brown's $4.6 billion budget, the largest ever submitted to a state legislature.

In a televised speech in San Diego in February, Reagan handled the subject in a characteristically visual way:

"Now I've been told that it's politically unwise to talk about (the budget), that for average citizens like us, four billion, six hundred thousand dollars as a figure is meaningless. Well it is, it's incomprehensible. So, I've been trying to get it down to pocket size, because that's where it is going to come from. . . .

"If I have here a four inch stack of thousand dollar bills in my hand, I would be a millionaire. That's a million dollars—that little handful. But if we had that budget piled up in front of us in thousand dollar bills, the pile would be more than one thousand five hundred feet high. . . .

"If you're an average family in California of four, your share of the ante in that budget is a little over a thousand dollars this year. Now I'm just foolish enough to think that the average Californian has some interest in what someone in Sacramento is going to do with his thousand dollars."

By now, the average Californian was listening closely as the candidate told him how Gov. Brown and his administration intended to spend his money with a budget "characterized by sloppiness, incompetency and a tendency to sell out the future—our future."

The candidate freely admitted that he was not a fiscal expert but had turned to "the most competent authority I could find on this budget—a man employed by the state to analyze the budget." That is how Alan A. Post, a legislative analyst for fifteen years, became one of Regan's most quoted authorities during 1966. He used Post's findings again and again to buttress his conclusions of "sloppiness and incompetency" while the Democrats writhed.

As an alternative, candidate Reagan suggested that "instead of harassing business and industry with regressive taxes, let's adopt a creative approach and ask how we can use government to further free the people to allow us to reach our fullest potential. *We have a leadership gap in Sacramento*. They abdicated their responsibility and they continue to seek the answer to every California problem in Washington."

Reagan hit hard at the political machinations of the Brown machine and the inevitable malpractices which mar an administration too long in office. His voice took on a lyrical note as he described his dream of a Reagan administration:

"Picture, if you will, an administration in our* state capital without any printed charts listing the minimum campaign contributions that will be acceptable from the state employees. Picture instead an administration that proclaims there will be no solicitation of campaign funds from state employees in any campaign, an administration not characterized by political hacks or hangers on, but one that will seek men to match our mountains.

"That will challenge the men and women of this state to give their time and talents in service to their state and to their fellow citizens and be proud to do so. Out of this great pool of technical skill and talents that is the body politic of California, there isn't any problem that we can't solve if we will refer it to the people and trust the people to find the answer.

"President Eisenhower asked, 'Does political experience automatically result in the creation of a statesman or does it just provide a backlog of men skilled in political give and take?' Well, politically experienced men drew up this budget with very little give—and a great deal of take. Now I'm not a politician and that's precisely why I ask your support, precisely why I'm doing what I'm doing in this point of time. I believe very deeply that the time has come for ordinary citizens to bring honor and morality and the clear fresh air of common sense to government."

It made sense. It had appeal. The average Californian was impressed, and said to his wife, "You know, this guy Reagan sounds like he might make a pretty good governor." The word began to get around, galvanizing his opponents into desperate action.

In late January, the anti-Reagan forces in the Republican Party finally persuaded Laughlin Waters to withdraw from the gubernatorial race and former Governor Goodwin Knight not to enter. This narrowed the field to two major candidates, Reagan and George Christopher, prompting Lawrence E. Davies, the *New York Times* correspondent in San Francisco, to write:

"This means, in the eyes of many observers, a contest of two philosophies—a battle between Ronald Reagan, the actor, with heavy conservative and right-wing support, and former Mayor George Christopher of San Francisco, generally pictured as a moderate.

"A straight fight between these two men, Christopher adherents contend, will enable the former Mayor to pin the right-wing label on Mr. Reagan and win the nomination at the June 7 primary.

* In Washington, D. C. as well as Sacramento.

"Reagan advisers call this stand ridiculous."

It was. Reagan had declared himself a candidate only after he had satisfied himself that he was acceptable to people in all wings of the GOP. He consistently refused to describe himself as a conservative, right-wing or Goldwater Republican. He shunned labels and hyphens. His initial campaign organization had liberals and conservatives, Rockefeller as well as Goldwater backers from the 1964 primary. The Christopher camp's logic was not compelling but the former mayor and his associates were obliged to try every possible ploy to warn and frighten the party about Reagan.

The Democrats helped as best they could, knowing that Reagan would be the tougher opponent (although they publicly pretended that Christopher was the man they feared). In late January, just a few days before Pat Brown announced for reelection, a statement by all Democratic county chairmen declared:

"Your probable opponent represents a philosophy so divergent from the mainstream of American democratic institutions as to make it imperative that we oppose him with our most able advocate, our best campaigner."

On February 15, Christopher received a boost when Sen. Thomas H. Kuchel, the GOP's top office holder who had won reelection by 727,644 votes in 1962, announced his support for the former mayor, calling him the leading "moderate" in the contest for the gubernatorial nomination. At a news conference in Los Angeles, Sen. Kuchel said that California needed a governor who would "inspire confidence in people, be unswervingly committed to law and order, believe in equal justice for all and be completely free of the taint of bigotry and hate."

In making the endorsement, the Senator described Christopher as "one who represents Republicans in the Lincoln tradition and the Eisenhower tradition. He is specific and speaks out boldly." Sen. Kuchel delivered his endorsement with a straight face. An ideologue, he apparently believed that Reagan was a willing captive of the right wing.

The very next day, the California (Field) Poll reported the following surprising figures:

Among Republicans:	
Reagan	38%
Christopher	35%
Undecided	27%

Among Republicans and Democrats:

Christopher	45%	Reagan	40%
Pat Brown	37%	Pat Brown	44%
Undecided	18%	Undecided	16%

This represented a gain of seven points by Christopher against frontrunner Reagan among Republicans since the last poll and a similar 7 percent increase by the former mayor over the actor in trial heats against Gov. Brown. However, this poll was received with considerable skepticism by many officials in both parties. The skepticism was confirmed within two weeks when the *New York Times'* political correspondent, David Broder,* wrote, "At least one private survey taken since the poll appeared Feb. 16 has indicated a 10 point advantage for Mr. Reagan" over Christopher.

George Christopher enjoyed another little surge in his campaign following his February 27 appearance before the Republican State Committee at Coronado, across the bay from San Diego. There, he matched oratorial skill with Ronald Reagan, surprising the 275 members of the committee in attendance. But as the *New York Times* reported:

"Mr. Christopher's stand-off with the actor in the applause rating on his speech failed to shake the view among Republican professionals that Mr. Reagan is the favorite in the primary. . . ."

Christopher's "victory" was easily explained: Reagan had a 102-degree temperature and a case of flu which kept him in bed during most of the weekend meeting. When he took his turn on the rostrum his face was flushed and his voice lacked its usual vibrancy. Christopher rightly took full advantage of his opponent's condition and seized the day.

Reagan was still not up to physical par one week later, on March 6, when he blew up publicly for the first and only time during the campaign. (He was still recovering from an eleven-day bout of flu and dysentery.) The setting was the National Negro Republican Assembly's California Convention in Santa Monica. There was an audience of more than one hundred. Reagan, Christopher and William Patrick were invited to present themselves and their views. In his presentation, Reagan said that while he agreed with the goals of the Civil Rights Act, it "was a bad piece of legislation" and that he probably would not have voted for it if he had been in Congress.

In their remarks, both Christopher and Patrick made subtle ref-

* Now with the *Washington Post*.

erences to Reagan's statement, playing to the all-black audience. Reagan became visibly more tense as the meeting progressed.

In the question-and-answer period toward the very end, a delegate said, "It grieves me when a leading Republican candidate says the Civil Rights Act is a bad piece of legislation."

At this, Reagan jumped to his feet, threw down some more cards and said loudly:

"I resent the implication that there is any bigotry in my nature. Don't anyone ever imply I lack integrity. I will not stand silent and let anyone imply that—in this or any other group."

In the ensuing hush, he stalked out of the convention hall.

It was just the kind of emotional outburst that an actor and alleged right-winger should never engage in. A Reagan man was quoted as saying: "A couple more like that and it's curtains."

There were no more "like that." Christopher, and Pat Brown after him, tried relentlessly to provoke a similar blow-up but to no avail. The combination of circumstances which had produced the walk-out never occurred again and the Reagan campaign swept on and up, leaving opponents waiting futilely for the candidate to err.

Reagan's explanation of the incident was straightforward. He had been stewing over insinuations by Christopher and Patrick that he was anti-black. "Bigotry," he said, "is something I feel so strongly about that I get a lump in my throat when I'm accused falsely."

Chapter Eleven

The Creative Society

On March 15, 1966 the Watts area of Los Angeles tragically erupted again, resulting in two deaths, about twenty injuries and forty-nine arrests. Incredibly enough, in the face of the massive 1965 Watts riots when thirty-five were killed and a thousand injured, Gov. Brown was out of the state and country when the latest outbreak occurred—although he had been informed of impending trouble by a black assemblyman.

Reagan denounced Brown for "flagrant dereliction of duty" by going on a trip to Greece after he had been told about a possible outbreak. He declared that the governor should have informed Mayor Sam Yorty and Police Chief William Parker of Los Angeles.

Brown replied, rather lamely, that the warning was one of twenty to twenty-five he had received, that it had not been specific as to time or type of incident and that he *had* albeit routinely, informed the National Guard.

Mayor Yorty, a just-announced candidate for the Democratic nomination for governor against Brown, stated that Gov. Brown had failed to tell him of the Watts rumor.

Reagan and Yorty continued to press Brown hard on this issue for the next three months.

Yorty's entrance into the Democratic primary, although dismissed as inconsequential at first, was to become increasingly significant. If nothing else, Yorty provided Reagan with some quotable language as the Democratic mayor accused the Democratic governor of "indecisiveness and monumental incompetence." Brown, in turn, called Yorty "a cruel, cruel man" and "a renegade."* At this point, Yorty trailed Brown among Democrats by 27.6 percent to 49.2 percent but the large number of undecided (23.2 percent) offered the scrappy mayor an inviting target for his anti-Brown vituperation.

There were other developments:

(1) At the annual convention of the ultra-liberal California Democratic Council, the largest of the party's unofficial organizations, Gov. Brown has booed when he defended President Johnson's Vietnam policy. In fact, when he continued to praise the President about 100 of the convention's 1,800 delegates walked out of the hall.

(2) When Jesse Unruh, Speaker of the California Assembly and the state's most powerful Democrat outside of the governor, was asked by a reporter how Brown was getting along, he replied: "Compared to who?"

(3) A black newspaper publisher and physician, Dr. Carlton B. Goodlett, filed for the Democratic nomination for governor, declaring:

"The Brown administration came into power in 1958 on a progressive and forward-looking Democratic program. During the ensuing years, Brown has given Californians an increasingly conservative and, in most instances, an undistinguished state administration. Brown has been a stumbling, gregarious and uninspiring Governor, who lacks both creative initiative as well as the will to put executive drive behind his legislative programs."

April is the month of conventions in California and it was the cruelest month for the fading aspirations of George Christopher. Republican liberals tried hard to counteract the certain endorsement of Reagan by both the California Republican Assembly and the United Republicans of California, the party's two largest unofficial groups. In late March the Republican Council of California endorsed Christopher. The Council was made up of a handful of liberal legislators and party leaders. Its announcement got one paragraph in the *New York Times*.

Two weeks later, the liberal California Republican League, one year old, about four thousand members strong, endorsed Christopher for governor after having denied Reagan permission to address the delegates at a morning session. The GOP front-runner had asked that the time of his appearance be shifted because a three-day cam-

* Yorty also said: "The Democratic voters deserve an alternative to the mercenary, corrupt, left-wing, entrenched Brown machine."

paign tour had been scheduled before the League had announced its candidates' session. The CRL's president, William P. Gray, turned down the request, but added graciously that he would be happy to acknowledge Reagan's presence.

However, Gray was careful not to allow Reagan's name to be placed in nomination, apparently because he had not addressed the convention. Not one CRL delegate raised his voice in protest, revealing a great deal about the liberal mentality and fondness for fair play.

Following the overwhelming vote for Christopher, William Patrick, the only rival permitted entry, held a news conference at which he angrily charged that the meeting had been "rigged" in favor of the winner. The charge was denied by Gray and Christopher.

And then it was Ronald Reagan's turn. The California Republican Assembly, with 11,500 members, and the United Republicans of California, with 7,500 members, both gave the actor ringing endorsements as their candidate for governor. The CRA, founded thirty years before, had gone conservative in 1964 after several decades of liberal leadership. UROC was founded before the 1964 campaign by a group of conservatives dissatisfied with CRA's liberal ways. Reagan received a hero's welcome at both conventions as he assailed the Brown administration. Christopher, in contrast, continued to make the same basic mistake by ripping into the radical right and candidates who refused to repudiate the radical right—an obvious swipe at Reagan. Christopher was jeered at the CRA convention, which was inexcusable. But the important point is that Christopher never comprehended that the great majority of Republicans were weary of attacks on other Republicans. When Christopher persisted in stomping Reagan rather than Brown, he sealed his fate and his defeat.

Two major issues emerged in May and were quickly picked up by an alert Reagan and his campaign team. In a 153-page report, the State Senate Subcommittee on Un-American Activities accused Clark Kerr, president of the University of California, of having permitted the infiltration of communists which had led to "left wing domination" of the Berkeley campus.

The Committee's major charges:

(1) President Kerr had allowed communist-oriented students and non-students to use campus facilities and become the nation-wide "focal point" of the anti-Vietnam war movement.

(2) Under President Kerr, the "campus sank to a new low" morally. Cited in the report were lewd dances featuring "debased

spectacles" and promiscuity, widespread intoxication and use of marijuana.

The Committee accused Kerr of "unconditional surrender" of leadership, adding:

"As the campus became more and more politicized by radical elements, what few rules remained were simply ignored. In the name of free speech, civil liberties and academic freedom, the campus at Berkeley has been harboring radicals who have no connection with the institution, and who are allowed to use the state facilities without paying any fees, and to plot acts of civil disobedience that are illegal by their very definition."

Kerr called the report "inaccurate" and "distorted" and challenged the senators to produce evidence of communists connected with the Bekeley campus.*

Reagan swiftly called on Gov. Brown to take immediate action "to restore the university to its once high standing." He kept up the pressure and a week later accused Brown of a "cover-up" in asking the UC Board of Regents, which included Kerr, rather than the state legislature, to investigate.

Even before the release of the Senate report, Reagan had been criticizing Brown, ex-officio president of the Board of Regents, for failing to exert leadership and take appropriate steps to correct the bad image of Berkeley across the country. Berkeley was to become a prime issue in the fall campaign and the one that elicited the most emotional response.

The second major issue was created when the State Supreme Court, by a five-to-two vote, overturned a state constitutional provision permitting owners of private property to sell or rent their real estate to whomever they wanted, without regard for race, creed, or color. The provision thrown out was the famous Proposition 14, approved in a statewide referendum in 1964 by a margin of two to one. The proposition had nullified the Rumford Act, prohibiting discrimination in property sales or rentals.

To Ronald Reagan the issue was clear. He approved Proposition 14 because it upheld "the right of a man to dispose of his property or not to dispose of it as he sees fit." The Rumford Act, he said, "by infringement on one of our basic individual rights, sets a precedent which threatens individual liberty."

---

* One obvious name was Bettina Aptheker, self-admitted communist and daughter of the leader communist theoretician in the United States, Herbert Aptheker. Bettina was a prominent leader in the Free Speech Movement along with Mario Savio and also ran for a campus-wide student office. It's unlikely that Kerr had never heard of her at *some* point.

He had been for Proposition 14 in 1964 before it had passed and he was still for it. In contrast, George Christopher loudly applauded the action of the State Supreme Court. Pat Brown did too, although not so loudly. He was adding up the issues and the votes, and too many of them appeared to be coming to rest in the other fellow's corner.

The Reagan bandwagon was now folling merrily along. In speech after speech, the candidate stressed his main theme —Sacramento extravagance and high taxes. He frequently extended his attack to blame Gov. Brown, as a prominent member of the Board of Regents, for the Berkeley demonstrations instituted by a "minority of malcontents, beatniks and filthy-speech advocates."

Gone was any trace of the tension and strain which had erupted at the March meeting with black leaders in Santa Monica. He looked good, somewhere in his early forties unless you got within five feet of him (he was now fifty-five). He sounded good, his resonant baritone never seeming to show any sign of strain. He openly enjoyed what he called the "mashed potato circuit" and even when the temperature soared into the nineties, as the *New York Times'* conceded, the candidate, "dapper in a black suit and pearl-gray tie, remained unruffled and unperspiring."

Potshots were occasionally taken. *Newsweek* reported that he wore pancake makeup. In a letter to the editor, Reagan rejoined that he had never worn it offstage or while making a speech, explaining, "You see, when I was younger, I could get along without it. And now it wouldn't help any."

The *Saturday Evening Post* began a long article: " 'Sure, he's drawing the crowds,' snorts one rival candidate for political office. 'So would Jayne Mansfield.' "

But even the veteran liberal columnist Marquis Childs was obliged to report, "Reagan seems likely to win the nomination for governor."

And although his critics often made fun of it, pretending not to understand what he was talking about, one of Reagan's major appeals was his Creative Society, which he formally discussed at the University of Southern California on April 19. To emphasize the importance of his subject, he spoke from a prepared text, one of only two times he did so in the primary.

After admitting that he was not a politician, Reagan asserted, "It's time now for dreamers—but practical dreamers—willing to re-implement the original dream which became this nation—that idea that has never fully been tried before in the world—that you and I have the capacity for self-government—the dignity and the ability and the God-given freedom to make our own decisions, to plan our own lives and to control our own destiny.''

He argued that we should not automatically turn to the federal government because "with every ounce of Federal help we get, we surrender an ounce of personal freedom. The Great Society grows greater every day—greater in cost, greater in inefficiency and greater in waste.

"What is needed," he declared, "is not *more* government, but *better* government, seeking a solution to the problems that will not add to bureaucracy, or unbalance the budget, or further centralize power. Therefore, I proposed a constructive alternative to the Great Society which I have chosen to call a Creative Society.''

He asserted that "there is no major problem that cannot be resolved by a vigorous and imaginative state administration* willing to utilize the tremendous potential of our people.''

He gave the assembled students several specific things that a Reagan administration would try to do:

(1) In the area of crime, give local communities the right to pass ordinances for the "protection of the people." Also, call upon the "best minds in the field of human relations and law and penology" for a study of our penal and parole systems.

(2) Create a joint committee of laymen and members of the Bar Association which would choose a panel of outstanding individuals from which the governor would be obliged to "appoint all judges," taking "judicial appointments once and for all out of politics.''

(3) As the best brains of the business community what is needed to make California attractive once again to industry—the state had fallen from sixth to thirteenth in attracting new industry in the last five years.

(4) Persuade business to evolve plans for creating job opportunities and a program of on-the-job training.

(5) Study the welfare program with an eye to reducing red tape and excessive regulations—and come up with a welfare rehabilitation program which would eliminate the dole as a way of life for certain citizens.

He mentioned voluntary programs that were working, among them:

(1) United Student Aid Funds, with 65,000 students on 700

* Or national administration, he would argue in 1980.

campuses who have borrowed $35 million, all of it underwritten by private citizens with no government participation at all.

(2) The cooperation of the Los Angeles Chamber of Commerce along with a group of black businessmen in Watts who put five thousand people in that area to work.

(3) A California B'nai B'rith Lodge which adopted a youth probation camp and, through a willingness to listen to the young men, reduced the period of time they must stay in camp by one-third.

San Francisco, he reminded them, when destroyed by fire was rebuilt by Californians "who didn't wait for urban renewal."

What is the Creative Society? He asked and answered himself.

"The Creative Society . . . is simply a return to the people of the privilege of self-government, as well as a pledge for more efficient self-government—citizens of proven ability in their fields, serving where their experience qualifies them, proposing common sense answers for California's problems, reviewing governmental structure itself and bringing it into line with the most advanced, modern business practices."

Looking straight out into the audience, he finished:

"This is a practical dream—it's a dream you can believe in—it's a dream worthy of your generation. Better yet, it's a dream that can come true and all we have to do is want it badly enough."

The students responded enthusiastically, clapping and whistling. But this was to be expected—they were young, idealistic. Young people will always respond to a challenge. But unexpectedly their parents, the older people, *also* responded, asking themselves whether this man Reagan was talking straight and whether this thing he called the Creative Society might get the government off their backs, if only a little bit, might lower their taxes, might make them feel the man in the street did matter, did count, could make a difference in what was going on around him. Was he kidding them, they asked themselves, or was he on the level? They looked and listened and wondered, and recorded their decision on June 7, 1966.

Chapter Twelve

Landslide I

George Christopher kept insisting that what he needed was a large turnout on Primary Day. The conservatives and the right-wingers, he declared, always showed up at the polls. If enough moderates and others (he never said left-wingers) swelled the number of Republican voters beyond the usual number, he had a fighting chance. Christopher got his wish. There was very heavy voting throughout the long sunny day, but as the sun sank in the Pacific, the former Mayor of San Francisco sank into political oblivion. Ronald Reagan won the GOP nomination for governor by better than two to one, carried fifty-three out of fifty-eight counties and immediately established himself as a favorite to beat Gov. Brown in the fall.

In the Republican primary (30,586 precincts reporting), the official returns were:

Ronald Reagan, 1,417,623
George Christopher, 675,683
Three others, 92,751

In percentages, Reagan received 65 percent of the Republican vote, Christopher only 31 percent.

In the Democratic primary, the returns were:

Edmund G. (Pat) Brown, 1,355,262
Samuel W. Yorty, 991,088
Four others, 234,046

In percentages, Brown received 52 percent of the Democratic vote, Yorty 39 percent.

Brown's slim margin over Yorty underscored Reagan's amazing showing. In a state where Democrats outnumber Republicans by three to two, Reagan had polled 62,000 more votes than Brown. (There is no crossing over in the California primaries.)

There is an old political formula in the Golden State: to win a general election, a Republican must get 90 percent of his party's votes plus about 25 percent of the other party's. Reagan and his advisers took a good look at the almost one million Democrats who had voted for Yorty plus the 234,046 who had voted for four also-rans and broke into broad grins. All they had to do was keep preaching unity among the Republicans (thereby holding on to the George Christopher voters) and go after those 1.25 million anti-Brown votes to win, but big, in November.

The consensus among the California and national press was that Reagan might very well do just that.

Los Angeles *Times:* "The whole thing spells trouble for Brown in his runoff battle with Reagan."

Time: "The Democrats . . . gave Governor Pat Brown his third-term nomination by a sufficiently meager margin to establish Reagan as an attractive even-money bet in November's general election."

Newsweek: "Out of these surprising margins of victory, observers last week spotted a new tide of conservatism—a deep, unsuspected current that could well carry the Republican movie star into the statehouse at Sacramento and stir up a new Goldwatery wave in the national GOP."

Columnist Doris Fleeson: "The California primaries have sung a song of social and political significance to the state and nation. . . . The primary returns certainly suggest that in California at least an underlying tide of dissatisfaction fed by historical and contemporary events is running against the Democrats."

Columnist William S. White: "The immense victory of Ronald Reagan for the gubernatorial nomination is in Party-power terms nothing less than an earthquake. Win or lose in the fall against the incumbent Democratic Governor, Edmund Brown, Reagan has put his brand deeply upon the GOP in the West."

Columnist John Chamberlain: "So it's Ronald Reagan versus Edmund (Pat) Brown in the big California stakes for governor next fall—and it says right here that Reagan is going to win. . . . In a year and a half of campaigning, which included many dangerous question-and-answer set-tos with critical reporters, Reagan did not make a single important slip."

New York Times columnist Arthur Krock: "The primary results in California . . . could . . . be a portent . . . that the voters are weary of the repetitious clichés and of the time-worn faces of those in office."

The media also condluded that Reagan's basic appeal was conservative.

Los Angeles *Times:* "A mood of conservatism swept over California politics and politicians in the major races at last Tuesday's election, according to an analysis of the recent surveys and results by the State Poll. Although there were other factors, this emerged as probably the single most important factor of the election."

Los Angeles *Herald-Examiner:* "Ronald Reagan is considered a conservative. And yet he scored a victory of landslide proportions without having had the experience of a veteran political campaigner."

Chicago *Tribune:* "Reagan's victory should silence further talk that voters have no use for anybody who has been devoted to conservative views on government policies."

David Broder, *New York Times:* "Reagan's sweeping victory . . . has given the national Republican party its sharpest tug to the right in two years and placed continued Democratic control of the state in clear jeopardy."

Pollster Lous Harris reported in *Newsweek* that "California is going conservative." Here are the highlights of Harris' significant poll:

(1) "Six out of every ten Republicans in California are conservative. Reagan won over 90% of this vote in the GOP primary."

(2) "Reagan made his most striking showing in the formerly moderate sections of Los Angeles and its suburbs to the east—in Riverside and San Bernardino counties, which now hold one-fourth of the entire state. . . . The bulk of his gain came from the new communities made up of elderly migrants from the Middle West and the young marrieds."

(3) "In 1928, Al Smith lost for President but brought out the big-city Catholic vote that provided a central pivot for Franklin Roosevelt's new majority in 1932. In 1948, Tom Dewey lost but brought into being new suburban Republican power which largely formed the basis of victory for Dwight Eisenhower in 1952.

"Now conservatives are hoping that when Barry Goldwater lost in 1964, he crystallized a new right-of-center vote in America. It may be too soon to say that the biggest state, often volatile, is the U.S. trend-setter; yet it is now possible this new conservative bloc could provide Ronald Reagan with victory in California in 1966—and in the nation in 1968 or 1972.''

Just how important California elections had become nationally was summarized by the liberal newscaster, Howard K. Smith, in a newspaper column just prior to the June 8 primary.

After a few statistics about the truly phenomenal size and growth of the state (''gross annual output of wealth now surpasses that of 100 sovereign nations . . . state's annual budget is exceeded only by budgets of the US, the USSR, Great Britain, West Germany and France . . .''), Smith made his most telling, and pragmatic point:

''There have been 17 presidential elections in the nation since 1900. In 14 of the 17 a New Yorker has been on one of the presidential tickets, because New York had more votes to be won than any other state. Well, the time has now come when it will be obligatory to have a Californian in every presidential race for the same reason.''

However, Ronald Reagan's thoughts were far removed from presidential races. He set to work immediately building an effective coalition, stating that he would go after everyone, including ''the independents because our cause crosses party lines.''

In Washington, D.C., Republican National Chairman Ray Bliss, no ideologue but a politican who loves a winner, said: ''The sizable majority by which Ronald Reagan won the gubernatorial nomination can now be blended into a united Republican drive for a complete victory in California in November. As national chairman, I urge all Republicans to unite behind him for governor. . . .''

Sen. George Murphy urged all Republicans to accept the primary results ''and work together for a restoration of sound and sensible government in Sacramento.'' Murphy had watched the primary from the sidelines but campaigned strenuously for Reagan and Finch in the fall despite a serious throat operation.

For once in California politics, people seemed to be listening to reason. In Los Angeles, within one week, the leading financial backers of Reagan and Christopher held a news conference at which they announced they were ''completely united'' behind Reagan. In attendance (for the liberals) were Thomas A. Pike, former Assistant Secretary of Defense under Eisenhower, and Leonard Firestone, of the tire manufacturing company; and (for the conservatives) Henry Salvatori and A. C. (Cy) Rubel.

Commented Salvatori: "The GOP, seldom united in recent years, has finally come through in one piece."

It was a shining hour for Salvatori and Rubel, who less than eighteen months before had told Ronald Reagan in his Pacific Palisades home that he was the *only* Republican who could unite the party behind him and win.

It was revealed at the news conference that George Christopher had spent about $450,000 on his primary campaign, almost as much as Reagan, who spent a little more than $500,000.

From San Francisco, Christopher said that while he would certainly *vote* for his victorious opponent in the fall, his active support would depend upon Reagan's position with regard to Sen. Kuchel's reelection bid in 1968. Translated, this meant that Christopher would vigorously back Reagan if Reagan would give him assurances that he would support Kuchel two years hence, Christopher was rightly concerned that GOP conservatives would challenge the very liberal Mr. Kuchel in the Republican primary and he wanted Ronald Reagan, as the new head of the party and champion of the conservatives, to prevent so unfortunate (to him) a happening.

Reagan's answer was unequivocating: No deal. He felt that governors should not take positions in primaries and besides, who could tell *who* the candidates would be in two years?

As a result, Christopher remained silent and still throughout the fall. The former mayor was also smarting from two Drew Pearson columns filled with "scurrilous charges" about him which he claimed had been distributed by Brown and Reagan partisans.

The columns rehashed an ancient story (twenty-eight years old) about legal troubles which Christopher's dairy had with the State Bureau of Milk Stabilization. Fuming and furious, Christopher lashed out at Pearson and wrote to California papers who normally carried his column. Pearson sued Christopher for $2.6 million, charging libel and interference with livelihood. Christopher responded with a $6 million countersuit.

Brown admitted that members of his staff had talked with Pearson before the columns were published. But when a police mug shot of Christopher began to circulate through the mails, the governor expressed his shock and declared that his staff had nothing to do with its distribution. Reagan made similar disavowals. Christopher, who has a short temper and a long memory, obviously used the incident as one more reason *not* to go all out for the man who put him out to political pasture.

In view of Christopher's attitude, it came as no surprise to anyone when Sen. Kuchel remained silent as to whether he would or would not endorse Reagan. In fact, however, Kuchel had already told the state chairman, Dr. Gaylord Parkinson, that if Ronald Reagan won the nomination he could not support him.

As important as Kuchel was, the real object of Reagan's and Brown's affection was the little maverick mayor, Sam Yorty—and the nearly one million votes he received.

Swallowing his pride and the many insults the Los Angeles mayor had aimed at him during the primary, Pat Brown said at a post-primary news conference that he would rate Yorty as a moderate. Said the governor pointedly: "I'm holding out an olive branch to every progressive and every moderate in California."

At a news conference held later the same afternoon, Reagan stated, "I think the Yorty people are a target for *our* attention, as evidencing dissatisfaction with the administration."

At his conference, Brown presented a brief preview of the coming campaign by describing Reagan as "the crown prince of the extreme right" and a man who "has taken the mantle of leadership from Mr. Goldwater." He added: "Like Barry Goldwater, he is the spokesman for a harsh philosophy of doom and darkness."

Retorted Reagan, "the governor is about two years behind. He's still running against Goldwater."

And when told that Brown had asserted that there is a white backlash in California, the Republican nominee for governor declared that he would not want to be the beneficiary of such a vote, and riposted:

"I think what took place yesterday was a *Brown* backlash."

With that Ronald Reagan was off to lay plans to visit the state's Republican congressional delegation in Washington, make a speech at the National Press Club in the nation's capital and drop in on a very distinguished senior Republican who resided in Gettysburg, Pa.

Chapter Thirteen

Common Sense and Nonsense

The old soldier was asked what advice he had given the youthful-looking nominee for governor.

"I just told him," replied the former President, "to start hitting, keep hitting and when he gets tired to hit harder."

Was his visitor a presidential possibility?

"Any Republican," he replied, "who wins a governorship and conducts it efficiently on the basis of the welfare of all the people—you can bet he will become a presidential possibility."

Did he support his visitor for governor?

"Well, I don't know too much about California, but Mr. Reagan is a man of great integrity and common sense and I know he's a Republican and I'm for all Republicans."

The general added that "the Governor and I—there, I'm calling him the Governor already—agreed that if the Republican Party has any label at all it ought to call itself the common sense party."

The visitor smiled broadly and contentedly because "common sense government" was exactly what he had promised he would bring to California if he were elected governor.

Reporters and photographers dutifully recorded the meeting between Dwight D. Eisenhower, thirty-fourth President of the United States, and Ronald Reagan, the gubernatorial candidate of California's Republican Party.

The *Washington Post* reporter wrote that "the 55-year-old actor, looking younger than the cloud-flecked springtime morning, wore a bright blue suit." He added, quite correctly, that a "picture with General Eisenhower is worth a thousand words in any political campaign."

The meeting had come about at the general's suggestion and the candidate had naturally accepted. In fact, the two men had known each other for many years. They had a fifty-five minute talk at the general's office at Gettysburg College and then lunch at the Eisenhower farm. It was all very cordial and significant for it canceled out the possibility that Sen. Kuchel or any other liberal Republican in California would criticize Reagan. He had received the Eisenhower blessing, and that was that. Ike's endorsement also spelled trouble for Pat Brown and his strategy of pinning the extremist-Birch label on Reagan. After all, how could the Democrats convince the California electorate that Reagan was a Birch captive after he had been endorsed by the man whom JSB leader Robert Welch had said was either "shallowly opportunistic" or "consciously serving the Communist conspiracy."

Following the meeting, some elements of the eastern press jumped to the conclusion that Reagan was trying to "moderate" his image. All too few bothered to draw the more obvious conclusion that Reagan was employing a shrewd political maneuver which defused two of the bigger bombs his opponents had intended to throw at him in his fall.

The following day, Reagan was the luncheon speaker at the prestigious National Press Club in Washington, D.C., graveyard of many an ambitious politican. Robert Donovan, Washington bureau chief of the Los Angeles *Times,* summed up his appearance:

"Ronald Reagan chided Governor Brown, the Great Society and Berkeley beatniks . . . at one of the largest National Press Club luncheons since the visits of Nikita S. Khrushchev and Fidel Castro.

"Suddenly a full-fledged political celebrity in Washington, the Republican nominee for Governor of California gave a witty, deft, engaging performance in his debut in one of the capital's chief forums."

Ted Lewis, Washington bureau chief of the New York *Daily News,* and a veteran reporter who had viewed hundreds of major candidates in a long and distinguished career, wrote:

"In the personality of Reagan there is exactly the sort of political appeal that kingmakers constantly seek. He is deeply serious about the need for change. He has a happy sense of humor. He is a family man, yet, like John F. Kennedy, drives the teen-agers to crazy leaping and squealing. At least, he did in making the Washington rounds today."

It only needs to be added that there were a lot of blasé, middle-aged politicians anxious to meet and be photographed with Reagan.

Columnist Richard Wilson revealed that the new candidate was of concern to the top Democrat of them all: "Even President Johnson pricked up his ears when Reagan came to town. The day afterward he called in Los Angeles Mayor Sam Yorty, presumably to explain to the conservative former Democratic Congressman why it would be desirable for him to swallow his distaste and support Brown against Reagan."

Back in California, Reagan began to lay plans for the fall campaign with his three top aides: Bill Roberts, thirty-nine-year-old partner of the Spencer-Roberts firm; Phil Battaglia, a young thirty-one-year-old lawyer who had performed so brilliantly during the primary that he was appointed campaign manager for the general election; and Lyn Nofziger, a forty-one-year-old political reporter for the Copley News Service. Roberts was a professional campaign consultant and a Republican with no particular ideology. But he had great confidence in Reagan. He had suggested that both Battaglia and Nofziger be hired.

Battaglia was a lawyer and former head of the Los Angeles Junior Chamber of Commerce. He had worked for Kuchel and Nixon in 1962 but was not active in the bitter Goldwater-Rockefeller primary in 1964. He was absolutely tireless and quickly secured the respect and trust of Ronald Reagan. Nofziger was rotund, balding, addicted to cigars and possessed of one of the sharpest wits in Washington where he had plied his writing trade. He had been offered and turned down countless jobs by various Republican organizations (including the Republican National Committee). He was finally persuaded by Bill Roberts, an old friend, to become press director for the Reagan campaign. A conservative, he became in short order a member of the inner circle around the candidate.

In addition, there were four other men who saw Reagan frequently during the fall whose opinion he respected:

Holmes P. Tuttle, sixty, one of the original group of wealthy Republicans who approached the actor in February 1965.

Ed Mills, sixty, a vice president of Holmes Tuttle Enterprises, who served as Southern California finance chairman, Mills had been active for Goldwater, Nixon, and Eisenhower.

Taft Schreiber, fifty-seven, vice-president of MCA, and agent for Ronald Reagan since 1938. He was vice chairman of the candidate's statewide campaign finance committee.

Neil Reagan, fifty-seven, the candidate's brother.

Mills and Schreiber, in particular, worked hard and long for Reagan, raising much of the $3 million which was to be spent in the fall.

The Reagan team patiently put together a unity team of Republicans. Caspar Weinberger, a former state GOP chairman and one of the party's leading liberals, was appointed a member of Reagan's steering committee. Also placed on the steering committee were: Dr. Gaylord Parkinson, the Republican state chairman and author of the famous Eleventh Commandment; State Senator John F. McCarthy, a former Rockefeller leader and minority leader in the Senate; liberal Robert T. Monagan, minority leader in the Assembly, and US Congressman Glen Lipscomb, chairman of the GOP congressional delegation and a conservative.

Several top Christopher supporters were brought aboard, including Marco Hellman, a noted San Francisco financier, who served as the former mayor's state finance chairman; Josiah P. Knowles, co-chairman of the Christopher campaign; J. Max Moore, one of the defeated candidate's closest personal and political friends; and Assemblyman George W. Milias, a top official in the Christopher drive.

With one notable exception, Sen. Thomas Kuchel, Reagan and his inner circle were uniting the GOP behind and with them.

Gov. Brown was having considerably less success with his fractious, fratricidal party.

His biggest problem remained Sam Yorty and the almost one million Democrats who voted for him. The governor did everything short of rolling a peanut down Wilshire Boulevard with his nose to please Yorty. They held meetings, conferred over the telephone, got their assistants together.

Enjoying to the fullest his position as the catch of the season, courted by both Brown and Reagan, Yorty declared that he *would* endorse Brown *if* the governor repudiated (1) the Democratic national committeeman, Eugene Wyman; (2) the State Democratic Chairman, Robert Coate; and (3) the ultra-liberal California Democratic Council. Yorty added that Brown would also have to give full support to President Johnson's Vietnam policy, sharply and constantly condemned by the CDC, whose support Brown desperately needed.

Brown sighed and went looking for other prominent Democrats. In early July, he held a news conference with Assembly Speaker Jesse Unruh and Senate President Pro Tem Hugh Burns, both of whom declared their "enthusiastic" support of the governor. Unruh and Brown had been at odds for several years because of the speaker's political ambitions which the governor had tried to thwart. Now, faced by the very real possibility of a Republican victory, they ostensibly joined forces, and Brown spoke confidently of a "new ball game."

The bonhommie did not last very long. One month later, on August 13, a sharp fight broke out in Sacramento over the choice of a new Democratic State Chairman. The two candidates were Mrs. Carmen Warschaw and Assemblyman Charles Warren. Nicknamed "the Dragon Lady," Mrs. Warschaw was favored by Unruh, Frederick Dutton who was brought in by the governor as his top campaign strategist, and Brown himself. Warren was backed by Don Bradley, Brown's official campaign manager, Lt. Gov. Glenn Anderson and most Democratic clubs.

Warren won by a vote of 447-443. Republicans were quick to made the obvious point that the governor couldn't control his own party.

At this same meeting of the State Democratic Central Committee, Brown shocked many liberals by announcing that he was going to appoint a bipartisan commission of "the state's most outstanding citizens to consider amendments to or a substitute for the Rumford Act," the state's open housing act.

There was some applause, but several delegates shook their heads and later sat silently during a standing ovation.

Remarked a black assemblyman from San Francisco, William L. Brown, Jr., "He sounded like Reagan."

It was an obvious and embarrassing retreat for Brown, who had pushed the Rumford Act through the state legislature in 1963. Brown's expediency was all the more apparent because it followed by one week the Republican state convention at which Reagan, in conformity with his principles, had promised to campaign for repeal and replacement or amendment of the Rumford Act.

The polls held little cheer for the embattled governor. The California Poll, conducted by Mervin Field, reported that Reagan was the favorite of 52 percent, Brown, 37 percent, with 11 percent still undecided. Field said that such an advantage had not been registered by any gubernatorial candidate since Earl Warren twenty years before.

At the Democratic state convention, Brown tried to split the Republicans, referring constantly to Kuchel, Christopher, Nixon and Knight as traditional progressives "with almost nothing in common" with Reagan. Earlier he had traveled to San Francisco to apologize personally to Christopher for the "scurrilous" Drew Pearson columns about the former mayor.

Within one week, Goodwin Knight announced that he had ac-

cepted an appointment as chairman of a Republican effort to elect
state legislators, adding:

"Electing Ronald Reagan governor without electing a Republican majority in the Legislature would be inexcusable. Since com-
pleting my term as governor in 1958, the Republicans have lost
control of the state government. Reapportionment gives us a golden
opportunity to recapture the Legislature."

As for the others, Christopher was locked in because of Ike's
endorsement and the unity actions of most of his top supporters.
Nixon was not about to pick a fight with Reagan, if for no other
reason than its adverse effect on Robert Finch, a friend and advisor,
who was running for lieutenant governor on the Reagan ticket. That
left only the self-isolated Kuchel, who was to say or do nothing for
either candidate in the fall.

In his quest for GOP votes, Brown even hired a campaign management firm which usually handled Republicans—Baus and Ross,
which ostensibly handled Barry Goldwater's successful presidential
primary in California in 1964. I say "ostensibly" because I was in
California in May 1964, as one member of the Goldwater team
brought in to save a faltering campaign. One of the major reasons
why Goldwater was in trouble and why eight of us were flown in
from national headquarters in Washington was the unaccountably
lackluster performance and incomplete planning of Baus and Ross.
When their appointment to assist Brown was announced, one political observer commented, "Now I *know* Reagan will win."

Something had to be done to help good old Pat Brown. The
gloom at the state AFL-CIO convention in early August was as thick
as Los Angeles smog on a bad day. It was clearly time for extreme
measures. Back in June, a Brown advisor had revealed that a team
of researchers was scrutinizing Ronald Reagan's career and background. Was a "smear" intended? Replied the advisor:

"The word 'smear' is used rather loosely. I gather every time
you analyze a man's character you'll have the word 'smear' thrown
at you. In my book the word 'smear' means something that is untrue.
I don't think we will hold back on the truth just because it might
be called a smear."

What was the truth? Pat Brown had revealed it the day after the
primary, referring to his opponent as "the crown prince of the
radical right."

The "proof" came in two parts. On July 28, State Controller

Alan Cranston* released a twenty-six-page report on the John Birch Society, charging that it was "riddled" with anti-Semitism. For four days, Cranston attempted to deliver personally a copy of his report to Reagan, following the Republican candidate up and down the state, complaining that Reagan was ducking him. At last they met at Los Angeles International Airport. Reagan accepted the report and commented, "You've made your grandstand play. Why don't you go out and campaign against Mr. Flournoy?" (The Republican nominee for state controller.)

After reading the report, Reagan referred reporters to his basic statement on the John Birch Society, in which he stated he would not seek its support, and added, "It's no secret that I deplore racism of any kind."

Democratic State Chairman Robert Coate quickly stated that Reagan's comments and his refusal to debate Cranston showed that the GOP candidate "is an apologist for and is supported by the John Birch Society. . . ." Within the next week, Coate said, Democrats "will complete and make public a profound document proving that Reagan is the willing associate and collaborator of some of the most obnoxious extremist causes in America."

The twenty-nine-page "profound document" was released on August 11 by Mr. Coate. It was entitled: "Ronald Reagan, Extremist Collaborator—An Exposé." It charged:

"That he (Reagan) has collaborated directly with a score of top leaders of the super-secret John Birch Society.

"That his campaign organization is riddled with members of the society.

"That he supports the programs, policies and projects of numerous extremist fronts.

"That the extremist money from California and eastern states is an important source of his campaign financing."

Among the supporting "evidence" were the following facts:

● Reagan had cooperated with Birchers in 1964 to keep the "ultra-right wing magazine," *Human Events,* financially afloat. *Human Events,* a weekly tabloid published in Washington, D.C., is about as ultra-right as *Reader's Digest.*

● Reagan was an advisor of the "extreme right" Young Americans for Freedom. YAF had several hundred distinguished Americans on its senior advisory board, including forty-three members

* Now a US Senator.

of the US House of Representatives and Senate, both Democrats and Republicans.

● Reagan had campaigned for Congressman John Rousselot, a prominent member of the JBS, in 1962 (see page 67 for an explanation of this old bromide).

● Reagan had appeared in 1961 in support of Dr. Fred Schwarz's "Christian Anti-Communism Crusade." Dr. Schwarz's book, *You Can Trust the Communists (To Be Communists),* is widely recognized as one of the best primers on communism published in the last twenty years.

Listed by Coate as members of what he called "Reagan's Rightist Brain Trust" were Patrick J. Frawley, Jr., president of the Schick Safety Razor Company, Henry Salvatori, Walter Knott, industrialist C. C. Moseley and Loyd Wright.

Reporters pressed Coate about Reagan's extremist connections. No, Coate did not believe that Reagan was a Bircher. No, he did not know of any ranking John Birch Society member who was a day-to-day advisor. No, he did not think that Reagan was bigoted. Yes, it was true that genuine conservatives supported Reagan but "they do not call the shots."

The same day Reagan held an impromptu news conference at the Century Plaza Hotel in Los Angeles where he was meeting with several Jewish business leaders, who did *not* refuse to meet the alleged "extremist collaborator." The GOP candidate said that it was "absolutely not true" that he was under the power or influence of extremist groups. The following day he called the leaflet a "smear" and a tactic used by the Democrats because Gov. Brown "does not dare campaign on the issues." He added that he would continue to "repudiate anyone or everyone who is a racist or bigot." Concluded Reagan: "The governor won't run on his record, so he has this phony issue. . . . Come October, they're going to come in dripping mud up to their elbows and say they've never seen such a dirty campaign."

Later, a close Reagan advisor commented: "Our feeling has been we are just not bothering to reply to this type of charge. They are trying to run our campaign for us. We are running against Pat Brown, not anyone else."

Right or wrong? Shrewd psychology or wishful thinking? The newspapers were filled for several days with Coate's charges as were radio and television news programs. The Democrats happily concluded that at last they had an issue and they trundled out the cannon. Pat Brown declared that "Reagan was a handsome, smiling puppet reading the script of the John Birch Society." Lt. Gov. Glenn Anderson called Reagan "unstable" and asserted that the Republican candidate had "been for almost every crackpot gimmick, every shallow fraud, every silly novelty that has been proposed." He said that "Reagan is about as conservative as the leader of a mob of self-appointed vigilantes."

Unruffled, Reagan kept hitting the Brown administration about taxes, spending, Berkeley, the need for morality in government. In short, he refused to panic.* He went right on being the calm, reasonable, persuasive candidate he had been throughout 1966. The people took one look at what the Democrats were saying about Reagan (puppet, unstable, extremist) and then a look at Reagan in person, on television, on a platform, in a parade, and decided that somebody had to be very wrong. As the election returns were to prove, the Democrats overdid it just as Rockefeller's people had back in the spring of 1964 when they kept implying that Barry Goldwater was unstable and an extremist who couldn't be trusted in the same room with an H-bomb (a major Rockefeller mailing piece in California was entitled, "Who Do You Want in the Room With the H-Bomb?").

The Democrats unveiled their big exposé and to their dismay the public yawned.

---

* His standard reply was: "We welcome anyone's inspection of our organization. No member of the John Birch Society will be found." But he also added, typically and fairly, "It never occurred to me to give a saliva test to the people who have supported me."

Chapter Fourteen

"A Prairie Fire"

Although each man had been campaigning since the first of the year, Ronald Reagan and Pat Brown were expected to observe an old political ritual by officially kicking off their campaigns on Labor Day, September 5. Obedient to custom as usual, the governor went to Los Angeles where he told a Catholic Labor Institute that his administration had a good record against crime. He accused the Republicans of trying "to peddle phony election-year statistics" about crime but openly revealed that all was not right by presenting a detailed anti-crime program of his own. Three of his proposals —tougher anti-pornography laws, more protection for citizens, and state assistance for local crime prevention agencies—echoed earlier Reagan suggestions.

The Los Angeles *Times* later asked editorially: "How much will (these proposals) cost and where will the money come from?

"A cost-conscious electorate is entitled to the answers.

"This is particularly so because on the same day he presented his crime program, Brown pledged to seek a reduction in property taxes. . . .

"Taxpayers should bear in mind that even if no new programs are instituted by the incoming administration, they still face a whopping tax increase next year—just to pay for expanding programs already underway."

The next day, Gov. Brown and Mayor Sam Yorty rode in a downtown parade marking the 185th birthday of Los Angeles. Just one thing marred this touching display of togetherness—the governor and the mayor rode in separate cars. Following the parade, Brown left to make a campaign speech in Ventura while Yorty

125

moved to the reviewing stand whose honored guests included—Ronald Reagan.

By now Pat Brown was beginning to feel like the Ancient Mariner, only he had trouble everywhere. Five days earlier, several disenchanted, disgruntled Democratic liberals (including Edward Keating, then publisher of *Ramparts* magazine) announced they would hold a statewide Conference on Power and Politics September 30 - October 1. The liberals described both Brown and Reagan as "know-nothings" and explained that a defeat of Brown "could reinforce the liberal wing of the Democratic Party." They stated that one of the major speeches at the conference would be made by Julian Bond, public relations director of the militant Student Non-Violent Coordinating Committee (SNCC), an invitation not calculated to soothe an already riot-shy state.

However, all was not doom and gloom for the beleaguered Brown. On September 2, the Field Poll reported that the gap between the two candidates had narrowed sharply since the last polling in June, immediately following the primaries. The Field results:

	September	Mid-June
Reagan	46%	52%
Brown	43%	37%
Undecided	11%	11%

A 15 percent advantage had been trimmed to only 3 percent. Field stated that Brown had won over a "significant portion" of the Democrats who voted for Mayor Yorty and other Democrats. He also reported that there had been a shift of Republicans who had backed George Christopher to Ronald Reagan.

Although cheerier news than Pat Brown had recently been getting, the poll still showed that in the more populous south Reagan held a sizeable 49 to 42 percent lead, with 9 percent undecided. Brown had to cut into that margin or suffer an overwhelming defeat. To do that, he had to spur his party to greater efforts than ever before. But as Gerald Hill, president of the ultra-liberal California Democratic Council, told a Los Angeles *Times* reporter, "It's true that fewer are sitting on their hands now than a month ago. The spirit is starting to pick up some. But the real damage to Brown is that so far the campaign has not excited the activists, who are the liberals."

Reagan had no difficulty in exciting his supporters on Friday, September 9 (the 116th Anniversary of California's entry into the

Union) when he formally launched his campaign in a speech at Los Angeles' Biltmore Bowl. The address was telecast over a statewide network. The hard news in his remarks was his promise that if elected governor he would appoint John McCone, former head of the Central Intelligence Agency, to head a "blue ribbon" commission to conduct a "fair and open" inquiry into University of California affairs.* That got the headlines. But what impressed those watching was the soundness of the Republican candidate's analysis of the state's major problems. He certainly didn't look or sound like an extremist as he asserted that he would (1) retain the state's system of unemployment insurance; (2) strengthen the system of social security by eliminating the earnings limitation on those who wished to augment their pensions and by extending coverage to everyone over sixty-five; (3) continue to oppose right-to-work laws "as too big a gun for the problems we seek to solve" but would push for a "secret ballot" on all union votes; (4) continue welfare aid to those in need but promised there would be "no pay for play."

The GOP candidate hit hard, although not by name, at Senators Robert Kennedy and Abraham Ribicoff for "insulting" Mayor Sam Yorty at a recent Washington, D.C., hearing through "an arrogant display of bad manners." He added that he hoped Sen. Kennedy would come to California on behalf of Pat Brown because "it would be interesting to have this citizen of Massachusetts, who serves as the Senator from New York, explain why he's qualified to tell us how to run the state of California." The audience roared their appreciation.

He also criticized two regents of the University of California, declaring that they violated an obligation "not to get involved in partisan politics." At an ensuing news conference he identified one regent as Frederick Dutton, serving as Brown's campaign manager, and the other as William Coblentz, who is "organizing university professors to help school the governor on the issues."

In that soaring lyrical style which many had come to expect of him, Reagan concluded:

"We can start a prairie fire that will sweep the nation and prove we are number one in more than size and crime and taxes. This is a dream, as big and golden as California itself.

"It's a dream that knows no partisanship. Millions of patriotic Democrats will join us bringing that dream to fulfillment because

* An irreproachable selection: Governor Brown had selected McCone to head an inquiry into the 1965 Watts riots.

they, too, believe in a 'Creative Society' mobilizing the full resources of our people, bringing the common sense of the people to bear on all the problems, restoring pride in ourselves, our government and our state and nation.

"We can 'get up astounding enterprises and rush them through with magnificent dash and daring.'

"William Penn said: 'If men be good, government cannot be bad.'

"Our people are good. Our government can be."

Pat Brown retorted that California's government had not only been outstanding but had won national recognition. As proof, he offered the "impartial" testimony of the first of a number of Great Society Democrats who were to visit the Golden State that fall: Interior Secretary Stewart Udall. After praising the conservation policies of California, Udall hinted broadly that if Ronald Reagan were elected governor, the state might not receive as much federal assistance.

"My department can help, as it is now helping with many of California's water problems," the Secretary of the Interior said. "But the help we can offer, under both existing programs and those yet to come, will continue to be effective *only* in the context of an imaginative, progressive, enlightened program of state leadership and action."

Udall announced that he would be back next week with Mrs. Lyndon Johnson, who would join Governor and Mrs. Brown in dedicating Point Reyes National Seashore and Scenic Highway One. Others scheduled to drop by, Brown aides announced, were Vice President Hubert Humphrey, Sen. Robert Kennedy and Agriculture Secretary Orville Freeman, all friends of Pat Brown.

In contrast, Reagan had declared back in June that he planned a campaign with only the help of Californians. "This isn't a case of Senator Goldwater or Nixon or anyone else," he explained. "I believe it's between the candidates and the people. I'm not going to ask any national figure to come in and campaign for us."

The governor's next major ploy was worthy of its setting. Speaking to a joint meeting of judges and lawyers at the state bar convention at the Disneyland Hotel on September 21, he asked that crime, the courts, the Rumford Act *and* the University of California be removed as issues in the campaign. "We need," said Brown, "sanity, clear thinking and an end to irresponsible rabble-rousing from any side."

And an end, as well, to four issues which were bothering the hell out of him, and the voters.

His call for an elimination of the Rumford Act as an issue followed by only six days a Field Poll which reported that 68 percent of the people favored either repeal or reform of the Act, and appeared on the *same* day as a State Poll which revealed that 72 percent of the people supported the right of a property owner to discriminate in any way he sees fit with regard to the sale or rental of his property.

To no one's amazement, Reagan declined to stop talking about the major issues of the campaign, which inevitably began to attract the usual procession of national columnists and reporters who made some not-so-usual conclusions.

Liberal columnists Rowland Evans and Robert Novak reported on September 24 that the "Birch issue indeed is dead. . . . Polls taken by both camps showed Californians—particularly the 60 percent of the state's population that lives in Los Angeles, Orange and San Diego Counties in Southern California—couldn't care less about the John Birch Society or right-wing extremism issue. What bothers them much more is the Negro revolution and high taxes."

Reporter David Broder of the staunchly liberal *Washington Post* wrote on September 18: "There is . . . coming into view—a man who is more old-shoe likable than Hollywood glamorous, more pragmatic than doctrinaire; a man with an open mind, an inquiring intelligence and a healthy ambition.

"His top political advisors believe this Reagan can be elected Governor of California and quite logically, become a strong contender for the 1968 Republican presidential nomination."

George Nobbe of the usually conservative New York *Daily News* wrote on October 2: "He can talk thoroughbred horses with grizzled ranchers, argue college morals with beatnik coeds, greet old movie fans, and put down hecklers with a pleasure that is obvious, all the while signing autographs—and without taking his eyes from the person who is talking to him.

"A sort of homey philosophy is woven into The Speech from start to finish and, if it sounds a little cornball, that's Ronald Reagan. . . .

"He insists he wrote The Speech himself, though he doesn't say just when, and the more you hear him give it, the more inclined you are to believe him, because it *sounds* like Ronald Reagan."

In the *New York Times* on October 2, Warren Weaver wrote of the "rather startling interpretation" Reagan placed on his lack of experience, quoting the candidate as saying:

"Nowhere in the state constitution does it say to be governor you have to be a professional politician, and I'm not. This country was created by ordinary citizens, not by politicians, to be run by ordinary citizens.

"I think it's time for ordinary citizens like you and me to bring some common sense thinking to all these problems that have been created in California in the past eight years by the professional politicians."

Inevitably, Hollywood got into the act—on both sides. Stars like Frank Sinatra,* Joey Bishop, Danny Kaye, Trini Lopez, Dean Martin, Keely Smith, Danny Thomas and Nancy Wilson entertained at Democratic fund-raising events. GOP events were treated to the likes of Walter Brennan, Buddy Ebsen, George Chandler and Andy Devine. In addition, such Democrats as Kirk Douglas, Burt Lancaster, Gene Kelly, Dan Blocker and John Forsythe appeared on television and radio, all uttering variations on this theme: "I could play a governor in a movie, but I don't have the ability to be one." Maybe *you* don't, but Ronald Reagan *does,* argued Republicans Pat Boone, Irene Dunne, Chuck Connors, Ruby Keeler, Fred MacMurray, Roy Rogers, Fess Parker and John Wayne.

Wrote AP film columnist Bob Thomas: "This autumn's outburst of political activity by actors is the greatest ever seen for a state campaign. The reason is both ideological and personal; aside from their political feelings, many actors feel strongly about whether one of their profession is or is not fit for high public office."

One voting bloc, in particular, shuddered at the possibility of a citizen like Ronald Reagan in the governor's mansion—organized labor.

Way back in July, labor columnist Victor Riesel wrote that the AFL-CIO planned to "raise at least $3 million inside labor alone for Brown's supreme conflict." At their state convention in early September, California labor leaders rammed through a special dues increase plus a call for a "voluntary contribution" of $1 per union member to build a $1.5 million war chest. Labor organizers were appointed for every congressional district. A massive voter registration drive was begun. Labor papers were filled with the full text of the Democratic exposé, "Ronald Reagan, Extremist Collaborator." Although Reagan protested that he was not anti-labor (after all, he had served six terms as president of an AFL union) and that he was *not* for right-to-work laws (he campaigned against them in

---

* In 1980, Sinatra attended the GOP National Convention as a guest of Reagan.

1958 when they were a major state issue), union leaders insisted that he was a front man for right-wing extremists who would block future economic and social gains for working people. The word had gone out from AFL-CIO headquarters in Washington: Get Reagan.

The White House concurred. And so Vice President Hubert Humphrey came, he saw, but he conquered very little. In a major speech in Los Angeles he contented himself with describing Pat Brown as "a big man with a big heart" who is "more than a shadow on any silver screen."

Humphrey instructed aides to strike from his prepared speech two full pages of wisecracks about Reagan, based on his movie roles and brief experience in politics. Some Democrats were beginning to conclude that they had been overemphasizing Reagan in the campaign. Others kept on beating the extremist drum. The disagreement was more evidence of a confused and cantankerous Democratic Party split four ways—among the ultra-liberals of the California Democratic Council (CDC), the Brown loyalists, the Unruh "power brokers" and the Yorty insurgents.

Then on September 28 a riot broke out in San Francisco. During the four-hour outburst a sixteen-year-old black boy was killed by a policeman. Governor Brown immediately called out two thousand National Guardsmen, moving swiftly to prevent any charge of negligence similar to that which he suffered during the Watts riot in March when he was touring Greece. Some Democrats said that Brown's acting with such dispatch reassured the voters. But all the stories rehashed the previous riots, including the Watts outbreaks of 1965 and 1966. Three weeks later, on October 19, violence exploded in Oakland, across the bay from San Francisco. Hundreds of juveniles smashed equipment at schools and grocery stores, assaulted teachers, threw gasoline bombs and called in false alarms. About thirty were arrested. The two racial outbursts jolted the people of northern California, which has traditionally considered itself the more enlightened half of the state.

During a televised joint appearance with the governor, Reagan said that he thought the new disorders were "an indication of a lack of leadership in Sacramento." Brown countered that he thought the riots were the action of an "extremist" minority. Most political observers agreed that they reinforced a growing conviction that it was time for a change in Sacramento.*

* One of the most effective Reagan slogans, used in Spanish-American areas, was "Ya Basta?" ("Had Enough?").

The October 11 California Poll, conducted by Mervin Field, confirmed the suspicion:

	Today	September	June
Reagan	46%	46%	52%
Brown	39%	43%	37%
Undecided	15%	11%	11%

Field concluded that "Brown's drive to close the gap on Ronald Reagan has apparently stalled." The governor was seven points down with less than a month to go. Significantly, according to Field, 16 percent of the Democrats were undecided on how to vote, and a "large majority of the Democrats who voted for Los Angeles Mayor Sam Yorty and others who contested Brown in the primary election are still not giving Brown their support."

The *New York Times* became so agitated that it wrote an unprecedented editorial concluding: "Governor Brown belongs at the State Capitol in Sacramento, dealing with the stubborn public problems he knows so well; Mr. Reagan belongs in the studios in Hollywood, gracing the movie and television screens he knows so well. On Nov. 8, Californians will, we trust, understand where reality ends and fantasy begins."

Ramparts magazine, another liberal publication, disagreed with the *Times'* definitions, editorially describing Pat Brown as a "lumpfish," who is "distinguished by his completely undistinguished appearance . . . enjoys mouthing platitudes . . . but his weak backbone keeps him from acting upon them. . . . When not drifting along with the prevailing currents, he enjoys floundering in a sea of expedience."

In contrast to such stormy seas, Reagan was enjoying smooth sailing.

In early October he received a warm endorsement from a formidable vote getter, Dr. Max Rafferty, State Superintendent of Public Instruction, who in June had polled the largest vote ever received by a candidate for nonpartisan office in California. His total of 3 million votes was more than the combined totals for Reagan and Brown. Rafferty sent education questionnaires to both candidates. Brown, well aware of Rafferty's conservative bent, refused to answer. Reagan's replies made it clear that he favored more local control over the schools and intended to meet with the Board of Regents to persuade them to adopt regulations which will prevent "treasonable and immoral conditions" within the university.

All the while, aides to Brown and Reagan had been trying to agree on a proper format for a full-fledged debate between the two candidates. When a debate had first been suggested in early September, Reagan said, "Sure, why not?" To some people's surprise, Brown also accepted. It was one of the governor's shrewdest campaign moves. In a face to face debate with a more eloquent and skilled speaker, Pat Brown had to score well—because he would be expected to be demolished. The situation was similar to 1960 when just about everyone (except Nixon and Kennedy) thought beforehand that Nixon, the man who had stood up to Khrushchev, would crush the less experienced JFK. When Kennedy more than held his own, millions of votes shifted. Brown hoped to pull off the same trick in 1966. But he wanted a little insurance and asked for a news panel format. Reagan preferred a straight debate. The air was filled with charge and counter-charge, accusation and counter-accusation. In the end, there was no debate, although the two men did appear together on three television programs. The consensus? Pat Brown did surprisingly well.

But there was no sign anywhere that he was pulling ahead of the Republican candidate. And it didn't look as though Reagan was going to make a serious mistake—like losing his temper and stalking out of a meeting. Well, they could always *try* to make him mad. Call him names, someone suggested, imply he's a bigot. That seems to get under his skin. Brown obliged.

On October 6, in Los Banos, Brown called Reagan "one of the most dangerous right-wing candidates this country has ever seen."

On October 7, in San Francisco, Brown said that members of the John Birch Society are "the storm troopers" of Ronald Reagan's "drive for governor."

But the governor outdid himself in a special television program that, for undiluted demagoguery, topped the Democrats' TV spots against Barry Goldwater in the 1964 presidential campaign. The thirty-minute film was called, "A Man Against the Actor," and was telecast one hundred times throughout the state in the final ten days of the campaign. In its most controversial scene, Brown was talking to a group of black children.

"You know," he told them, "I'm running against an actor . . . and you know who it was who shot Abe Lincoln, don't you?"*

---

* The Democrats made a one-minute TV "spot" of this scene and saturated the state with it in the last week.

All it lacked was a doctored film clip of Ronald Reagan playing John Wilkes Booth. But the Democrats had again misjudged the gullibility of the California electorate. Reagan ordered a poll which showed that the voters were not impressed by so obvious a smear. The results on November 8 proved that the public had reacted against the marksman rather than the target.

Another sample of Democratic subtlety was a leaflet distributed among union groups which shrieked, "The Target Is Your Family." It charged that Reagan favored up to $1,000 a year tuition at state colleges (not true), opposed accepting federal aid to education (not true), had supported the idea of a voluntary social security system (Reagan was for a voluntary option, not system), and opposed further land acquisition for public recreation (not true).

As he had for ten long months, Ronald Reagan stuck to the issues.

On October 1, in San Diego, Reagan called for tuition at the University of California, warning that the alternative might be a cutback in the entire "higher education program."

On October 9, in San Mateo, he asked Democrats to join with him to restore balance to the two-party system. In a rare reference to the Vietnam war, he said: "Rank and file Democrats don't believe we should stop bombing in North Vietnam when the weapons to fight in South Vietnam are coming from North Vietnam." To Democrats, he said: "There is only one way to get your party back and that is to throw that gang out of Sacramento."

On October 13, in Riverside, Reagan hit hard at Brown's call for a commission to examine the Rumford Act, which he once supported. "This plot is so obvious," stated Reagan, "that many good people asked to serve on the commission refused and it took him weeks to round up a commission. It's too late and too little." Reagan reiterated his position that a property owner should have the right to sell or rent to whomever he pleased.

On October 23, in Concord, Reagan called for a "yes" vote on Proposition 16 (CLEAN) so "we can have a mandate from the people" on the subject of obscenity. (Proposition 16 was a measure on the ballot which would have redefined what is obscene material and written the new definition into state law. It also would have set up new and tougher procedures for prosecution of those dealing in obscene material. The public favored Proposition 16 by two to one according to the State Poll.) Reagan emphasized that as governor he would guard "against any kind of book burning."*

Bobby Kennedy came to California in late October and was greeted by signs saying, "Carpetbagger," "Beware, This is Yorty Country," "Aren't Two States Enough?" The Senator called Gov. Brown, who traveled with him during his two day trip, "an inspiration to the rest of the nation." But he was careful to make no direct attack on Reagan.

Newspapers began to publish their endorsements. The Los Angeles *Herald Examiner* (a Hearst paper, daily circulation 724,273) endorsed Pat Brown, saying that "although we have disagreed with Gov. Brown on many occasions, and if he is re-elected there no doubt will be other differences of opinion, we believe the over-all record of his administration warrants his re-election." Smaller papers like the Riverside *Press Enterprise,* the Palo Alto *Times* and the Redwood City *Tribune* also endorsed Pat Brown with but-studded editorials.

But the important endorsement, the Big One, is that of the West Coast's publishing goliath, the Los Angeles *Times* (daily circulation 812,147, Sunday 1,149,295), which on October 16 declared:

"The *Times* earnestly believes that the election of Ronald Reagan as governor, and Robert H. Finch as lieutenant governor, will be in the best interests of California."

The long editorial made the following points:

Reagan has "steadfastly ignored attacks upon his personal integrity and personal motives," comporting "himself with dignity and courage in the face of brutal name-calling and guilt-by-association tactics."

Reagan has announced he will "draft the best brains in California" to assist him in drawing up programs in finance, law enforcement, agriculture, welfare and other complex areas.

Reagan has pledged himself to bring about "a more constructive relationship between government and business."

He has asserted he will replace welfare spending with "welfare investments" to rescue "discouraged men from the economic junkheap."

He approves the legitimate use of "Negro political and economic power," but not repressive "black power," to win deserved benefits.

* Despite the polls, Proposition 16 was rejected by more than 600,000 votes on election day.

He will solicit the best financial advice to devise a tax revision program.

It was a thoughtful editorial, one which the editors of the *Times,* an increasingly liberal although traditionally Republican paper, had obviously considered very carefully. They knew that what the *Times* said carried great weight. And so it did.*

In the last two weeks, both sides unleashed a television blitz, accounting for much of their $3 million election budgets. (This figure does not include the $3 million or so spent by labor on Brown.) The Brown forces scheduled 2,000 spot announcements on radio the next-to-last week and 2,500 spots the final week. On major TV stations there were twenty to forty spots a week. The Reagan schedule included four hundred TV spots up to one minute long during the next-to-last week, a five-minute program every night on each of the thirteen key TV stations, and a one-hour "telethon" in San Francisco.

Labor tried desperately to counter-attack but even among blue-collar workers Ronald Reagan buttons could be found. One poll in mid-October showed that Reagan enjoyed 38 percent of the vote in the factories and mills populating the Los Angeles industrial complex. It must have been very frustrating, for as the labor editor of the Los Angeles *Herald Examiner* wrote: "In money and manpower, unions have what must be a modern record invested in the fortunes of Pat Brown."

In one last desperate attempt to prove that there *was* a deliverable labor vote, Walter Reuther, president of the United Auto Workers and number two man in the AFL-CIO, came to town on October 28 to work some political magic. Reuther flourished all the old clichés: Reagan was "unreliable." "He sold out for 30 pieces of silver as the paid propagandist of General Electric." What happens on November 8, the labor leader warned, will influence the bargaining posture of every union because "we do not operate in a vacuum."

Another visitor to California was to make far more difference: Stokely Carmichael, the leader of the Student Non-Violent Coordinating Committee, who spoke before twelve thousand cheering students on the Berkeley campus of the University of California. If Reagan had a speechwriter and if this ghost had tried his very

---

* Other newspapers that endorsed Reagan included the Oakland *Tribune* (owned by former US Senator William Knowland), San Jose *News* and San Diego *Union.*

best, he could not have written a speech more calculated to help the GOP candidate.

On October 29, nine short days before election day, Stokely declared that the only way to stop the war in Vietnam was for young Americans to say "to hell with the draft."

"And I am saying, 'To hell with the draft!' " he shouted. He added that the Vietnam war was "murder of women and kids" and that American black soldiers there are "nothing more than black mercenaries."

Significantly, Reagan had tried to prevent that which he must have suspected would be to his political benefit. He sent a telegram to Carmichael in New York asking him to cancel the trip and asked Brown to join him in the request. Caught in the middle again, Brown refused and lamely said he deplored Carmichael's appearance. Good old Pat Brown had done it again, or rather had *not* done anything again. Following his appearance, Brown condemned the SNCC leader's "to hell with the draft" speech and then added, incredibly enough: "Black power and the white backlash are now working strangely hand-in-glove to defeat me." Speaking on CBS-TV's *Face the Nation,* Reagan stated that he didn't think there was a white backlash in California "except in the mind of someone who wants to use it in a political sense." He added that if there was a backlash, it wasn't racial but only "a backlash against what seems to be a breakdown in law and order."

Still another visitor never arrived: President Lyndon Johnson, scheduled to spend two full days stumping California with the slumping Brown. However, after a two-week tour through Asia, a little summit meeting with our Asian allies in Manila, and a flying visit to the front in Vietnam, the President returned to the United States in very late October more tired than he cared to admit. It was announced, almost immediately, he was not going to campaign (it was even denied that he had ever planned to campaign although that was not true) but instead would be going into the hospital in a few days for minor surgery. Two weeks later he was operated on for removal of a noncancerous polyp from his throat and repair of an incisional hernia in his abdomen.

By now, Pat Brown wished that he too could go into the hospital, but he had the last few weary days of a frustrating campaign to endure.

The last Field Poll showed:
Reagan   46%

Brown	41%
Undecided	13%
The last State Poll reported:	
Reagan	49%
Brown	43%
Undecided	8%

Brown said he found the figures "very encouraging." Reagan's managers, Bill Roberts and Phil Battaglia, tried to control their jubilation. It was obvious that, barring another San Francisco earthquake, their man was going to win by as much as 500,000 votes and maybe more.

On Monday, November 7, the last day of the campaign, Brown flew from a breakfast rally in Los Angeles to a midday rally in San Francisco to a late afternoon event in San Jose. Reagan undertook a flying tour of six airport rallies from Sacramento to San Diego. The preceding Thursday he had been showered with confetti and cheered by thousands during a downtown parade in San Francisco—Pat Brown's home town. At every stop on that last day, the candidate cautioned the happy, sign-waving crowds against "overconfidence," asking them to turn out themselves as well as their friends and neighbors, in full force on the morrow.

They did.

Chapter Fifteen

Landslide II

The last polls showed Reagan five to six points ahead of Brown, with as many as 13 percent of the people undecided. The Reagan camp translated these figures into a very solid 500,000 plurality. Pat Brown stubbornly insisted that he would win by 300,000 votes—the memories of his one million vote victory over William Knowland in 1958 and his 200,000 vote win over Richard Nixon in 1962 obviously etched in his mind. Brown's managers, clinging to outdated political clichés, expressed the hope that election day would bring "Democratic sunshine" and a large turnout which would help the governor because of the three-to-two registration edge Democrats enjoyed.

With the dawn of November 8, 1966 came cloudy, dripping skies over much of Southern California—which should have meant a lighter turnout and an advantage for the GOP. But, in fact, new voting records were set or threatened throughout the state with 79.19 percent of those Californians registered voting. By the old clichés, this should have meant a plus for the Democrats. But it was not to be in 1966 as Ronald Reagan and company won every major state office but one, reduced the Democratic majorities in the Assembly and State Senate to prosciutto-thin margins and picked up three new Republican Congressmen.

The results of the gubernatorial contest:

| Ronald Reagan | 3,742,913 | 57% |
| Pat Brown | 2,749,174 | 42% |

It was a million vote victory, less 6,261. The Republican candidate carried fifty-five out of fifty-eight counties, losing only Ala-

139

meda (by less than 2,000), Plumas (by less than a hundred) and San Francisco, Pat Brown's home county (by about fifty thousand votes). All three are in the North. Reagan piled up huge totals in Los Angeles County (over a 350,000 vote plurality), Orange County (a 180,000 vote plurality) and San Diego County (a 110,000 vote plurality). He received 60 percent of the Los Angeles vote and even 51 percent of the San Francisco Bay area vote, despite losing the city of San Francisco. Reagan garnered 57 percent of the votes of people with middle incomes—14 percent more than Nixon had in 1962. He received 65 percent of the non-black vote. As expected, Brown got an overwhelming 95 percent of the black vote but, according to pollster Don Muchmore, this was "not a significant change from 1962." Brown also got 76 percent of the Spanish-American vote, traditionally Democratic.

All observers agreed that Reagan's awesome margin was due to almost every one of the "undecideds" going for him rather than Brown. Clearly, Ronald Reagan had convinced them that he and his Creative Society would do more for California.

Other state-wide races:

For Lieutenant Governor:

Robert H. Finch (Rep.)	3,834,978
Glenn Anderson (Dem.)	2,578,887

Bob Finch, forty-one, campaign manager for Dick Nixon's presidential try in 1960, and campaign manager for George Murphy in his successful senatorial drive in 1964, had been in trouble since the primary. Although popular with all shades of Republicans and many Democrats, Finch had not generated any appreciable enthusiasm. As the campaign entered its last month, some polls showed him 15 percent behind the lackluster Anderson, who had handled so ineptly the Watts riot in 1965. But Reagan needed a *Republican* lieutenant governor whose duties in California go far beyond the usual ceremonial functions in most states. In the last three weeks, therefore, the campaign's emphasis was shifted to a Ronald Reagan—Bob Finch theme. Over $300,000 was spent on TV spots and billboards promoting the "team." Reagan and Finch campaigned together. When Reagan was not there, Sen. Murphy was, calling on voters to back Finch. In addition, Finch had almost total newspaper support and it is generally agreed that editorial recommendations influence voters far more on lesser offices. A top campaign strategist told me flatly: "Finch would not have won without Reagan."*

> *For Secretary of State:*
> Frank M. Jordan (Rep.)   3,481,016
> Norbert S. Schlei (Dem.)   2,777,445

Jordan was an incumbent, having served as secretary of state for twenty-four years.

> *For Controller:*
> Houston L. Flournoy (Rep.)   3,186,455
> Alan Cranston (Dem.)   3,125,070

Cranston, the man who had tried to present a JBS bouquet to Reagan, must have been particularly distressed to lose to Flournoy, a liberal professor-assemblyman.

> *For Treasurer:*
> Ivy Baker Priest (Rep.)**   3,203,367
> Bert A. Betts (Dem.)   3,069,660

> *For Attorney General:*
> Thomas C. Lynch (Dem.)   3,375,334
> Spencer Williams (Rep.)   2,901,840

Incumbent Lynch was the only Democrat to win a statewide office. Pollster Muchmore attributed Williams' defeat to the fact that he trailed Lynch "by such a wide margin among those registered voters who characteristically vote." As they did for every other Republican, the bulk of the undecided's swung to Williams but they could not overcome Lynch's advantage among those who knew how they were going to vote. Williams was subsequently appointed Health and Welfare Administrator by Reagan.

In the state legislature, the Reagan landslide reduced the Democratic majority to two in the Senate and four in the Assembly.

---

* As can be seen, Finch received 92,000 more votes than Reagan. His winning margin was much greater than Reagan's because his opponent, Anderson, pulled 171,000 less votes than Brown.

** The attractive gray-haired Mrs. Priest was Treasurer of the United States under President Dwight D. Eisenhower.

Because of reapportionment, there were elections for all seats. The breakdown:

Before Nov. 8, 1966:
Senate   26 Democrats
                  14 Republicans
Assembly   49 Democrats
                  31 Republicans

After Nov. 8, 1966:
Senate   21 Democrats
                  19 Republicans
Assembly   42 Democrats
                  38 Republicans

In national offices, the Reagan sweep carried three new Republicans into Congress: Robert Mathias, former Olympic champion, Jerry Pettis, and Charles Wiggins. That they won because of Reagan can be seen in their winning percentages, which were 6 percent, 9 percent and 11 percent, respectively, behind the man at the top of the ticket. Reagan carried thirty-one out of thirty-eight congressional districts and received a greater percentage of the vote than the GOP candidate in twenty-three out of thirty-eight districts. The new line-up was Democrats twenty-one seats, Republicans seventeen.

The governor-elect was elated understandably, as were his campaign workers who jammed the Biltmore Bowl for a victory celebration. When Pat Brown conceded late Tuesday night, pandemonium ensued. As the band played, a surging crowd knocked over two policemen and a huge "Reagan for President" banner was unfurled.

The next day at a news conference, the governor-elect disavowed any presidential ambitions but acknowledged that as the leader of a state with forty electoral votes he would probably play a "significant" part in the 1968 national campaign. A few days later, when *U.S. News & World Report* asked if he would "object" if Republicans asked him to try for the presidential nomination, Reagan replied:

"You dangle something there that is the supreme honor that can come to any citizen of the United States. Let me put it this way: I will do nothing to encourage such a thing. I will even discourage it, because I've been handed a great responsibility here as Governor of California, and I have nothing else in mind but getting at this job."

On election night, Reagan was asked about the meaning of his victory and replied: "It seems to be all over the country. The people seem to have shown that maybe we have moved too fast, and want to pause and reconsider the course we've been following."* Later for *U.S. News & World Report,* he became more specific:

"For me, the vote reflects the great concern of the people with the size and cost of government.

"There were disturbed, too, by our runaway crime rate and the excessive cost of welfare. There was a belief that, as far as welfare is concerned, we were not curing the problem—weren't helping people to help themselves. We were just building up a whole segment of society that was coming along for a free ride.

"And, of course, the demonstrations and riots at the University of California at Berkeley had people deeply disturbed."

As a Republican governor with a Democratic legislature, he was asked, will you have trouble putting your program across? He replied:

"If you have a sound program that the legislators know will benefit the people, they will go along. We've got quite a record here in California of legislators crossing party lines for the good of the people."

Reagan sounded rather naive but within three days of his election, both Jesse Unruh, Speaker of the Assembly, and Attorney General Thomas Lynch, a Democrat promised the governor-elect their cooperation. Lynch specifically contradicted widely-circulated reports that he had hinted he might resign because of "white backlash" in the campaign. Lynch emphasized he had no such intention and that his only remark about backlash had been an offhand remark about not wanting to be associated with "white backlash" in *other* parts of the country.

As part of his running start to get at the job, Reagan appointed Phil Battaglia his executive secretary and A. C. Rubel chairman of

* President Johnson had predicted that there would be "minimal" Democratic losses in the House, if any losses at all, but in fact the 1966 elections were a nation-wide rejection of the Great Society. In the House, Republicans picked up a net gain of 47 seats. In the Senate, there was a net gain of three seats for the GOP. Republicans picked up a net of eight new governorships, bringing the count to 25 Republicans, 25 Democrats. But Republicans reigned in states with a total of 293 electoral votes—with 270 needed to elect a President. In the state legislatures, Republicans gained 677 seats, controlling both houses in 16 states, the Senate in 18 states and the lower house in another 22 states. Nationwide, Republicans received 54.1% of the popular vote, based on returns for Senate or Governor or for House seats where there were no statewide races. GOP analysts stated that one more election year like 1966—with its "minimal" losses for the Democrats—and LBJ would be back on the ranch, permanently.

a "Major Appointments Task Force," to screen prospective appointees to the more than thirty-one department directorships and thirty-one deputy directorships which constituted the bulk of the governor's patronage. Lyn Nofziger was made director of communications. Other staff appointments soon followed. A week later, after a very brief four-day vacation, Reagan spoke at an Associated Press Managing Editors convention in Coronado. There, the governor-elect asserted that he would consult with the people in his administration to bring about not centralized but grassroots government.

"The time has come," he said, stressing a by-now familiar theme, "to reimplement the original dream that resulted in the forming of this nation—the idea never fully tried in the world before—that you and I have the capacity for self-government—the dignity and the ability and God-given freedom to make our own decisions, plan our lives and control our destiny.

"People," he said, "would like a government that lectures less and listens more."

The job of his administration, he explained, "will be to provide the leadership and to restore to the people, through their city and county governments, the power and authority to solve those problems, or to share in their solution with the state government."

Could it be done? Did the people *want* it to be done after so many years of depending upon federal or state or local government to solve, if they could, all economic and social problems? Was Ronald Reagan the right man to undertake so monumental and revolutionary a task? Was *anybody* the right man?

One Reagan intimate suggested part of the answer when he said:

"The man will be the most unique political animal in history. Nobody has any strings on him."

It would take, assuredly, a man without strings, without obligations but with convictions and courage, to implement a Creative Society in a world seemingly ready to accept the proposition that that government is best which governs most.

PART THREE

THE GOVERNOR

Chapter Sixteen

"A Cause to Believe in"

The tall, erect, suntanned man, immaculate in a dark blue suit and muted tie, waited for the waves of applause to subside. The sky was blue, the sun bright, the audience expectant. They had said he could not win the nomination. He had proved them wrong. They had said he could not win the general election. He had proved them wrong. Now they were saying that he could not govern. He intended to prove them wrong once again.

"To a number of us, this is a first and hence a solemn and momentous occasion, and yet, on the broad page of state and national history, what is taking place here is almost commonplace routine."

So Ronald Reagan, the thirty-third Governor of the State of California, began his inaugural address on the morning of January 5, 1967, on the west steps of the gold-domed State Capitol in Sacramento.

During his twenty-seven-minute speech, which was constantly interrupted by applause and several times by cheers, Governor Reagan outlined what he hoped he and the people would do together for their state. It was all based on the premise that "freedom is a fragile thing and is never more than one generation away from extinction. It is not ours by inheritance; it must be fought for and defended constantly by each generation."

The new governor asserted that "the path we will chart is not an easy one. It demands much of those chosen to govern, but also from those who did the choosing. And let there be no mistake about this: We have come to a crossroad—a time of decision—and the path we follow turns away from any idea that government and those who serve it are omnipotent.

"It is a path impossible to follow unless we have faith in the collective wisdom and genius of the people. Along this path government will lead but not rule, listen but not lecture. It is the path of a Creative Society.''

He did not confine himself to rounded generalities but offered pointed proposals:

''We will propose legislation to give to local communities the right to pass and enforce ordinances which will enable the police to more adequately protect these communities.

''I pledge my support and fullest effort to a plan which will remove from politics, once and for all, the appointment of judges.*

''We can and must frame legislation . . . to protect (our young people) from the . . . harmful effects of exposure to smut and pornography.

''Lawlessness by the mob, as with the individual, will not be tolerated. We will act firmly and quickly to put down riot or insurrection wherever and whenever the situation requires.

''We seek reforms that will, wherever possible, change relief check to paycheck. . . . (But) only private industry in the last analysis can provide jobs with a future. Lieut. Gov. Robert Finch will be liaison between government and the private sector in an all-out program of job training and education leading to real employment.

''On the subject of education . . . hundreds of thousands of young men and women will receive an education in our state colleges and universities.

''We are proud of our ability to provide this opportunity for our youth and we believe it is no denial of academic freedom to provide this education within a framework of reasonable rules and regulations. Nor is it a violation of individual rights to require obedience to these rules and regulations or to insist that those unwilling to abide by them should get their education elsewhere.''

The audience of nearly twenty-thousand erupted into loud applause and cheers. Berkeley was ninety miles away.

''It seems to me that government must accept a responsibility for safeguarding each union member's democratic rights within his union. For that reason we will submit legislative proposals to guarantee each union member a secret ballot in his union on policy matters and the use of union dues.''

At last he came to the most tangled problem of all—the cost of government—and he told the thousands before him and the millions

* Before he left his Sacramento office in late December 1966, lame-duck Governor Brown filled 80 vacancies on the California judicial bench.

watching him on television and listening to him on radio the un-compromising truth: the State of California was in serious financial trouble. The budget for the year ending July 1967, was $4.6 billion and despite a bookkeeping gimmick of using fifteen months revenue there would still be a deficit of $63 million. The budget for 1967-68 would be several hundred million dollars more and with "projected increases plus funding for property tax relief which I believe is absolutely essential . . . our deficit in the coming year would reach three-quarters of a billion dollars. . . ."

Reagan gave it to them cold-turkey: "We are going to squeeze and cut and trim until we reduce the cost of government. It won't be easy, nor will it be pleasant, and it will involve every department of government, starting with the governor's office."

Nor did he rule out the possibility of taxes, saying that he would turn to "additional sources of revenue . . . if it becomes clear that economies alone cannot balance the budget."

He exhorted the people to join with him, explaining, "This is not just a problem for the administration; it is a problem for all of us to solve together. I know that you can face any prospect and do anything that has to be done as long as you know the truth of what you are up against. . . ."

The new governor paused and looked behind and above him.

"If, in glancing aloft, some of you were puzzled by the small size of our state flag . . . there is an explanation. That flag was carried into battle in Vietnam by young men of California. Many will not be coming home. One did—Sergeant Robert Howell, grievously wounded. He brought that flag back. I thought we would be proud to have it fly over the Capitol today. It might even serve to put our problems in better perspective. It might remind us of the need to give our sons and daughters a cause to believe in and banners to follow."

A veteran legislator seated on the broad platform whispered to a friend: "By God, he's going to do *exactly* what he said he was during the campaign!"

But first there was a four-day "fiesta," which included the dramatic oath-taking ceremony shortly after midnight, January 2, in the rotunda of the Capitol; a San Francisco Symphony concert; a prayer breakfast; a civic luncheon given by the Sacramento Chamber of Commerce, and a grand ball at the State Fairgrounds, which attracted more than five thousand people. Explained Richard (Sandy) Quinn, who coordinated the many activities, "Governor Reagan wanted an inauguration that would *establish* some traditions for the

first state in the nation.'' The *New York Times* summed up: ''Never
before, observers of the political scene said today, has a governor
been inaugurated so thoroughly and with such pageantry.'' The
governor clearly liked Quinn's coordination for he appointed the
thirty-one-year-old former press secretary to Sen. George Murphy
his appointments secretary.

At the ball, comedian Danny Tomas introduced the governor
by saying: ''The people of California have given you a four-year
contract. And if it pleases God, it will be renewed and I hope the
residuals are wonderful.''

By then, Reagan had begun to grapple with the residuals of the
Brown administration, which were *far* from wonderful.

The budget estimates given the new administration by the old
administration called for expenditures of $4.8 billion, *excluding any
new programs,* for the fiscal year starting July 1, 1967. Revenues
were divided in this manner: $3.2 billion from the general fund,
which finances most of the state's operating activities; $1.1 billion
from ''special funds,'' intended for such things as highway construction and wild-life conservation; and $519 million from funds
raised through bond issues to finance California's water project,
construction at the University of California and similar projects.

There was an estimated gap of $500 million between revenues
and expenditures in the general fund. Cash in the special and bond
funds could *not* legally be used to fill the general fund gap. The
new administration had to act, and fast, because it was required by
state law to submit its budget to the state legislature by no later than
January 31—less than four weeks away. Although the new director
of finance, Gordon Smith (a former vice president with the well-
known management firm, Booz, Allen and Hamilton), had been
analyzing the budget since early December, he and his team were
unfamiliar with many of the intricacies of the state budget. More
time was what they needed and did not have.

At first glance, it might seem no arduous task to trim drastically
a $3.2 billion general fund budget. But almost two-thirds of this
sum was payments made to counties and communities for such
activities as public education and welfare. Most of these subsidies,
as *Fortune* magazine pointed out, ''were required either by provisions in the state constitution or by statute, and could not be reduced
without repealing existing laws.''

Any trimming in this area was also blocked by the firm promise
Reagan made during the campaign that he would provide *more* state
assistance to local governments so that they could reduce property

taxes—the major source of their income. The state's 3.7 million homeowners had huzzahed Reagan for his commitment to reduce the nation's highest property taxes. He could not now ignore that commitment, which he would do if he attempted to reduce state subsidies.

What was left, then, on which the budget cutter could practice his skill? About $1.15 billion in the state government's operating expenses. The two largest items were $464 million for higher education (chiefly at the University of California and state colleges) and $193 million for care of the mentally ill. They were sacred cows invariably revered by all, but Reagan and his advisers were determined to practice austerity, no matter what happened. And almost everything did.

The University of California had requested a record $278 million for 1967-68. Gordon Smith and his budget team recommended that this be cut by $82 million—more than 25 percent of the total. A good part of the difference, Reagan suggested, about $20 million, should be made up by charging annual tuition for Californians (out of state students already paid tuition of close to $1,000 annually). The governor's proposed tuition was $250 to $280 for the University of California and $150 to $160 for the state colleges.* In addition, he asked the UC board of regents to use the $20 million contingency fund to pay some of the university's bills.

If Ronald Reagan had dropped an H-bomb on Berkeley he could not have enraged the academic community more. UC President Clark Kerr flew back immediately from a trip in the Far East to declare that any such cut would force the university to turn away 22,400 qualified students from its nine campuses in September.** Franklin Murphy, chancellor of the University of California at Los Angeles (UCLA), normally thought of as friendly to the new administration, said: "I must state plainly that I do not intend to preside

* At his first news conference as governor on January 10, Reagan said: "There is no such thing as *free* education. The question is who pays? I think there is nothing wrong with young people being responsible for a part of the cost." He suggested that some "who come to agitate, not to study," might have second thoughts about demonstrations if they invested their money in tuition.

** Less than two years earlier, the California Coordinating Council for Higher Education (*including Clark Kerr among its members*) concluded that the policy of free tuition at all state institutions ought to be changed. A major reason for the finding was that 20% of the students at the University of California come from households with an annual income between $14,000 and $20,000. Another 18% come from families whose income exceeds $20,000 annually. It was clearly unreasonable to ask the California taxpayer to help subsidize the education of those who could pay their own way.

at the liquidation or substantial erosion of the quality which fifty years of effort have created at UCLA.'' The governor was hanged in effigy at Fresno State College, his home in Pacific Palisades was picketed, and protest rallies were held, among other locales, at Long Beach State College, Valley State College and San Jose State College.

On January 20, the UC Board of Regents met for the first time under the Reagan administration. They deferred action on tuition and displayed little interest in reducing the budget request. But they *did* fire Clark Kerr as president of the University of California by a vote of fourteen to eight. Another H-bomb had been dropped with Ronald Reagan widely assumed to be the bombardier who pressed the release button.

While it is true that Reagan was sharply critical of Kerr during the gubernatorial race, it is *not* true that he led a Board of Regents vendetta against the UC president. In the first place, the Board of Regents had almost fired Kerr two years before because of his indecisive handling of Mario Savio and the Free Speech Movement at Berkeley. Only Gov. Brown's personal intervention at that time had saved Kerr.

Secondly, the board was made up of twenty-four prominent Californians—sixteen of whom had been appointed by Gov. Brown and Goodwin Knight (this group voted nine to five for dismissal). The other eight were members of the board because of their public office. They were: Gov. Reagan, Lt. Gov. Robert Finch, Assembly Speaker Jesse Unruh, State School Superintendent Max Rafferty, State Agriculture Board President Allan Grant, Theodore R. Meyer, president of the San Francisco Mechanics Institute, and Chairman of the Board of Regents, Harry R. Haldeman, president of the University's alumni association, and Clark Kerr.

Two members were absent and did not vote: Max Rafferty and Clark Kerr.

Late Friday night, January 20, following the firing of Clark Kerr, Reagan stated that ''the matter of a vote of confidence was brought up by Dr. Kerr, not the board. His request came as a complete surprise to all of us.''

The following day, Kerr retorted: ''The governor's statement is completely false. I never have asked for a vote of confidence and I didn't yesterday.''

Somebody was lying—or standing on their semantic rights.

Board chairman Meyer set the record straight on January 23, although his statement has not received the attention it should from academicians more eager to cry "McCarthyism!" than to find the truth. Here is what Mr. Meyer said, as reported in the *New York Times:*

"Dr. Kerr's status has been the subject of discussion and speculation for several years. His relations with the Regents were adversely affected by his handling of the Berkeley campus disorders in the fall of 1964. They deteriorated further as a result of his action the following spring in announcing his intended resignation to the press without consulation with or notice to any of the Regents. Some subsequent events did not improve the relationship. The resulting uncertainty and controversy have been harmful to the university in many ways."

Before the January 20 meeting, Meyer said, he and Mrs. Dorothy Chandler, the board's vice chairman, met with Dr. Kerr *at the president's request* (emphasis added).

"He told us," said Meyer, "that he could not carry on effectively under existing conditions, and that if the question of his continuance in office was likely to come up at any board meeting in the near future, he thought the Regents should face up to it and *decide it now one way or the other"* (emphasis added).

Meyer said that he and Mrs. Chandler asked Dr. Kerr whether he would be willing to resign, and the reply was no. Following the fourteen-to-eight vote "to terminate Dr. Kerr's services as President," Meyer and Mrs. Chandler again visited Dr. Kerr. They told him of the vote and of the Regents' "hope that before it was made public he would reconsider his refusal to resign.

"He said that he would not do so and that the board must take the responsibility. Under these circumstances, the question whether Dr. Kerr requested a 'vote of confidence' or a 'clarification of his status' appears to be *more a question of semantics than one of substance"* (emphasis added).

In addition, Mrs. Randolph Hearst, another regent and wife of the newspaper publisher, said, "Kerr delivered an ultimatum to the Regents to the effect that they must either give him a vote of confidence or release him from the office of president. . . . This action was initiated in no way by the Regents."

Dr. Kerr did not call Meyer or Mrs. Chandler or Mrs. Hearst liars nor challenge their public statements, although he did continue to insist that he was a victim of "politics."

Indeed, he was—his own.*

In the meantime, Reagan and his team pressed on with their austerity program. The governor called on all state agencies to begin implementing a 10 percent reduction in their operating budgets and he imposed a freeze on all state hiring to halt replacements or additions to California's 165,000 civil service employees.

"No department can expect to have a free ride," he declared. "We are running tens of millions of dollars behind the budget that was approved for the present fiscal year ending June 30. . . . We are in the way a family sometimes gets—outgo is far in excess of income. We just kid ourselves if we go on with a kind of fiscal sleight of hand."

On January 31, Gov. Reagan submitted to the legislature a 1967-68 budget of $4.615 billion—down about $250 million or 5 percent, from what he estimated the state would have spent by the end of the current fiscal year, ending June 30, 1967. Despite the cutbacks, he said that California would still face a deficit of $240 to $150 million. He added he would submit tax increase proposals shortly.

The night before, in a televised "Report to the People," Reagan declared that under Pat Brown the state "had been looted and drained of its financial resources in a manner unique in our history. Not since the bleak days of the Depression," he charged, "when California was forced to such desperate measures our credit was affected for decades—have we faced such a dark picture." He reported that "California, for the last year, has been spending $1 million a day more than it has been taking in."

Reagan added that new or increased taxes in the amount of $240 million would be needed "just to balance the budget . . . if all the economies we've proposed are put into effect."

Democrats in Sacramento were shocked—by the governor's use of the shibboleth, "looted," and his talk about a tax increase. Assembly Leader Jesse Unruh, who had derided Brown in private and in public for years, allowed as how he was "very distressed" about the governor's language. "The governor," he said piously, "certainly couldn't have meant the dictionary application of the

* It was later reported that *before* his removal as president, Clark Kerr had accepted the part-time chairmanship of the Carnegie Study of the Future of Higher Education, a project expected to take three or four years to complete. In this context, Kerr could force a vote of "confidence" or "status," knowing that he had a first-rate job waiting for him. An anti-climactic note: on April 10, it was announced that Kerr would take a part-time teaching and research post at Berkeley in the fall of 1967.

word 'looting.' That implies criminality. I certainly *hope* that isn't what he meant."

At his weekly news conference, Reagan expressed regret at having used the word "looted," describing himself as "addicted" to using the simplest words instead of terms such as "profligate" in his public speeches. He admitted that it was a "bad choice of words . . . and I'm sorry; I do not mean to imply any criminality."

But he insisted on making his point: The state was "going in the hole" financially, money had been spent and the fact "that the money was nonexistent was concealed from the people."

The determined Reagan administration continued to apply the brakes of the toboggan, effecting savings in large and small ways and, even more important, doing their utmost to convince the state employees that they meant it.

In the first six months, for example, the new administration:

(1) Sold the *Grizzly II,* the state Convair used by Brown, for $217,000, and ordered state officials to travel by commercial plane.

(2) Reduced out-of-state travel by state officials and employees by 74 percent.

(3) Froze purchase of new automobiles and equipment by department heads and consolidated motor-pool operations for a 15 percent saving in gasoline buying.

(4) Banned fancy-colored brochures and reports by departments and ordered them to use mimeograph machines. (Savings: $550,000 annually.)

(5) Scheduled the closing of eight of the state's forty-one conservation camps, centers for fighting fire and erosion.

(6) Reduced the state civil service by 2,550 full-time employees (out of a total of 165,000).

(7) Canceled a proposed ten-story office building (cost: $4 million) as "unnecessary."

(8) Eliminated $750,000 from the budget for a new governor's mansion. A private group was raising the funds to build an official governor's mansion in accord with the principles of the Creative Society. The Governor and Mrs. Reagan moved out of the old mansion on March 1, 1967, for a simple reason: it was a fire trap.

(9) Initiated a review of telephone use which was designed to save $2 million annually.

Many state agencies reported sizeable cuts in their annual budgets. The Office of Consumer Counsel reduced its budget by 77 percent. Other offices were not so successful. The State Supreme Court could only cut its budget $5,000, $129,000 less than the economy goal assigned it. State colleges cut their budget $4 million, $33 million less than what the administration had hoped to effect.

One major obstacle in the way of the Creative Society was the attitude of the state's bureaucracy, typified in this comment by an old Sacramento hand to a *Fortune* reporter: "We have been through this kind of thing before, though never quite so deep a cut. What you do is make temporary cuts in your operating expenses, while keeping your crews and your equipment intact. That way you can hold down costs for a single year, while making no real reduction in your program."

What the old hands didn't realize was that Ronald Reagan was serious about Operation Austerity—it was not a publicity gimmick, nor was his suggestion that state employees volunteer to work without extra compensation on Lincoln's and Washington's Birthdays, thus saving the state about $7 million. However, the proposal went over like a wooden (George Washington) nickel. Union leaders protested. The Democratic-controlled legislature took a long-week-end holiday, including Lincoln's Birthday, although Assembly Speaker Jesse Unruh and Senate President Pro Tem Hugh Burns, both Democrats, agreed at their weekly news conference that there was nothing wrong with inviting state employees to work on holidays. Said Burns: "I could think of many requests that would be much worse than working one day on a holiday. For instance, a cut in pay. . . ." Only a tiny percentage of the 165,000 state employees showed up on the two holidays, but Gov. Reagan had made his point with the public, most of whom *did* work on Lincoln's and Washington's Birthdays.

In late March, the governor submitted a revised budget for 1967-68 of $5.06 billion—$434 million more than he had asked for in January. Of this $440 million increase, $170 million represented the first installment on his promise to expand state aid to local districts, providing relief to payers of property taxes. Another $75 million resulted from the unexpected rise in Medi-Cal costs (Medi-Cal is the state's program which provides medical care for indigents under sixty-five in collaboration with the federal Medicare law). Total expenditures came to $184 million more than the actual spending under Pat Brown's last budget—"the smallest increase," as Minority Leader Robert Monagan put it, "in any year since I have been in office." It represented an 8 percent increase over the 1966-67 budget which had been 16 percent higher than the preceding year's.

To acquire the needed extra revenue and balance the budget,

Gov. Reagan called for a tax increase of $946 million. He tapped just about everyone, proposing raises in personal income taxes, the sales tax, excise tax on cigarets and liquor as well as raises in the tax on corporate net profits and on banks. Reagan, the alleged captive of Big Business, "could not have gone any heavier on bank and corporate income taxes," conceded former Finance Director Hale Champion, a liberal Democrat.

Reagan also added $38 million to the appropriation for higher education—with some $20 million going to the University of California. That meant a total of $216.5 million for UC—a figure which was raised to $230.1 million in the final budget version. The Regents added another $20 million from the contingency fund.

In his original message of January 31, Reagan had proposed 10 percent cuts in operating expenses for almost all state agencies. His March message restored about $55 million of that money but left a reduction in operating expenses of $127 million—"the largest economy accomplished in the history of California state government," Reagan maintained. It was over 8 percent not a bad performance by an administration which was told it couldn't be done.*

In mid-March, Operation Austerity collided with the last remaining program in which substantial savings could be made: the Department of Mental Hygiene. Reagan announced that nearly three thousand positions in the mental hospitals and elsewhere in the department would be eliminated and that eight mental health clinics would be closed. Annual savings to the state: $20 million.

The outcry was almost louder and longer than that raised about the firing of Clark Kerr in January. There were references to "the Snake Pit" and "the Middle Ages." But the governor's staff had discovered that the patient population in the state's mental hospitals had declined 40 percent in the last four years and there had been *no* comparable reduction in hospital personnel. Critics replied that the 40 percent reduction in patient population had not resulted in a like reduction in work load. Under the proposed new standards, they argued, staffing would be only 67 percent adequate for the mentally ill and 63 percent for the mentally retarded. The sum of $100,000 was sought to pay for anti-Reagan TV commercials and newspaper ads. Newspapers sympathetic to Reagan began wavering.

---

* In August, Reagan used his shears once again by trimming $200 million from Medi-Cal for 1967-68, explaining that the program had run up a deficit of $130 million during its first 16 months. The governor emphasized that no basic health and life-saving services were eliminated, and that the program would still pay out $600 million to about 1.5 million needy Californians.

The Los Angeles *Times,* however, backed the governor, describing his economy move "as a step in the right direction—and one that makes abundant good sense." But a poll showed that 58 percent of the public opposed the governor's economy stand on mental health, while only 23 percent favored it.

As a result, the closing of five clinics was put off for one year. The Department of Mental Hygiene, the governor announced, had full authority to halt all cuts "if at any time it appears that patient care will suffer."

The mental health issue might have damaged Reagan and his drive for economy badly if it had not been for a fifteen-minute "Report to the People" carried over twenty-two TV stations in California. His explanation of why he had reduced the staff of the Department of Mental Hygiene neutralized much of the antagonism. Although it did not swing a majority over to his side, his report convinced the people once again that Ronald Reagan was doing *his* best to represent *their* best interests.

On June 30, Deadline Day, Governor Reagan signed a budget for 1967-68 of $5.07 billion—then the largest state budget in US history. At the very last moment, he trimmed $43.5 million from such departments as the University of California, state colleges and mental hygiene. Although there had been protests and sarcastic remarks about the "economics" of the Creative Society, the Senate approved the budget by thirty-one to eight, the Assembly by sixty-four to fifteen. The wide margins reflected the increasingly persuasive voice of the new governor.

A month later, Reagan signed a $900-plus million tax bill which was then the largest state tax increase in US history. The money was needed to balance the budget, pay off a $194 million debt left over from the previous administration and finance a reduction in property taxes for elderly homeowners—a modest $25 million start on his promise to provide relief for all owners.

Unruh and other Democratic leaders had earlier suggested that income taxes be deducted directly from paychecks but Reagan successfully opposed this move toward withholding. He insisted that taxpayers should be kept "painfully" aware of the cost of government by paying their income tax once a year.

In signing the tax bill, the governor emphasized that "the people of California are still paying too much for government, but I'm optimistic that in the next year we can reduce the cost of government."

Throughout his first year in Sacramento, Reagan did not flinch, regardless of the issue.

For four years, Pat Brown postponed executions in the hope that capital punishment would be abolished by the state legislature. No action was taken and when Ronald Reagan took office there were sixty convicts waiting to be led into the gas chamber. Amid midnight vigils and passionate speeches, the new governor declined to stay the execution of Aaron Mitchell, who died on April 12. Reagan explained that the death penalty is a deterrent to capital crimes and that until the courts acted he would be obliged to obey the law. Soon thereafter the courts stayed the sentences of the next two men scheduled for execution.

As liberal columnist Roscoe Drummond wrote: "This is another example showing that, however much one may disagree with him, Reagan thinks for himself and is capable of standing by his own decisions whatever the political pressures."

Equally controversial was the bill liberalizing the state's abortion laws. Emphasizing that the bill was "by no means perfect," Reagan reluctantly signed it on June 16. The statute legalizes abortions when the child's birth would endanger the physical or mental health of the mother, in cases of statutory rape involving a girl under fifteen years of age, and when pregnancy resulted from forcible rape or incest. The statute replaced one that permitted abortions only to save the mother's life. The bill passed the Assembly by forty-eight to thirty and the Senate by twenty-one to seventeen after considerable pressure had been brought to bear against its passage by the Catholic Church and other organizations.

Clark Kerr, taxes, the budget, mental hospitals, capital punishment, abortion laws, *Grizzly II*—all these dramatic issues were the visible tip of the iceberg. Beneath the waterline, invisible and generally unknown to the public, was the far greater part of the Creative Society. Much of it revolved around nearly two hundred businessmen, on loan for six months from their companies and corporations, who were probing every aspect of state government, seeking to improve the efficiency and economy of operations. These men, all executives with salaries up to $100,000 a year, were donating their time. They were living in cramped hotel rooms in Sacramento and other cities throughout the state. One group was studying California's tax structure. Another was checking buying and housekeeping practices at state institutions. Another was inquiring into state relief rolls and alleged "welfare frauds."

Their examinations and recommendations would determine in

great measure the success or failure of Ronald Reagan's belief that "government *can* be run by the people and run with common sense answers to the problems of government and run with common sense business practices."

Was such government possible in the modern America of the 1960's? Equally important, did the people *want* such government?

Chapter Seventeen

The Reagan Record: 1967—1974

A pattern was established in the first year which Gov. Reagan consistently followed during his eight years in Sacramento:

Cut and trim government wherever possible, keep government income and outgo in balance, use business and professional experts to make government more efficient and effective and don't be afraid to make unpopular decisions if necessary.

It is, clearly, the pattern he will follow in Washington, D.C., as President.

The remarkable Reagan record as Governor of California from 1967 through 1974 is there for all to examine. According to the Los Angeles *Times,* Reagan left office "an accomplished practitioner in the art of government, a proven administrator and a polished and potent force in conservative national politics."

His two successful terms were built on:

(1) Attracting top people from the private sector, men and women, to administer his programs. Most political commentators agreed with columnist Neil Peirce that "most Reagan cabinet and staff appointees were of high caliber."

That same commitment to quality carried over to his appointments to the judiciary. Reagan installed a system which prescreened candidates for judgeships and then had them evaluated by committees made up of members of the bar, judges and laymen. Said the *San Francisco Chronicle:* "By almost all testimony, from enthusiastic friends as well as reluctant critics (Reagan) has made first-class appointments to the bench." The *Washington Post's* Lou Cannon concurred: "Friends and foes alike agree . . . that his judicial appointments were of high quality."

(2) Using the Task Force approach to solving problems, with

heavy reliance on citizen participation. Reagan Task Forces produced (a) recommendations that saved the state more than $200
million through improved management techniques; (b) the compre-
hensive Welfare and Medi-Cal reform programs; (c) the stimulus
for a greatly expanded program against drug abuse; and (d) recommendations to improve the management of school districts and
education in general.

(3) Involving his cabinet intimately and constantly in the deci-
sion-making process. As *Time* reported: "As a rule, Reagan made
no important decision without first discussing it at his almost daily
cabinet meeting or probing for more facts in lengthy sessions with
agency heads and other experts."

Bill Clark, who served as cabinet secretary in the first Reagan
administration, instituted the mini-memo to help the process. The
one-page memorandum was divided into four parts: issues, facts,
discussion (pro and con), and recommendation. They had to be one
page, no more and no less. At first, Clark acknowledged, there were
frequent objections that complicated topics could not be condensed
to one page.

"But it was found that almost any issue can be reduced to a
single page," he said. "At times if the governor wanted to go into
more depth, he would request more detailed reports. He's a late-
night reader."

Generally, eight to twelve issues were taken up at each cabinet
session with Reagan making the decision then and there. Clark
lauded the governor's "incisive" manner. "He has the ability,"
the former cabinet secretary asserted, "to digest material quickly
and to ask vital questions." More often than not, he put what became
his trademark—"OK, RR"—on the bottom of the memos.

To those who criticized the system, Clark had a ready reply:
"Everyone wants to see the Governor, but the only way he can
operate efficiently is to ration his time. Otherwise, chaos would
exist."

Quite the opposite of chaos was maintained during the Reagan
years. Pat Brown had eight agency chiefs overseeing the state's
twenty-three departments. Reagan reduced their number to four at
the suggestions, among others, of Richard Krabach, then Ohio's
finance director, who told Reagan how Ohio had cut five thousand
new jobs and lowered state costs 9 percent after GOP Gov. James
A. Rhodes took office.

All four of California's agency chiefs were business executives
who earned far more in the world of business than they made in

state government. For example, Reagan's first finance director, Gordon Smith, commanded a salary of more than $100,000 in 1967 in business, but his state salary was $30,000—a significant pay cut.

These men reflected Reagan's determination to put $100,000-a-year men into $25,000-a-year jobs—not to fill top state posts with people wanting a 100 percent salary hike at the California taxpayer's expense. Such officials also showed Reagan's ability to persuade outstanding men and women to make sizeable personal sacrifices for the goal of a better California.

One of the most important sacrifices was made by H. C. (Chad) McClellan, a Los Angeles businessman who resigned as president of his paint company to become head of a nonprofit organization called the Management Council for Merit Employment Training and Research.

What he did was truly remarkable. McClellan persuaded more than 2,600 companies in the Los Angeles area to cooperate in a job-training and job-finding program for residents of Watts, the same Watts which erupted into such terrible violence in 1965. At that time, statistics showed about 25,000 unemployed people in Watts. Immediately following the riots, McClellan, a former president of the Los Angeles Chamber of Commerce, swung into action and within eighteen months, 17,500 unemployed had private enterprise jobs. Here was the Creative Society in action.

One of Gov. Reagan's first acts was to ask Chad McClellan to extend his operations throughout California. At no cost to the state (the program was funded by individuals and foundations) McClellan created "skill centers" which provided short-time training for factory employees in Los Angeles and set up similar centers in San Diego, the San Francisco Bay area and Fresno. Chad McClellan is a most unusual man, as revealed in this story about a meeting between the Los Angeles businessman and a hundred young blacks from Watts, which Reagan likes to tell:

"McClellan appeared personally before that group of young men. Everyone had a jail record—young men who admitted they had led in the riots but had turned around and organized themselves actually to curb disorder in the future. And this was a group of fellows who, if you sent them to Vietnam, you would not have to send weapons. McClellan challenged them to take jobs. Of the 100 of them, 82 accepted the challenge.

"And today they are working in private enterprise jobs with records of no tardiness, no absenteeism. Some of them even are moving up with promotions."

As columnist Victor Riesel put it: "The governor sees the business community—and not the federal government—as the salvation of the black community—from Watts to Harlem."

Reagan realized that despite his one million vote victory, he would have to work with a skeptical, even hostile, Democratic legislature to get his programs enacted. He began regular breakfast meetings with legislators and adopted the rule that any legislator could see him within twenty-four hours of making the request.

The governor was not above some low-key lobbying. He and Mrs. Reagan invited a small group of legislators and their wives to have dinner at the governor's residence twice a week. They maintained the schedule until they had hosted every member of the Senate and the Assembly, and their spouses. The evenings were kept carefully bipartisan.

Dinner was elegant with candlelight and California wine. Cocktails were served by Orientals in native costume. Conversation was kept flowing by the always gracious Nancy Reagan. Upon the completion of dinner, the evening took an unexpected turn. The governor would rise and say, "Gentlemen, let's go downstairs." There the men were confronted by a gigantic electric train set covering nearly one-half of a large recreation room, an upright piano and a pool table. Taking off his tux, the governor would run the trains while a senator would strike up a tune on the piano and an assemblyman would send a cue ball hurtling into the racked balls.

After such an evening, it was difficult for legislators to describe Ronald Reagan as an extremist or know-nothing. In fact, several liberal Democrats began to admit that they *liked* him.

His performance in dealing with the legislature caused Julius Duscha of the *Washington Post* to write, "Reagan demonstrated . . . that he has what it takes to be effective in dealing with a legislative body."

There was no scandal during the Reagan years—no "Scam" or "Gate" of any kind. He set a high standard through his own personal integrity which was matched by those who served under him. James Dickenson of the *Washington Star* wrote that Reagan "left office with the reputation of a man of principle who kept his word when negotiating with his foes."

As Tom Goff, the Sacramento bureau chief of the Los Angeles *Times,* summed it up in 1974:

"Reagan singlehandedly browbeat the legislature into making welfare law reforms which appear to have ended a cost and caseload spiral that threatened the fiscal soundness of the state.

"The size of state government, measured in buildings and number of employees, has been held almost to a standstill.

"There is solid evidence that Reagan, particularly through his vetoes, has been an effective brake in keeping government spending from accelerating at an even more rapid rate.

"More subtly, perhaps, Reagan's presence—often a nagging presence—has made the people of California far more aware than ever before of their state government, the things it is doing and not doing, the money it is spending.

"Finally he has proved that a general shaking up of the government establishment . . . can be beneficial in the long haul."

And the people liked what he did as their governor. When he left office, the California Field Poll reported that Ronald Reagan had a three-to-two approval rating among the electorate—a higher popularity rating than any of his predecessors.

That popularity was reflected in his 1970 reelection campaign. He defeated Democrat Jesse (Big Daddy) Unruh, the powerful former speaker of the California Assembly, by 3,380,122 to 2,879,630—a popular margin of 500,000 votes. It was a solid victory if not by the overwhelming majority some overconfident Republicans had predicted. In the campaign, *Newsweek* described Reagan as "one of the most brilliantly gifted politicians anywhere in the U.S. today—a campaigner unmatched for sheer star quality since the depature of Dwight Eisenhower and the arrival of the Kennedys a decade ago." After his defeat, Unruh paid Reagan this grudging tribute: "As a governor, I think he has been better than most Democrats would concede and not nearly as good as most Republicans and conservatives might like to think. As a politician, I think he has been nearly masterful."

Here are the highlights of the eight-year Reagan record:

Spending. When he took office, Reagan discovered California was spending a million dollars more each day than it was taking in. When he left office, he turned over to his successor, Jerry Brown, a surplus of $554 million. Under Reagan, California's bonds were upgraded to the highest possible rating, Moody's Triple-A, for the first time in thirty-one years—a rating that saved millions of dollars in interest charges. Editorialized the *San Francisco Examiner:* "We exaggerate very little when we say that (Reagan) has saved the state from bankruptcy."

Taxes. Reagan was the biggest tax-cutter in the state's history, enacting over $5.7 billion in tax relief. Measures included: (1) the first comprehensive property tax relief program in the state's history, totalling $2.4 billion; (2) abolition of the personal property tax on household effects, for a total of $895 million in tax relief; (3) providing renters with $230 million in state income tax relief; (4) reduction of the business inventory tax by half.

He consistently fought to limit the power of government to tax its citizens, including such actions as: (1) signing a law prohibiting a city from levying an income tax on nonresidents who work in the city; (2) signing into law a measure restoring direct voter control of school tax ceilings; and (3) vetoing a bill which would have permitted school districts to levy an additional tax without voter approval.

He climaxed his tax limitation efforts in 1973 by sponsoring Proposition 1, an amendment to the state constitution which would have eventually placed a ceiling of 7 percent on the income tax that California could levy on its citizens.

Although the measure lost—gaining 46 percent of the vote—columnist M. Stanton Evans concluded that Proposition 1 "spawned a series of parallel efforts in 20 other states, transferring the momentum of political agitation on such issues away from the spenders and towards the savers."

With the success of Howard Jarvis' Proposition 13 in California in June 1978, and passage of similar measures in twelve out of sixteen other states in November 1978, Ronald Reagan's 1973 initiative can be called the birth of the tax limitation movement in America.

The cost of government. Due to inflation, the constant demands of a Democratic legislature and new bookkeeping methods, the state's annual budget went from $4.6 billion to $10.2 billion during Reagan's eight years in office. Most of this increase was caused by new or expanded state programs ordered by the federal government over which Gov. Reagan had no control. A fairer criterion is the state's operations budget, which in eight years increased from $2.2 billion to $3.5 billion, two-thirds of it due to inflation.

Reagan fought the big spenders all the way, vetoing 994 bills. Only one veto—a nonspending item—was ever overridden.

The Los Angeles *Times'* Goff wrote, "There is solid evidence that Reagan, particularly through his vetoes, (was) an effective brake in keeping government spending from accelerating at an even more rapid rate."

U.S. News & World Report commented: "Most agree that if Reagan had not pursued a policy of 'squeeze, cut and trim,' California's taxes and spending would be much higher than they are today.''

Welfare reform. By 1971, the annual cost of California's welfare system was $3 billion. The welfare caseload was increasing at a rate of up to forty thousand a month, totalling some 2.3 million people in March 1971.

Confronted by this crisis, Reagan formed the Welfare Reform Task Force, which after five months of study proposed a series of far-reaching but sensible changes. The governor put together a reform package that became law and ultimately transformed public welfare not only in California but across the nation. Among the changes:

(1) Penalties were stiffened for welfare fraud; (2) financially able parents were required to support minor children who left home and went on welfare; (3) recipients with jobs were removed from the welfare rolls when their outside income exceeded 150 percent of their basic needs; (4) adult children were required to contribute to the support of their aged parents on welfare; (5) the power of counties to make absent fathers pay for the support of their families was broadened; (b) able-bodied recipients were required to take job training or work on public works projects at least four hours a day.

The results were startling. By September 1974, the total caseload had dropped by approximately 350,000, shrinking the Aid to Families with Dependent Children (AFDC) rolls from nearly 1.7 million to 1.3 million. The tax dollar savings were equally dramatic—about $1 billion in two years. And the Reagan administration was able to raise the benefits to those in true need—those without any outside income—by 43 percent.

Welfare reform was not some fleeting success. Commented his successor, Gov. Jerry Brown, several years later: ''The Reagan welfare program is holding up, and considering today's high unemployment, it is amazing that it has kept welfare down as much as it has.''

The program would not have become law without Ronald Reagan's personal and persistent involvement. Alan A. Post, then the legislative analyst and a highly respected expert in state government who was a frequent Reagan critic, told the Los Angeles *Times* in 1974 about the welfare bill: ''It would not have happened if the governor had not pushed for it . . . if the governor's real concern had not turned the program around.''

What actually happened is that there was some horse trading between the governor and Bob Moretti, the new Democratic Speaker of the California Assembly, breaking a long impasse between the state's executive and legislative branches on the welfare issue. Moretti agreed to more stringent regulations if Reagan would go along with increased benefits for the truly needy. It was the kind of compromise that Reagan was more than willing to make. It is the kind of "compromise" we can expect from him as President.

The size of government. Under Reagan, the number of state civil service employees (excepting higher education where the governor has only indirect control) remained virtually the same, rising from 108,090 to just 115,090. But the workload often increased—by 30 percent, for example, in the Department of Motor Vehicles and 25 percent in the Department of Public Works.

Crime. Reagan signed more than forty anticrime bills, ranging from the capture of criminals to their imprisonment and punishment. He created the first-ever Inter-Agency Council on Drug Abuse, which coordinated federal, state and local programs. He established the nation's first computer crime information hook-up. He supported numerous measures to strengthen criminal penalties, including the reestablishment of capital punishment for the most serious of murder offenses.

"I believe," he explained, "that capital punishment is a deterrent to the most violent crimes, that it is a measure of self-defense for society to make certain that people who commit the most heinous crimes will not be able to repeat them."

Education. College violence was born on the Berkeley campus of the University of California in 1964. As governor, Reagan signed into law legislation tightening laws against unlawful assembly, making it illegal for anyone kicked off a campus during a disturbance to return within seventy-two hours, classifying the placing of a bomb that results in a death as first-degree murder, suspending state financial support for students convicted of campus disturbances, and making it a crime to coerce by threats the officials or teachers at any educational institution.

In so acting, Reagan was not seeking to deny academic freedom to anyone but to protect the rights of the law-abiding majority on campus against the revolutionary minority.

As a result, while Columbia, Harvard, Cornell, Kent State and the University of Wisconsin were erupting in 1969 and 1970, experiencing mass destruction and even deaths, campuses in California remained open because of the firm stand of Reagan and college presidents like Dr. S. I. Hayakawa of San Francisco State University, now the junior Senator from California.

At the same time, Governor Reagan did not stint on funding for education, considering it an important investment in the state's future. For example:

• Aid to the state university system rose from $240.1 million to $493.2 million, an increase of 105.4 percent, while enrollment increased 43.9 percent.

• Support for the state college system increased from $167.7 to $490.2 million, an increase of 192.3 percent, while enrollment rose 78.4 percent.

• Spending for community colleges went from $74.4 million to 314.8 million, an increase of 323 percent, while enrollment increased 83.5 percent.

• Aid to the primary and secondary school system, grades K-12, increased from $1.154 billion to $2.371 billion, an increase of 105 percent, while enrollment went up 5 percent.

Gov. Reagan worked hard to reverse the trend to centralize authority over education at the state and federal levels. He sought to emphasize the joint cooperation of teachers, parents and local school boards. To this end, he did the following:

• Sponsored and signed the Teacher Preparation and Licensing Law of 1979, which permitted school boards to choose their school district superintendents on the basis of management ability instead of teaching credentials.

• Signed legislation revising teacher tenure law, making it possible to weed out incompetent teachers.

• Signed a law prohibiting school districts from requiring students to be bussed for any purpose without the written permission of the parents.

• Signed a law requiring that textbooks be available for public display and inspection in at least fifty locations and for at least sixty days before adoption.

• Signed a law requiring parental involvement in the development of sex education courses and in the testing of pupils on their personal beliefs or practices.

Energy. When the energy crisis hit in late 1973, Reagan acted quickly and decisively. He implemented an odd-even gas sales system, authorized toll-free lanes on the San Francisco-Oakland Bridge for car pools, ordered a 10 percent reduction in automobile mileage by state vehicles, consolidated motor pool operations for a 15 percent savings in gas buying, and deferred the nitrogen oxide control program for 1966-70 cars, saving an estimated 100 million gallons of gasoline a year.

Both then and now, Ronald Reagan has a simple suggestion on how to make US energy independent: "Get the government out of the energy industry and turn it loose in the marketplace."

Consumer affairs. In 1970, Reagan consolidated all of the various state consumer protection bureaucracies into a single Department of Consumer Affairs—the first such agency in the nation. The move eliminated waste and gave consumers a single department to deal with.

Specific accomplishments included: (1) Conducting over 133,000 investigations, handling nearly 82,000 complaints, and taking over 55,000 disciplinary actions in one year; (2) introducing the One-Stop Complaint Form, coordinating fifteen state agencies handling consumer complaints; (3) supporting the establishment of a Division of Auto Repairs to crack down on unscrupulous practices; and (4) signing the law preventing property insurers from summarily cancelling fire, homeowner and personal property insurance policies without good cause.

Minorities. Because he is a conservative, Ronald Reagan is sometimes described as insensitive or indifferent to the needs and aspirations of minorities. Such a description falls far short of the truth. He has long been concerned with discrimination and with ensuring that everyone has an equal opportunity to advance. But he does not believe in throwing federal, state or local money at the problems of minorities. He sees economic growth and jobs as the answers.

Therefore, as governor, he strove to strengthen private business in minority areas, encourage economic growth, discourage wasteful government spending and needless regulation, and increase educational opportunities. For example, he:

● Signed a law which established a uniform state code for factory-built, pre-fabricated housing and permitted inspection at the factory rather than the construction site. The first such act in the nation, it was copied by almost thirty states within two years. The law reduced the cost of new low-cost housing for lower-income people.

● Developed a State Plan for Employment Opportunity, under which jobs for minority youths, who represented 20 percent of California's 28,000 apprentices, would be significantly increased.

● Signed legislation—the first of its type in the nation—providing tax incentives to private lending institutions to make real estate loans to low income families in inner city neighborhoods.

● Signed legislation—the first of its kind in California —establishing a state scholarship program for vocational education students.

• Created the Career Opportunities Development Program to develop new employment and career possibilities in the state civil service for disadvantaged and minority persons, and to eliminate unnecessary eligibility tests that barred their advancement.

• Signed legislation significantly expanding bilingual study programs to ensure Hispanic students' proficiency in English.

• Made available, for the first time in the history of the state, a Spanish translation of the California Driver's Handbook.

One-fifth of Reagan's first hundred appointments were minority citizens. He appointed the first black ever to head a California department as well as numerous minority community members to policy-making posts on boards, commissions and the judiciary. He named more Hispanics to important state positions than any California governor before him.

Wilson Riles, California's highest-ranking black official, defeated a conservative incumbent, Max Rafferty, to become State Superintendent of Public Instruction in 1970. When he took office, Riles told the *New York Times,* he expected problems from a governor who seemed to sport the same philosophy as Rafferty.

Riles asked for an appointment with Gov. Reagan and got it. He said he did not want his office to become politicized and Reagan agreed. He said he would like personal access to Reagan "if I saw a problem developing," and the governor promised to give him full access.

Several times over the next four years, Riles took positions contrary to those of Gov. Reagan. He always found the governor receptive to hearing an opposing view and sometimes even willing to accept it.

Concluded Riles about Gov. Reagan: "He did his homework, and he was well-organized. He was an administrator in the sense that he set the policies and directions and chose good people to carry them out."

Women. Without fanfare, Reagan worked constantly to eliminate economic and legal barriers against women. He signed laws (1) prohibiting discrimination on account of sex in employment, real estate transactions and the issuance of insurance; (2) establishing the right of a married woman to obtain credit in her own name; (3) allowing married women to buy and sell securities without their husbands' consent; (4) increasing the penalties for rape and the use of firearms in a rape; and (5) providing for the development and improvement of child care centers.

Environment. Under Reagan, California adopted the toughest anti-smog laws in the country and the strongest water pollution control law in US history. A total of 145,000 acres, including forty-one miles of ocean frontage, were added to the state park system. Two underwater park preserves off the coast were set aside. Bike trails, boat harbors and urban parks were improved. A major bond issue for park development was backed.

At the same time, he vetoed a 1971 bill which would have practically eliminated the internal combustion engine after January 1, 1975, and opposed regulations of the Environmental Protection Agency (EPA) that would have caused significant social and economic disruption in the state.

Some think that Reagan's finest hour as governor came on the issue of the Dos Rios dam, a proposed 730-foot structure on the Middle Fork on the Eel River, one of California's few remaining wild rivers.

According to reporter Lou Cannon of the *Washington Post,* "nearly everyone assumed that a decision (in favor of the dam) was a foregone conclusion." The Army Corps of Engineers and the state water bureaucracy favored the dam.

Opposed were Norman (Ike) Livermore, Reagan's director of resources, and some other aides, a few conservationists from Round Valley, which would have been flooded by the dam, and some Indians, first herded into the valley by Army troops in the late nineteenth century.

Round Valley contained gravesites of the Yuki Indian tribe, said some archeologists. The gravesites and some of the valley land are ours by treaty, argued the Indians, and their plea proved decisive.

"We've broken too damn many treaties," said Reagan in turning down the Dos Rios dam. "We're not going to flood them (the Indians) out."

The Reagan record set an example for the rest of the nation. Officials from New York, Illinois and West Virginia adopted some form of California's welfare program. Robert Carleson, Reagan's welfare reform chief, went to Washington, D. C. to head up a drive to help other states institute California's welfare system.

California's concept of treating the mentally ill with an expanded system of community mental health programs became a model for other states, as did the innovation of allowing conjugal visits for prison inmates with good behavior records.

In all of these programs, Ronald Reagan strove to bring government under control, to put a limit on how much personal income government takes in taxes. As he said:

"This idea will become a reality. It must prevail because if it does not, the free society we have known for 200 years, the ideal of a government by consent of the governed, will simply cease to exist."

PART FOUR

THE PRESIDENT

Chapter Eighteen

Off and Running

Six months after his retirement as Governor of California, Ronald Reagan was broadcasting a five-times-a-week radio commentary on more than three hundred stations, writing a weekly column for more than two hundred daily newspapers, making speeches from Los Angeles to Miami and proclaiming that the Republican Party must raise an ideological banner "of bold colors and no pale pastels." He was deeply concerned about the $50 billion deficit that Republican President Gerald Ford had incurred as well as Ford's avid pursuit of detente, including the adoption of the SALT accords and his plan to turn the Panama Canal over to Panamanian dictator Omar Torrijos, a self-avowed Marxist. Still, his basic impulse was to give Jerry Ford a chance. He did not relish the idea of running against an incumbent Republican President, even an appointed one. He saw himself, in the words of his long-time secretary, Helene von Damm, "as a party unifier, not a party divider." So he hesitated about declaring his candidacy for President, as he had once before.

In 1968, Reagan made a very belated bid for the Republican presidential nomination, delaying his formal announcement until the convention actually opened in Miami. He offered a rather naive explanation: "The office seeks the man, the man doesn't seek the office."

Frustrated friends hired F. Clifton White, the man behind Barry Goldwater's nomination in 1964, to put it together for the reluctant Reagan. But White was too late: Nixon, along with Goldwater and Sen. Strom Thurmond, was busy throughout 1967 and 1968 locking up the South—and the nomination.

Nevertheless, Reagan made an impressive showing in Miami. He waited in his trailer outside the convention hall while Clif White brought the key Florida delegation to see him. Some of the women delegates, *Newsweek* reported, were weeping because they wanted to vote for Reagan but were bound to Nixon.

He made an eleventh hour appeal to Strom Thurmond and "did everything but get down beside the couch and pray" for his support, he later told aides. "Son," responded Thurmond, who had firmly committed himself to Nixon, "you'll be President some day, but this isn't your year." He even scared Nixon's delegate hunter, John Sears, who estimated that Reagan was very close to breaking open the convention.

But it was a classic case of too little too late, and Nixon won on the first ballot with 692 votes while Gov. Nelson Rockefeller received 299 and Reagan 182.

It was far from an ignominious defeat, as *Human Events* pointed out.

"Because Reagan came very close to unravelling Nixon's majority strength in the South, Nixon felt constrained to concentrate his attention on keeping his Southern support.

"He could do this only by issuing ironclad assurances to delegates such as Senators Strom Thurmond and John Tower that he would do his utmost to guide the Republican party in a starboard direction. Thus, even in losing, Reagan managed to win a victory for conservatism."

Eight years later, he was almost but not quite ready to admit that the man must seek the office.

In July 1975, after several months of indecision, he gave permission to an old friend, Sen. Paul Laxalt of Nevada, to form a "Citizens for Reagan" committee, to see if there was significant national support for a Reagan run for the Presidency.

The soundings were good, the polls were promising and the money was there to finance a campaign. And on November 20, 1975, at the National Press Club in Washington, D.C., Ronald Reagan announced he was a candidate for the 1976 Republican Presidential nomination. He said:

"The American dream has somewhere been mislaid. We have to hope and believe the loss is temporary. Millions of Americans across this land still live by that dream and are determined to keep and expand their freedom and independence. They know that to do this they must reduce the power centralized in Washington.

"Over these past ten months going to almost every part of this country I've seen this in the faces of our citizens and heard it in their voices. We hunger for a sense of mission; to have once again a pride in our capacity to perform great deeds.

"Our children have heard too many political and economic myths in too many classrooms and all of us have heard too much of political demagoguery. The people are the best agents of their own destinies. Armed with the truth they will meet any challenge and make any sacrifice. . . .

"The hour is late for turning our nation toward a new, constructive course; to make government again our servant and to bring back to a human, understandable scale control by us of our own destiny. I am convinced that the great strength of the American people still glows and can be reignited to the beacon of freedom it once was. . . .

"I make one promise and one only to the people of America—Republicans, Democrats and Independents—and I make it also to myself. The principles I believe in and which I'll be discussing in these coming months will not be changed or compromised to meet so-called political realities."

The people liked what they heard. A Gallup poll in late November, following the Reagan announcement, showed that Reagan had surged ahead of President Ford among Republicans and independents. Reagan outpolled Ford among Republicans by 40 percent to 32 percent—compared to a Ford advantage of 48-25 percent in mid-October. Among independents, the Reagan lead was 27-25 percent, compared to a Ford lead of 26-20 percent in October. When an NBC pool matched Reagan and Ford against potential Democratic candidate Hubert Humphrey, Reagan led 48-44 percent while Ford trailed by 44 to 46 percent.

The New Hampshire primary on February 24, 1976, was the first in the nation and a key contest although only twenty delegates were involved. Reagan had the backing of Gov. Meldrim Thomson publisher William Loeb of the *Manchester Union-Leader* and other key Republicans in the Granite State. The early polls had him comfortably in the lead.

Then the Ford people resurrected an old speech in which Reagan had proposed transferring $90 billion worth of federal programs to the states. There were broad hints that things like social security, veterans benefits, and welfare payments would be slashed if Ronald Reagan became President.

Reagan was placed on the defensive. Doubts were raised about his ability to occupy the White House. In a gross overreaction, his campaign staff, led by John Sears, pulled Reagan out of New Hampshire in the last several days, neglecting to tell him that his lead in the polls had evaporated.

Reagan received 49.4 percent of the popular vote, and lost New Hampshire by a razor-thin 1,587 votes. A lot of Republicans, looking at the broad political and local media support that Reagan enjoyed, understandably reacted: "If he can't win in a state like New Hampshire, he's not going to make it."

It was a heart-breaking loss. A switch of only eight hundred votes in the state's nonbinding primary would have produced the headline, "Reagan Beats Ford," and established momentum for later primaries.

Much later, Reagan learned that he did in fact get more votes than Ford in New Hampshire, but they didn't count. Here is the story: The Ford people entered twenty-one candidates for the twenty-one delegate slots. The Reagan people entered twenty-four, because three pro-Reagan delegates qualified at the last moment and would not withdraw. Voters were instructed to vote for the official slate, but at least 5 percent of the Republican voters went for all twenty-four Reagan delegates.

New Hampshire law provides that if you vote for more than twenty-one delegates, your entire ballot is invalidated—even in the popular vote contest between Ford and Reagan. As a result, some three thousand New Hampshire ballots were thrown out, along with a winning margin for Ronald Reagan in the nation's first primary.

Ford won succeeding primaries in Florida, Illinois (Reagan's birthplace) and Wisconsin, establishing himself clearly as the frontrunner. At that point, Reagan took off his boxing gloves, jettisoned the Eleventh Commandment ("Thou Shalt Not Speak Ill of Any Other Republican") and began hitting the President hard on Panama, détente, deficit spending and other issues.

He also broke an embargo placed on TV speeches by campaign manager John Sears, who had feared they might remind voters of Reagan's Hollywood background. Sears' strategy had, in fact, deprived Reagan of his most powerful weapon. It was a little like forbidding Joe Louis to use his right hand in the ring.

With the guidance of Sen. Jesse Helms and his aide Tom Ellis, Ronald Reagan gave a brilliant TV performance on the eve of the March 23 North Carolina primary. As a result, he beat Ford decisively in the Tarheel State, filled up his nearly depleted treasury with $1.4 million and began an amazing comeback. Reagan shut out the President in Texas on May 1, winning all ninety-six delegates. All of a sudden, a lot of observers began saying that Reagan could go all the way.

In state primaries and conventions across the country, Reagan's forces showed ever-increasing strength. By the end of May, Reagan and Ford found themselves in a virtual deadlock for the nomination.

The climax, although it was not totally clear then, came with the June 8 primaries in California, Ohio and New Jersey. Reagan knew he had little chance in New Jersey, but potential strength in Ohio with ninety-seven delegates at stake. California, with its 167 delegates in a winner-take-all primary, was absolutely critical.

Reagan thought he was well ahead in his home state until "we let ourselves get scared by a Field Poll that had me behind. Two days before the primary," he recalls, and after extensive campaigning in California, "we realized the poll was phony as a three-dollar bill. So we went into Ohio for one day and, good Lord, we came out with 40 percent of the vote. I'm convinced we could have won Ohio."

As it was Reagan received only six delegates to Ford's ninety-one in Ohio. But the Reagan team still believed they could win the nomination with 1,140 votes on the first rollcall by picking up a fair share of the uncommitted delegates in the East. They miscalculated, Reagan later admitted, the political power of the Presidency.

"We saw Pennsylvania go from 95 (for Ford) down to 76, and in Kansas City it went back to 93. I hadn't realized until we began dealing with those uncommitteds . . . there are still old-fashioned machines with that kind of power. . . . In those areas where people are told how to vote, we lost."

By late June, the delegate advantage was shifting slowly but inexorably to President Ford. Something dramatic had to be done. Sears persuaded Reagan to announce before the convention met (an historical first) that his running mate would be Sen. Richard Schweiker of Pennsylvania, a Republican moderate. Reagan hoped to persuade the media that he was not beaten and to pry loose delegates from Pennsylvania and other Northeast states, Schweiker assured Reagan that he could deliver the urgently needed votes.

Schweiker overestimated his persuasive powers and underestimated the determination of the GOP establishment to stick with Ford, a predictable moderate conservative, over Reagan, a westerner with few commitments to them.

Many grassroots conservatives were furious at the choice of Schweiker—calling John Sears a "Svengali" and worse. Reagan himself put the choice and Sen. Schweiker into perspective, writing to one of his most faithful supporters:

"I didn't pull the Senator out of a hat. His seat mate is our chairman, Paul Laxalt, who, on the basis of their relationship, attests to his integrity and character. . . . We found ourselves in agreement in our opposition to amnesty for draft-dodgers and deserters, abortion on demand, forced busing, gun control, détente, and the Helsinki pact. We support the death penalty and a stiffer anti-crime program, as well as prayer in the schoolroom. Senator Schweiker has introduced a constitutional amendment to restore prayer and Bible reading in public schools. His record on national defense is sound, and he believes we must once again become number one in military strength."

Reagan went on to say that rather than just talking about party unity, he was really doing something about it "without sacrificing (conservative) beliefs and principles."

But the Schweiker gambit was to no avail. Reagan lost his party's nomination to Ford by 1,187 delegate votes to 1,070. It was no disgrace. He would have been the first candidate in 92 years to take the nomination away from an incumbent President. The next morning, over breakfast with Senator Laxalt, Ron and Nancy Reagan talked about what a wonderful once-in-a-lifetime experience it had been. As *Newsweek* reported, Laxalt cautioned them: "These are strange times. Anything could happen." The Reagans laughed.

That night after Gerald Ford had accepted his party's nomination, he called Ronald Reagan to the platform, which was normal, and then asked him to say a few words, which was not. Reagan gave a rapt convention and tens of millions of listeners a little sample of what they would have heard if he had been nominated. His brief remarks, delivered without notes or a teleprompter, were agreed to be the rhetorical highlight of the 1976 convention:

"Someone asked me to write a letter for a time capsule that is going to be opened in Los Angeles a hundred years from now, on our Tricentennial. . . .

"Riding down the coasts in an automobile, looking at the blue Pacific out on one side and the Santa Ynez Mountains on the other, I couldn't help but wonder if it was going to be that beautiful a hundred years from now as it was on that summer day. . . .

"Let your own minds turn to that task. You're going to write for people a hundred years from now who know all about us. We know nothing about them. We don't know what kind of a world they'll be living in.

"Suddenly I thought of the problems of which the President spoke here tonight; the challenges confronting us; the erosion of freedom that has taken place under Democratic rule in this country; the invasion of private rights; the controls and restrictions on the vitality of the great free economy that we enjoy. These are our challenges that we must meet.

"And then again there is that challenge of which he spoke, that we live in a world in which the great powers have poised and aimed at each other horrible missiles of destruction, nuclear weapons that can in a matter of minutes arrive in each other's country and destroy virtually the civilized world we live in.

"And suddenly it dawned on me, those who would read this letter a hundred years from now will know whether those missiles were fired. They will know whether we met our challenge.

"Whether they had the freedom that we have known up until now, will depend on what we do here. Will they look back with appreciation and say, Thank God for those people in 1976 who headed off that loss of freedom; who kept us now a hundred years later free; who kept our world from nuclear destruction? And if we fail, they probably won't get to read the letter at all because it spoke of individual freedom and they won't be allowed to talk of that or read of it.

"This is our challenge. And this is why we're here in this hall tonight. Better than we've ever done before, we've got to quit talking to each other and about each other and go out and communicate to the world that we may be fewer in numbers than we've ever been, but we carry the message they're waiting for."

Following the convention, columnist Patrick Buchanan postmortemed that Reagan should have started hitting Ford earlier and harder, especially at the GOP convention. Columnist M. Stanton Evans agreed, arguing that Reagan's top operatives backed away from a battle on the issues at Kansas City that could well have tipped the balance to Reagan.

Human Events pointed to the paradox between the delegates adopting a staunchly conservative platform and rejecting a staunchly conservative candidate. In this writer's opinion, Republicans narrowly picked Ford over Reagan in Kansas City because they are loyalists to a fault. They like Jerry Ford. They knew him, they were comfortable with him, they felt he had earned the nomination. That kind of loyalist sentiment was to work powerfully in Reagan's favor at the 1980 GOP convention.

In the fall, contrary to some reports and to Jerry Ford's own recollection, Ronald Reagan worked hard for the Republican ticket from top to bottom.

He campaigned in twenty-five states with a schedule as heavy or heavier than it had been during the primaries. He did a series of TV commercials for national use, ranging from five to thirty minutes in length. He delivered a thirty-minute national telecast, which netted about $1 million for the Ford-Dole campaign. He signed a fundraising letter which collected more than $1 million for the Republican ticket.

"The President and I appeared together," recalls Reagan, "at a closed circuit TV fund-raising dinner in Los Angeles, which was the largest in the nation and collected the most money."

Theoretically, Reagan could have done more, but it took the Ford campaign staff nearly a month to make any specific request of him and by then the former governor was committed to helping many other Republican candidates. Significantly, neither Reagan nor any of his chief political aides were invited to Vail, Colorado, where President Ford and his staff held a campaign planning meeting immediately after the Kansas City convention.

In light of these facts, the blame for any under-utilization of Reagan in the 1975 presidential campaign lies with the man who won the nomination, not the man who lost it.

Over the next two years, Ronald Reagan resumed his stump speaking, his daily radio commentary and his newspaper column. His call for less government and more individual freedom became more popular than ever. By mid-1977, he was receiving about two hundred speaking invitations a week.* He could have easily settled into senior statesman status (he was, after all, now past sixty-five although he did not look or act within a decade of it), but something new had been added, after all these years. He wanted to be President.

He smarted over his narrow nomination loss to Gerald Ford. He felt that Ford's advantages of incumbency were not only enormous but unfair. And he believed strongly that he could have beaten Jimmy Carter.

He told Albert Hunt of the *Wall Street Journal* in August 1977 that he would not make any decision until after the November 1978

---

* The *Wall Street Journal* estimated that his net worth in July 1980 was more than $2 million, up from $1.5 million at the end of 1975.

elections. But, he added: "If circumstances are such that I honestly believe I offered the best opportunity to achieve what I believe in, I suppose I'd do it again."

There was not really much "supposing." He was campaigning and raising money for Republicans from California to New York. He formed Citizens for the Republic (CFTR) with nearly $1 million left over from his 1976 campaign—the money came in too late to be spent. Under the expert hand of his longtime aide, Lyn Nofziger, CFTR distributed funds to Republican candidates, held training schools around the country and provided a holding area for a number of old and new Reagan advisers, including pollster Richard Wirthlin and foreign policy consultant Richard Allen, a hardliner on Soviet Russia and national defense.

In the fall of 1978, he spoke in twenty-six states, making a total of eight appearances, even one for liberal Republican Sen. Charles Percy of Illinois, who needed to revise his reputation as a high spender. (Percy won, narrowly.)

After the elections, he spent a fast-paced week in Europe, visiting Great Britain, France and West Germany. He met with Dr. David Owen, the British Foreign Minister; Oliver Stirm, French Secretary of State for Foreign Affairs, and West German Chancellor Helmut Schmidt. He visited Berlin, along with US Ambassador William Stoessel, who told Reagan, according to the Los Angeles *Times,* it is important that American political figures keep reminding Berliners the US has not forgotten them.

Upon his return he gathered his advisers at his home in Pacific Palisades to discuss 1980. They agreed his age wouldn't be a problem unless he acted old. His "right-wing" image wasn't a problem either, they decided, in the conservative climate of 1980 as long as he came across as a thinking conservative. At the end of the session, according to *Newsweek,* Reagan gave the word: the man would seek the office.

Reagan went to work immediately. In January 1979, he spent three days on Capitol Hill in Washington, D.C., visiting Republicans of all philosophical persuasions, ranging from liberal Charles "Mac" Mathias of Maryland to conservative Barry Goldwater of Arizona. As columnists Jack Germond and Jules Witcover of the *Washington Star* reported, his strategy was to enlist key 1976 supporters of President Ford to convince possible opponents for the presidential nomination (and GOP delegates) that the Republican establishment was now on his side. Ford's reluctance to encourage any effort on his behalf (he was making an estimated $1 million a year in speaking fees and other activities and obviously enjoying a leisurely life in Palm Springs, California) created a political vacuum which Reagan easily filled.

Liberal columnist Mary McGrory summed up the campaign at this point: "If he looks 'pretty damn young' and he sounds pretty damn moderate, who is going to stop Ronald Reagan?"

In plain fact, it was not so much a matter of Reagan sounding more moderate as the nation becoming more conservative as a result of failed liberal policies and programs over a period of thirty and more years.

In the summer of 1979, the inflation rate hit 13.5 percent. Jimmy Carter admitted to a budget deficit of $61 billion. Three years of the Carter presidency, Reagan pointed out in a message to a Young Americans for Freedom convention, "has brought us the fall of Afghanistan, the give-away of the Panama Canal, the sell-out of Taiwan and the collapse of Iran." He mentioned the conservative victories around the world—in Sweden, France, Australia, New Zealand, Canada and Great Britain. He pointed out that Margaret Thatcher led her Conservative Party to victory behind the simple slogan: "Britain's better off with the Conservatives."

Ronald Reagan declared that "all of us should be prepared to tell everyone who will listen, 'America is better off with the conservatives.' "

In March 1979, Sen. Paul Laxalt announced the formation of the Reagan for President Committee at a crowded news conference in Washington, D.C. In 1976, Laxalt had been a lonely Washington voice for Reagan's presidential hopes—practically the only Member of Congress, besides Rep. Philip Crane of Illinois, to support the former California governor. This time, he was personally joined by half a dozen Senators and Congressmen and distributed a list of over 250 prominent Republicans as founding members of the Committee. Included were such Ford administration officeholders as former Treasury Secretary William Simon, former Secretary of Agriculture Earl Butz, former HEW Secretary Caspar Weinberger, and former Interior Secretary Stanley Hathaway. The announcement, it was stressed, was not a formal declaration of candidacy by Reagan, who sensibly wanted to delay his official entry until later in the year. In the meantime, the Committee could legally begin lining up delegates and raising money.

Sen. Laxalt concluded his remarks by saying of Reagan:

"He is the man who pioneered the concept of putting responsible restraints on government—an idea whose time has come today with the public's resistance to excessive taxation, irresponsible spending, and oppressive regulation of our lives.

"We pledge our support and commit our efforts to Governor Reagan because we believe he is the most able man in America today to inspire our people, to deal with problems and not shrink before them, and to restore the United States to a respected role in the affairs of the world."

Many Americans agreed with Laxalt and the Reagan for President Committee. In April, the Yankelovich survey for *Time* showed Jimmy Carter and Ronald Reagan in a deadheat—44 percent to 44 percent. Ten months earlier, a similar Yankelovich poll gave Carter a 3 percent lead. Reagan was the clear favorite among Republicans in the *Time* survey, only former President Ford giving him any serious opposition.

Obviously, Republicans and Americans in general were not impressed by the usual objections to Reagan—that he was too old, too conservative and not smart enough.

The obvious rejoinder to the former was: Too old for what? At issue, after all, was a candidate for President, not the decathlon. It was true that if elected, Reagan would, at sixty-nine, be the oldest man ever to assume the Presidency: William Henry Harrison was sixty-eight when he entered the White House in 1841.

But the post-World War II world was dominated by giants like Winston Churchill, Charles de Gaulle, Konrad Adenauer, Francisco Franco, Mao Tse-tung and Dwight Eisenhower, all of whom were older than Reagan when in charge. When asked about his age, the governor often retorted: "You know, I was in the Orient last year. They thought I was too young."

In October 1979, he underwent a full physical examination, including a treadmill stress test, and passed with flying colors. His vital statistics are as follows: height, six-feet-two, weight 185 pounds, blood pressure 130/80. He had successful prostate surgery in 1967 and receives shots for a chronic allergy. He has a hearing loss in both ears from a gun being fired near his head in a 1930's film, but requires no hearing aid. He is nearsighted and wears contact lenses. He does not smoke and limits his drinking to an occasional cocktail or glass of wine.

He keeps fit by exercising every day with an exercise wheel he carries in his luggage. He is an excellent horseman and swimmer. He has been an outdoor man all his life. At his ranch, Rancho del Cielo, some thirty miles from Santa Barbara, California, Reagan likes nothing better than to work with his hands. He remodeled, almost single-handedly, the two-bedroom Spanish style ranch home in which he and Nancy spend their weekends and vacations. He also built a fence around their home out of old telephone poles and constructed a rock patio. This isolated mountain home two thousand feet high (its name is Spanish for "ranch in the sky") is Reagan's special retreat where, he explains, "just getting here overnight somehow makes a difference inside me."

As for Reagan being too conservative, Louis Harris (who started out as John F. Kennedy's personal pollster) discovered that the majority of the American people liked the former governor's philosophy.

By 54 percent to 34 percent, reported Harris, a majority of Americans did not go along with the contention that Reagan "is too conservative to be trusted as President."

By 58 percent to 34 percent, a majority of Americans felt Reagan "has a highly attractive personality and would inspire confidence as President."

By 59 percent to 29 percent, a majority of Americans felt that Reagan "is right to want to get government out of business so that free enterprise can operate freely."

And by 53 to 34 percent, a majority of Americans felt that "Reagan is no ordinary politician, because he really wants to cut federal spending and cut back the federal bureaucracy."

As to intelligence, Reagan was smart enough as Governor of California to earn the plaudits of such unconservative media as *Newsweek,* which described his two administrations as "on balance successful years running the nation's largest state—a passage in which he balanced a deep-red budget, held down employment by the state, pared the welfare rolls, and in other ways demonstrated his competence to govern."

The key word is "competence." Observers were agreed that Gov. Ronald Reagan was an effective, competent administrator with conservative principles who made those principles work.

There were some problems with the emerging Reagan campaign in mid-1979 but they lay, not with the candidate, but with his staff. At the core of all of them was the cool, pragmatic, always confident John Sears. It was really very simple: Sears insisted on running the campaign his way while other Reagan aides objected to his front-runner strategy, which severely restricted Reagan's personal appearances and conservative rhetoric.

As a result, Lyn Nofziger, a former newspaperman who first worked with Reagan in 1966 during his initial campaign for governor, resigned in August, while still pledging his support for Reagan for President. Earlier in the year, the campaign had lost another talented political operative, David Keene, who had run Reagan's Southern operation in 1976. Keene bucked for a major role in 1980, but was offered liaison with Capitol Hill. Invited to become national director for George Bush's presidential campaign, Keene hesitated and then accepted, insisting he still held Reagan in the highest esteem.

Reagan was never really comfortable with Sears, reportedly commenting that the thirty-nine-year-old Washington lawyer looked you in the necktie knot when he was talking to you. But he valued highly his political acumen as did Reagan adviser Mike Deaver, who recommended Sears as the 1980 campaign manager over the objections of Nofziger and Sen. Paul Laxalt. Ironically, Sears soon threatened to quit unless Deaver did. Deaver went voluntarily in the fall, leaving the campaign securely in the hands of John Sears. The only person left from Reagan's days as California governor was chief-of-staff Ed Meese.

The stage was set for his formal entry into the 1980 race. In a significant act that showed he would not concede any part of the nation in his quest for the Presidency, Ronald Reagan flew to New York City and there, on November 13, 1979, announced his intention to seek the Republican nomination for President of the United States. He delivered his remarks to a packed ballroom at the New York Hilton Hotel and over a special network of TV stations that reached an estimated 79 percent of the American people. (All three of the major TV networks refused to sell him time for a half-hour program.)

He pledged: a federal tax cut along the lines of the Kemp-Roth bill . . . an orderly transfer of federal programs to the state and local levels along with the funds to pay for them . . . a revitalized energy program based on increased production of oil, natural gas, and coal . . . the development of a long-range diplomatic strategy to meet the challenge of the Soviet Union . . . statehood for Puerto Rico . . . a North American accord among the US, Canada and Mexico within which each nation would develop its full potential in resources, technology and foodstuffs.

He concluded.

"In recent months leaders in our government have told us that we the people have lost confidence in ourselves; that we must regain our spirit and our will to achieve our national goals. Well, it is true there is a lack of confidence, an unease with things the way they are.

"But the confidence we have lost is confidence in our government's policies. Our unease can almost be called bewilderment at how our defense strength has deteriorated. The great productivity of our industry is now surpassed by virtually all the major nations who compete with us for world markets. And our currency is no longer the stable measure of value it once was.

"But there remains the greatness of our people, our capacity for dreaming up fantastic deeds and bringing them off to the surprise of an unbelieving world. When Washington's men were freezing at Valley Forge, Tom Paine told his fellow Americans: 'We have it in our power to begin the world over again.' We still have that power. . . .

"I believe this nation hungers for a spiritual revival; hungers once again to see honor placed above political expediency; to see government once again the protector of our liberties, not the distributor of gifts and privileges. Government should uphold and not undermine those institutions which are custodians of the very values upon which civilization is founded—religion, education and, above all, the family. Government cannot be clergyman, teacher and parent. It is our servant, beholden to us."

On television, Ronald Reagan paused and then, looking directly at his audience, sounded the theme which has consistently been at the center of his personal philosophy and public career:

"A troubled and afflicted mankind looks to us, pleading for us to keep our rendezvous with destiny; that we will uphold the principles of self-reliance, self-discipline, morality and—above all —responsible liberty for every individual; that we will become that shining city on a hill.

"I believe that you and I together can keep this rendezvous with destiny."

Chapter Nineteen

Winning the Nomination I

It was a crowded field. Vying for the Republican presidential nomination, besides Reagan, were Sen. Howard Baker, the Senate minority leader; former Gov. John Connally of Texas; Sen. Robert Dole of Kansas, the 1976 vice presidential nominee; Congressman Philip Crane of Illinois, an articulate conservative; Congressman John Anderson of Illinois, a no-less articulate liberal; and Ambassador George Bush, also of Texas by way of Connecticut. Perhaps never before has a political party had seven more experienced and impressive candidates for the nation's highest office.

All analysts were agreed that Reagan was the strong frontrunner with Baker his most serious opposition. Despite his impressive record and speaking ability, Connally was not catching on in the polls. Dole was poorly organized and often abrasive in his campaigning. Crane's chance would come only if Reagan faltered badly. Anderson was too liberal for at least two-thirds of the party he wanted to lead. And while George Bush had a great resume and was campaigning hard, he had not won an election since 1968 when he was reelected to Congress from Houston.

Reagan was unquestionably the man to beat by virtue of (1) his near capture of the presidential nomination in 1976; (2) his experienced campaign team; (3) his ability to raise funds; (4) his conservative stand on the issues which matched so well the mood of the American people; and (5) his matchless speaking style. William F. Buckley, Jr., no mean rhetorician, referred to Reagan's "singular polemical skill, his capacity to penetrate bad arguments and leave his political enemies twisting slowly, slowly in the wind."

The first test came on January 21 with the Iowa precinct caucuses. Confident of his popularity and support among longtime backers, Reagan barely campaigned in Iowa. He refused to participate in a Republican debate in Des Moines, just two weeks before the caucuses. It was a "Rose Garden" strategy, generally followed by incumbent Presidents and carefully plotted by John Sears.

But when the Iowa Republican caucuses were through voting, George Bush had defeated Ronald Reagan by 31.5 percent to 29.4 percent. It was a startling upset by the near-unknown Bush. It prompted a former Reagan aide to remark: "A Rose Garden strategy only works when you have a Rose Garden."

Reagan's own polls later showed that 60 percent of Iowa didn't realize he had been there, which is not surprising. Bush spent thirty-one *days* in the state, Reagan only 41 *hours*.

Columnist William Safire of the *New York Times* wrote that Reagan "needed the shock of his loss to remind him that the business of a challenger (to the President) is to challenge, and that a candidate cannot win a nomination by playing not to lose it."

Knowing he was on the spot, John Sears proposed changes in the campaign staff, starting with the removal of Ed Meese. But Reagan didn't buy it. Instead, he brought in William J. Casey, former chairman of the Securities and Exchange Commission and an old acquaintance, to manage the campaign, leaving the day-to-day strategy to Sears. The normally unflappable Sears was furious, but decided that without him, Reagan could not make it and stayed on.

But it was only a matter of time until John Sears would go. He had made several serious mistakes, including gross overspending (the Reagan campaign had spent nearly two-thirds of its federally limited $18 million budget by late February), undercutting old Reagan friends and advisers and, the most serious of all, underestimating Reagan. Sears came to think that he was indispensable to the campaign, that, in effect, he and not Ronald Reagan was the candidate. The steady stream of stories, columns and telecasts about John Sears throughout 1979 and early 1980 created the erroneous impression in many minds that Reagan was merely a puppet manipulated by Sears.

Knowing that he had to win New Hampshire, Reagan abandoned Sears' "imperial strategy" and plunged into twenty-one days of intense campaigning that would have done in a man of thirty-five. He agreed to debate in New Hampshire, not once but twice. After the first debate, his polls told him that he came across well. The second debate was the turning point in New Hampshire and, it could be said, the entire primary campaign.

Reagan challenged Bush to a two-man debate on January 29, and the *Nashua Telegraph* newspaper agreed to sponsor it. Two days before the debate, the Federal Election Commission ruled that the paper's sponsorship constituted an illegal political contribution. Reagan offered to split the $3,500 debate cost with Bush, who refused, so Reagan paid the entire bill.

The other candidates began complaining about being excluded. Sears suggested that the two-man debate be expanded to include everyone. Reagan's people began inviting the other candidates to come. Bush told the press that he would reluctantly agree to a six-man debate, but later complained he did not know that invitations were in fact being extended by Reagan to the other candidates.

Saturday night, Reagan, Howard Baker, Robert Dole, Philip Crane and John Anderson arrived at the Nashua High School gym and went into an anteroom to discuss how to proceed. Bush arrived separately and was invited to join the others. He declined—a fatal mistake. He later explained the thought he might be walking into a trap. When Reagan appeared on stage with the other four candidates, he argued for a six-man forum—the same forum that Bush had publicly agreed to.

Moderator Jon Breen, editor of the *Telegraph,* declared that the format could not be changed at the last moment. And then came the famous scene, as reported by *Time:*

Reagan grabbed the mike. Breen ordered the power to be cut off. Reagan shouted with impressive raw anger, "I'm paying for this microphone, Mr. Breen!" Someone yelled at Breen from the audience: "Didn't you ever hear of freedom of the press?" Bush sat shaken and silent. At last, he said confusedly, "I was invited here by the editors of the Nashua newspaper. I am their guest. I will play by the rules, and I'm glad to be here."

A Baker aide said of Reagan: "He was terrific." Reagan's own comment: "Maybe the people like to see a candidate sometimes not under control." The other candidates bitterly accused Bush of excluding them.

An exhausted Bush flew home to Houston that weekend while Reagan campaigned in the New Hampshire snow right up to primary day. It was a telling contrast for a campaign in which Reagan's age was supposed to be a handicap.

In what had been billed as a close contest in New Hampshire, Reagan buried Bush by more than two to one, collecting as many votes as his six GOP rivals combined. The figures: Reagan 50 percent; Bush 23 percent; Baker 13 percent; Anderson 10 percent;

Connally 2 percent; Crane 2 percent; and Dole less than half of one percent.

Reagan won everywhere. He won three quarters of the vote in heavily blue collar, industrial Manchester. He beat Bush 60 to 14 percent among French Canadians, an important ethnic group in New Hampshire. He won nine to one in the small cities, two to one in the rural areas, three to one in the towns. He had a two to one edge over Bush among Protestant voters and better than a three to one margin among Catholics. He also defeated Bush 39-15 percent among white collar voters.

The afternoon of the New Hampshire voting, Reagan called in Sears and handed him a press release announcing his resignation. Sears was stunned but professed not to be surprised. Two days later, he held a new conference in Washington, D.C., in which he tried to defend his management of the campaign. It was not a very politic performance for so talented a politician. Sears later visited former President Ford, hinting he might be willing to help a Ford challenge to Reagan. His visit lent credence to the charge by conservatives that he was only a "hired gun."

Explained Reagan about Sears' departure: "John is a fine strategist, but there was a gap in administration, a lack of communication between the headquarters and the field. We just had a disagreement about that."

Sen. Paul Laxalt was more blunt about Sears' departure: "It's a good development. Now we can change the grand strategy and run a grassroots campaign."

Which is precisely what Ronald Reagan did throughout the March primaries, campaigning so effectively that before the month's end, Baker, Connally and Dole had all withdrawn from the nomination race.

He talked simply and directly about the major issues of the day:

● Inflation. "Government causes inflation and government can make it go away" by cutting taxes 30 percent over the next three years and turning welfare administration and funding over to state and local government.

● Energy. "The energy industry today is virtually nationalized. . . . If we turn both (energy and agriculture) loose in the marketplace, they will produce the food and fuel we need."

● Foreign affairs. The Soviet Union "has one course and one course only. It is dedicated to the belief that it is going to take over the world." One Reagan passage that always sparked thunderous applause: "The President said we must ratify the SALT II treaty because no one will like us if we don't. He said we should give away the Panama Canal because no one would like us if he didn't. It is time to tell the President, 'We don't care if they like us or not. We intend to be respected throughout the world.' "

● Social issues. He opposed the Equal Rights Amendment, abortion on demand and the legalization of marijuana. He supported a constitutional amendment to permit voluntary school prayer.

Republicans liked what they heard, very much.

On March 4, Bush narrowly defeated Anderson in Massachusetts by 1,200 votes, with Reagan a close third, a remarkable showing in such unfriendly territory for the man from California. The percentages were: Bush 31 percent; Anderson 31 percent and Reagan 29 percent. The same day, Reagan topped Anderson in Vermont by 31 percent to 30 percent, with Bush third at 23 percent. A discouraged Howard Baker, who ran a distant fourth in both states, withdrew the next day, March 5.

On March 8, Reagan decisively whipped John Connally in South Carolina, 54 to 30 percent, with Bush trailing far behind at 14 percent. Connally had invested an estimated $1 million in the South Carolina primary and campaigned extensively alongside the highly popular Sen. Strom Thurmond, but to little avail. Reagan beat his rivals in all six of the state's congressional districts, winning all twenty-five of South Carolina's delegates to the GOP national convention.

The next day, in Houston, John Connally announced that he was giving up his quest for the Republican nomination, declaring that Ronald Reagan was "still the champ."

The Baker and Connally withdrawals along with the dip in fortunes of Bush produced a number of stories about the possibility of former President Gerald Ford getting into the race. Unnamed aides kept saying that Ford wanted to run, but Ford himself was more equivocal. Behind his sudden interest was his fear that Reagan might blow a golden Republican opportunity to regain the White House along with his long-standing resentment against Reagan for allegedly not campaigning "hard enough" for him in 1976.

Ford went so far as to say publicly that he doubted Ronald Reagan could defeat Jimmy Carter in November. To which Reagan had the perfect rejoinder: "I never lost a Presidential race to Jimmy Carter."

On March 11, Reagan swept primaries in Florida, Alabama and Georgia, defeating George Bush by two to one in Florida, three to one in Alabama and five to one in Georgia. He won 105 of the 114 delegates from the three states. Reagan won right across the ideological spectrum in Florida, receiving 68 percent of the conservatives, 46 percent of the moderates and even 41 percent of the liberals. Anderson was a distant third in Florida and Georgia, receiving 9 percent of the vote in each state.

On March 15, it was revealed by the *New York Times* that John Connally had persuaded Gov. William Clements of Texas and Gov. James Rhodes of Ohio not to back former President Ford's entry into the race for fear of splitting the party.

Two days later, Ford announced he had made "a final and certain decision" not to seek the 1980 Republican presidential nomination. "I am not a candidate. I will not be a candidate," he said from his California home after several hours of discussion with his advisers. "I will support the nominee of my party in every way and with all the energy I have." He said that his becoming a candidate "might further divide my party."

Ford and his advisers were realists. They knew that the only way Ford could beat Reagan (given the Californian's long lead) was to challenge him directly in primary after primary. That meant lots of money and a national organization, neither of which Ford had. Many of his 1976 supporters were already working for Reagan, Bush or other candidates. On paper, and late at night, it looked as though Ford might pull it off. But in bright daylight, with the turndowns of key governors like Clements and Rhodes, a Ford challenge looked like what it was—a losing proposition.

On March 18, Reagan soundly beat John Anderson in Illinois, his home turf, by 48 to 37 percent, with George Bush a distant third at 11 percent. Congressman Phil Crane received only 2 percent of the popular vote in what was also his home state. It was an important victory for the former California governor for it demonstrated conclusively that he could win in a major industrial state. Reagan also showed his broad-based appeal, getting 40 percent of the independents to Anderson's 47 percent. Among voters who described themselves as moderates, Anderson barely edged Reagan 45-41 percent.

As in New Hampshire, Reagan used a TV debate in Illinois to undercut his most serious challenger—John Anderson. The liberal Congressman was moving up in the polls, but Republicans were upset over his seeming refusal to pledge loyalty to the party. It all came together in the debate when Reagan leaned toward Anderson and asked in mock sorrow: "John, would you really find Ted Kennedy preferable to me?'' The audience roared with laughter as Anderson sat frozen-faced and refused to answer.

Illinois was Reagan's seventh victory in eight primaries, and he began to turn his attention more and more to the general election and his probable opponent, Jimmy Carter. Campaigning in New York, Reagan reaffirmed his overall support for Israel and criticized the White House for supporting a UN resolution condemning all Israeli settlements in occupied areas, including Jerusalem. Carter later repudiated his support of the resolution, calling it a mistake by the State Department.

On March 25, Reagan narrowly lost to Bush in Connecticut (where the former UN ambassador grew up) by 34 to 39 percent. Anderson got 22 percent. The same day, Reagan emerged with a runaway victory in the New York delegate contest, with ninety-one to Bush's six delegates, one for Anderson and nineteen uncommitted.

On March 31, Robert Dole, who had formally withdrawn on March 14, threw his support to Ronald Reagan, assuring the farmers of Kansas and other midwestern states: ''I know from my own conversations with Governor Reagan that he will bring to agricultural America a combination goal of faith, hope and parity.'' (A humorous reference to Reagan's alleged ignorance of parity. Reagan had ducked a question about the subject a week earlier because he basically favored free market rather than government-guaranteed parity for farm prices.)

April was a cruel month for Phil Crane and John Anderson, who dropped out of the Republican race, leaving only George Bush to challenge a serenely confident Ronald Reagan.

Anderson had been saying for months that Wisconsin was the key state for him—that within its progressive boundaries his ''new coalition'' politics would produce a significant victory. He made a point of seeking crossover votes from Democrats and liberal independents, campaigning with special energy on college campuses. He spent more time and more money ($456,000) in Wisconsin than any other candidate.

On April 1, the voters of Wisconsin played an unpleasant joke on John Anderson—they gave the Republican primary to Ronald Reagan, who received 40 percent to Bush's 31 percent. Anderson came in third with 28 percent.

What's more, an ABC poll of voters leaving the polling places found Reagan capturing 36 percent of those who voted Republican but called themselves Independent—only 3 percent less than Anderson. Bush got 22 percent of this group. According to ABC, Reagan led his two competitors in every bloc of the electorate except "upper income" voters.

Significantly, among crossover Democrats, Anderson received only 44 percent while Reagan got 23 percent and Bush 31 percent. Reagan ran strongly in Wisconsin's small cities, rural areas and suburbs, and among Slavic groups. He beat Anderson and Bush by almost two to one among blue-collar workers, which was no great surprise. He was the first Republican candidate in memory to take his campaign into Serb Hall, an ethnic Democratic stronghold in Milwaukee.

The same day in Kansas, Reagan won 63 percent of the primary vote to Anderson's 18 percent and Bush's 13 percent.

Columnist Anthony Lewis of the *New York Times* wrote: "The returns from Wisconsin are significant, new evidence for a simple proposition: Ronald Reagan has a very good chance to be the next President of the United States."

He was referring to the thousands of Democrats who crossed over to vote in the Republican primary. In fact, Reagan received more popular votes than President Carter—361,643 to 349,299.

Five days later, former President Ford gave an interview in which he said Ronald Reagan would almost certainly be the Republican presidential nominee in 1980 and, in contrast to statements he made a month earlier, stated that public opinion polls would show that Reagan could defeat Carter in November. He added that he and Reagan would meet soon to "discuss certain things—productive and constructive."

Within twenty-four hours, a Yankelovich survey for *Time* revealed that a Reagan-Carter race was almost even with the former California governor one point ahead. But the same poll showed that Carter would handily beat Bush and Anderson by nine and thirteen points, respectively.

By April 15, the *New York Times* estimated that Reagan had 561 delegates with 998 needed to win the nomination. Bush had only 85 while Anderson had 59, with 151 uncommitted, pledged to others or in doubt.

In the middle of such plenty, the Reagan campaign was nearly starving because it was so close to exceeding federal spending limits. The staff had been cut by more than one-third since January. The payroll was sliced in half, with many workers agreeing to work without pay. Advertising expenditures were reduced sharply. The governor's campaign trips were curtailed and tailored to provide access to "free" media coverage rather than the usual grassroots campaigning. Bay Buchanan, the national treasurer, reported that by the end of March, the campaign had spent "a little more than $14 million" of the $17.7 million allowed by the Federal Election Commission.

There were also some misstatements by the candidate which gave the news media an opportunity to resurrect the old question, "Is Reagan smart enough to be President?"

After meeting with two retired military officers, Reagan got the mistaken impression that Vietnam veterans were not eligible for GI Bill educational benefits and said so loudly and incorrectly at a rally in Nebraska. CBS and the candidate got into a hassle over how much of a tax cut John F. Kennedy had asked for while President. For months, Reagan had been calling for a 30 percent tax cut over three years, citing the success of a similar JFK tax proposal. Not so, said CBS, citing the Treasury Department, the 1964 tax cut was only 19 percent. *Time* reported that the "actual Kennedy tax cut was only 20 percent."

The facts are that the 1964 cut was 23 percent in the top bracket and 30 percent in the lowest bracket. Commented columnists Rowland Evans and Robert Novak: "Computing the size of the Kennedy tax cut has become an exercise in how to make Reagan look bad."

But the candidate often brought it on himself, relying upon facts and figures he had personally acquired over his many years of writing his own speeches while on what he called "the mashed potato" circuit. He was not helped by uncertain staff work. Aide Peter Hannaford said of the Reagan brain trust: "We're like an amoeba. We're constantly dividing and re-forming into policy groups. We operate a lot by conference telephone calls." Finally, the campaign hired a seasoned PR man, James Brady, formerly with John Connally, to provide the governor personally with up-to-date, accurate briefings.

Meanwhile, more and more Republicans were climbing aboard the Reagan bandwagon. On April 16, leaders of New Jersey's Republican Party gave the governor pledges of support that translated into at least fifty-five of the sixty-six delegates available in the state's June 3 primary. State GOP Chairman David Norcross, a moderate Republican who backed President Ford in 1976, said he was convinced Reagan could beat Carter because he was "offering the kind of economic policies that make sense."

A day later, Congressman Philip Crane withdrew from the GOP race, and endorsed Reagan. The move had been expected for weeks.

His "early-bird" candidacy (Crane announced in the summer of 1978) never got off the ground.

Thirty-six Members of Congress, including Minority Whip Robert Michel of Illinois and Richard B. Cheney of Wyoming, who served as chief of staff for President Ford, endorsed Reagan.

Ohio Gov. James Rhodes invited state GOP leaders to Columbus where he endorsed Reagan, who flew in to receive the good news personally.

One day later and just before the Pennsylvania primary, Howard Baker got out of a Tennessee sickbed to fly to Springfield, Pennsylvania, to endorse Ronald Reagan. It is time, explained Baker, for Republicans to "rally around the nominee."

George Bush campaigned hard and long in Pennsylvania. He spent an estimated $800,000. His paid staff outnumbered that of Reagan by more than three to one. He desperately needed a win in Pennsylvania to stay alive. His only primary win had been in Connecticut. Reagan had won every other primary up to Pennsylvania.

Reagan concentrated on picking up delegates rather than going all out against Bush in the popularity contest out of choice and necessity—he just didn't have the funds to match the former ambassador.

As a result, on April 22, Bush beat Reagan by 53 to 46 percent in the Keystone State, but Reagan picked up an estimated fifty of the states eighty-three delegates. Reagan and Bush ran neck and neck in Philadelphia while Bush carried the four surrounding counties and Pittsburgh. Reagan ran better in the middle of the state.

Reagan brushed aside the Bush victory as the result of a million dollar campaign his opponent had waged in Pennsylvania. "What happened," he said, "was that George mounted a very massive campaign in the last few weeks and proved that advertising does pay."

On April 24, John Anderson, who had been hinting for weeks about an independent candidacy, dropped the other shoe and formally withdrew from the Republican race, declaring as an "independent" for the Presidency. He had competed in nine Republican primaries and won none.

Anderson explained that a committee headed by New York media consultant David Garth would study whether an independent candidacy was practical, whether he could get his name on enough state ballots to stand a real chance of winning and whether enough money could be raised to conduct a national campaign. He left little doubt that he expected the exploratory committee would soon give him a green light. In the meantime, he scheduled the first trip of his new campaign to New York, West Virginia, Michigan and Massachusetts.

If elected, Anderson promised a "national unity" administration, composed of leaders of both parties, which could work with a Republican or Democratic Congress.

The same week, President Carter tried and failed to free the American hostages in Iran through a special military strike force. The aborted attempt, which cost the lives of eight American servicemen, was initially supported by his political opponents. Sen. Kennedy cancelled a campaign appearance, commenting, "Whatever our other differences, we are one nation in our commitment to the hostages, our concern for their families and our sorrow for the brave men who gave their lives trying to rescue their fellow citizens."

Gov. Reagan said it was "a time for us as a nation and a people to stand united."

Bush said he completely supported Carter's actions, but added that if the President had acted sooner, "the hostages would be out of there and the U.S. would not be subject to this dwindling respect."

This rare unanimity immediately disappeared when President Carter announced that he would resume campaigning because the major problems facing him were "now manageable enough for me to leave the White House." Carter had said in December that he would not debate Kennedy or Jerry Brown or campaign until the American hostages in Iran were released.

Kennedy suggested that the President's decision was politically motivated by his losing five out of the last seven Democratic primaries or caucuses.

Reagan called Carter's handling of the Iranian crisis "a national disgrace" and derided the President's decision to resume campaigning. "If he feels freed," commented the governor, "I wonder if he feels the hostages now somehow are freed?"

Columnists Germond and Witcover of the *Washington Star* described the Carter decision as "an exercise in Orwellian logic." Orwell would have understood, they wrote, when President Carter referred to the fiasco in the Iranian desert as an "incomplete success" when it was in fact "a complete disaster."

On May 3, in Texas, Reagan beat George Bush in his home state by only 51-48 percent, a much closer margin than the Reagan campaign had expected. Bush even held an early lead. However, the governor picked up sixty-five of the eighty Texas delegates. Bush outspent Reagan by more than six to one and campaigned intensively during the last week, concentrating on Houston and Dallas. Once again, a heavy last-minute advertising blitz clearly helped Bush's strong showing.

But George Bush could not begin to match Ronald Reagan's overall strength across the nation. The following Tuesday, on May 6, Reagan won more than one hundred delegates in Indiana, North Carolina and Tennessee. He beat Bush 73-16 percent in Indiana, 66-22 percent in North Carolina and 74-18 percent in Tennessee.

Practical politicians continued to join the Reagan team. Gov. James Thompson of Illinois, a Republican moderate, endorsed the ex-California governor, describing him as "the overwhelming choice of my party." Sen. Jacob Javits of New York, a bona fide Rockefeller liberal, asserted, "I'm not a cheerleader for Reagan, but I can support him." Could Reagan carry New York? asked columnist William Safire. The state went for Nixon by over 12 million in 1972 and for Carter by under 300,000 in 1976. "Reagan is convinced," Safire wrote, "it is worth a serious try."

Chapter Twenty

Winning the Nomination II

A new ABC-Lou Harris poll, released in early May 1980, showed that Ronald Reagan had emerged as the candidate most likely to win the 1980 presidential election. The survey revealed that the American electorate had become increasingly favorable to the Reagan candidacy.

By 52 to 47 percent, a majority of the voters denied the proposition that "if elected President, Reagan will be nearly 70 years of age when he takes office and that is too old considering how hard it is to do that job." The previous October, a substantial majority, 61-36 percent, agreed with the statement.

By 53-42 percent, a majority felt that Reagan "has the personality and leadership qualities a president should have."

The most negative rating was the 68-27 percent majority who felt that Reagan "seems to make too many off-the-cuff remarks which he then has trouble explaining or has to apologize for making."

On May 13, Reagan won decisively in two more states, beating Bush by 48-41 percent in Maryland and trouncing him by 78-16 percent in Nebraska.

On May 15, the *New York Times* estimated that Ronald Reagan had 937 of the 998 delegates needed to capture the Republican presidential nomination. George Bush had a very distant 196 delegates. Time and money had just about run out for the former UN ambassador. Reagan could lose the Michigan primary the following week and still win the nomination by winning enough delegates in Michigan and Oregon.

And so it happened. With the enthusiastic personal support of Gov. William Milliken, Ambassador Bush captured the May 20

Michigan primary handily, winning 50 percent to Reagan's 32 percent. But Reagan picked up twenty-nine Michigan delegates and eighteen more in Oregon where he swamped Bush by 54-35 percent. Those gains, coupled with twenty-five other delegates won the previous weekend in Virginia, Delaware and Hawaii, clinched the nomination for Reagan.

Which is what CBS and ABC reported on the night of George Bush's Michigan victory, shocking the Bush campaign, which was savoring its sweet win. The TV networks' projection of Reagan as the Republican presidential nominee was the final blow to George Bush's faint hopes.

On May 26, after several days of agonizing reappraisal, George Bush, in a hotel ballroom in Houston, conceded the 1980 Republican presidential nomination to Ronald Reagan, ending his two-year quest. Bush had long hinged his candidacy on a strong finish in California, New Jersey and Ohio on June 3. But he needed $1.25 million to go into those three states, and his campaign was some $300,000 in debt.

"I see the world," he said, "not as I wish it were but as it is. I have never quit a fight in my life. But throughout my political career, I have always worked to unite and strengthen the Republican party." He sent a telegram to Gov. Reagan, congratulating him on a "superb" campaign and offering his "wholehearted support" in the fall campaign.

In California, Reagan called Bush "a superior campaigner" and said he was "most grateful for his expression of support for my candidacy and for his pledge to work for unity in the party."

When asked if his decision not to continue, as many supporters had urged him to do, was because he had hopes of being Ronald Reagan's running mate, Bush responded simply, "No."

Columnists Germond and Witcover put the Bush defeat into perspective, writing that there "has been a fundamental truth about the Republican contest all year . . . the party never really wanted an alternative . . . it wanted Reagan."

Ronald Reagan went on to win by enormous margins every remaining primary, including California, New Jersey and Ohio. In all, he won twenty-nine of thirty-three primaries. He won 60 percent of the popular vote, receiving 7,607,305 votes. Bush won 24 percent or a little over 3 million. Other candidates or uncommitted received 16 percent or just over 2 million. During the seven months of his campaign, Reagan visited 318 cities and towns and traveled 166,450 air miles, an average of 855 miles a day since he declared his candidacy in November.

While campaigning in Ohio, Reagan gave the voters a little taste of his fall campaign, hitting hard at President Carter, urging his audiences to turn the Democrat out of office "because we can't afford four more years of what we've had." He recited the nation's problems from inflation and unemployment to a depressed steel and coal industry, arguing, "All of these have been gifts of this administration—these are all man-made creations of the leadership we lack in Washington, D.C."

Reagan spent the next six weeks before the Republican convention beefing up his staff, overseeing the writing of the party platform and mulling over his vice presidential choice. He said over and over that he would pick someone who was philosophically compatible with him.

The most frequently mentioned were Sen. Howard Baker, George Bush, and Congressman Jack Kemp. Others on the list included Sen. Richard Lugar of Indiana, Congressman Guy Vander Jagt of Michigan, former Treasury Secretary William Simon and Sen. Paul Laxalt of Nevada.

Some old faces reappeared in the campaign along with new ones. Lyn Nofziger came back as director of communications. Mike Deaver returned as a senior adviser. William Timmons, who had served as head of congressional liaison under Presidents Nixon and Ford, was hired as political director. William Casey remained as overall campaign manager as did chief-of-staff Ed Meese. The top staff was rounded out by Richard V. Allen, director of foreign affairs and national defense; Martin Anderson, director of domestic policy, and Richard Wirthlin, director of polling.

All of these men, with the exception of Timmons and Casey, had known and worked with Reagan for years. They were generally conservative in philosophy and temperament, a remarkably homogeneous group, who worked together with little outward friction and competition—now that John Sears was gone.

On June 5, Ronald Reagan traveled to Rancho Mirage, California, to meet with former President Gerald Ford. The two men held a private ninety-minute meeting and then emerged to answer questions from the press. Ford did most of the talking.

"I feel very strongly we have to make a change in the White House," said the former President. "I am convinced Governor Reagan can be elected." He said that Carter's economic policies were a "catastrophe" and a "disaster," describing the Democrat's economic record as the worst since Herbert Hoover. "It is vitally important for me to campaign wholeheartedly on Ron Reagan's behalf."

Reagan responded that he was "honored and delighted" at the former President's endorsement and commitment to campaign for him.

Despite their previous antipathy, reporter Lou Cannon of the *Washington Post* wrote that "both men expressed apparently genuine regard for each other." Ford said he thought Reagan had moderated his position on several issues and that he agreed with most of what Reagan had been saying during the 1980 primary campaign.

Ford firmly ruled himself out as a vice presidential possibility on the grounds that such a selection would violate the US Constitution, which requires that the President and Vice President have different states of residence. Although he did not say so then, it was known that Ford favored George Bush as Reagan's running mate.

Most of the Republican Party's leaders agreed with Ford. A UPI survey of Republican state chairmen and other Republican National Committee members in late June gave Bush fifty-eight votes, Senator Baker twenty-two and Congressman Kemp seventeen. But a poll of delegates to the 1976 Republican National Convention gave Kemp a narrow margin over Baker—28.3 to 27 percent. Bush trailed in third with 19.6 percent. *Human Events* reported in late June that Reagan's own regional directors and state chairmen favored Kemp by an "impressive majority." Bush was their second choice.

As to whom the American people favored for their President —Ronald Reagan or Jimmy Carter—the June polls put the former California governor firmly in front for the first time.

A *New York Times*-CBS survey reported: Reagan 47 percent, Carter 37 percent, Don't know 16 percent. In a three-man race, the results were: Reagan 41 percent, Carter 30 percent, John Anderson 18 percent, Don't know 11 percent. Reagan's lead extended across all age groups, all income levels and most education levels. Carter's strongest support came from blacks and people with low incomes and low education levels.

A *Newsweek* poll conducted by Gallup showed a much closer race: Reagan 45 percent, Carter 43 percent, Don't know 12 percent. In the three-man race, it was Reagan 40 percent, Carter 36 percent, Anderson 19 percent, Don't know 5 percent. *Newsweek* reported a dramatic increase in the positive view of Reagan as a leader. He was seen as forceful, consistent on the issues and able to handle both the nation's economic problems and, to a somewhat lesser degree, delicate matters of foreign policy as well.

As the Republican convention, scheduled to open July 14, neared, public attention shifted to the party platform which was built from Reagan blueprints. The principal on-site architects were Sen. Jesse Helms of North Carolina, an uncompromising conservative, and Congressman Jack Kemp of New York, hardly less conservative but willing to give a little here and there.

As a result, the 1980 GOP platform called for a 30 percent tax cut in accord with the Kemp-Roth plan; the systematic reduction of federal rules and regulations over business and industry; and emphasis on production rather than conservation to handle the energy crisis; the denationalization of social welfare and public assistance programs; free enterprise zones in the inner cities to attract capital, entrepreneurs and jobs; a constitutional amendment banning abortion on demand; the support of equal rights for women but not support for the Equal Rights Amendment; the building of new weapons systems to help the US achieve military superiority; the continuation of the volunteer army but with sharply increased salaries and other benefits; strong support of Israel and the Republic of China on Taiwan; a North American accord between the US, Canada and Mexico; a sharp buildup of conventional armed forces like airplanes and ships.

It was a conservative platform passed by a conservative national convention for its conservative nominee. But the nominee went out of his way in Detroit to reassure various special interest groups that he was very much aware of their needs and aspirations. He told a group of women delegates that he would fight discrimination based on sex and would promote equality of opportunity if he were elected President.

He pledged to black delegates that he would deliver American blacks from the "bondage" of welfare and sponsor measures aimed at building up the black community's prosperity. He was asked if he would back an invitation to Benjamin Hooks of NAACP to address the Republican convention. Reagan had upset many blacks, and other Americans, by going on a vacation in early July rather than speaking at the annual NAACP convention. The Reagan staff readily admitted they had goofed in not calling the NAACP invitation to the governor's attention until too late. Asked if he would ask Hooks to speak, Reagan responded: "I don't have that right, but I'm hoping that he will." After Reagan's remarks, Hooks was invited to make a speech, and did so, in prime time.

So did Congressman John Rhodes of Arizona, the House Minority Leader; Henry Kissinger, the former Secretary of State; Sen.
Barry Goldwater, the 1964 standard bearer; Don Rumsfeld, the
former Secretary of Defense; Congressman Guy Vander Jagt, the
chairman of the Congressional Campaign Committee; Sen. Richard
Lugar of Indiana; and former President Gerald Ford, who on Monday
night delivered one of the most dynamic and eloquent speeches of
his long career, setting the convention, and Reagan himself, to
wondering if maybe the best ticket in 1980 wouldn't be Reagan
and . . . Ford.

For the next two days, as *Time* put it, "some of the coolest
operators in US politics clung to the heady notion that they could
somehow restructure the American presidency in a mere 36 hours."
In the end, they failed because of the pressures of time, because of
the gut feeling of Gerald Ford that shared responsibility "wouldn't
work" and because Ronald Reagan realized that he would have to
give up some part of his constitutional authority to make the deal.

Here is how the deal didn't happen: All Tuesday morning, July
15, party leaders visited with Reagan in his sixty-ninth floor suite
in the Detroit Plaza Hotel. Almost all mentioned Gerald Ford as a
vice presidential candidate. Reagan decided to take up the possibility
directly with the former President.

They met Tuesday afternoon for about sixty-five minutes in
Reagan's suite. According to *Newsweek,* Reagan said to Ford: "I
would like you to serve on the ticket with me, to run against and
hopefully defeat Carter. I know it's a difficult decision for you.
Likely, it will involve some sacrifices. I think a lot's at stake as far
as our country is concerned. Would you give it some consideration?"

Ford raised three questions: Whether a former President could
fit into the Vice Presidency, whether the staffs of the two men could
work together, and how to handle the Twelfth Amendment to the
Constitution, which says that if the candidates for President and
Vice President come from the same state, the electors from that
state couldn't vote for both. On the latter point, Reagan gave Ford
a copy of a legal opinion he had commissioned, suggesting that
Ford could shift his legal residence from Rancho Mirage, California
to Vail, Colorado, or even back to Michigan. Ford agreed to consider
Reagan's offer overnight, but said, "I don't think it will work."

All day Wednesday, July 16, Reagan and Ford aides met in near
continuous session, trying to work out an arrangement. The Ford
team consisted of Alan Greenspan, Henry Kissinger, Robert Barrett

and John March, all of whom had worked in the White House. The Reagan team consisted of William Casey, Ed Meese and Richard Wirthlin, none of them with White House experience. Only Casey had headed up a federal agency—the Securities and Exchange Commission. In the afternoon, the Reagan team presented a two-page memo which outlined in general terms the powers Ford might have. They included daily supervisory authority, but not veto power, over the National Security Council, the Office of Management and Budget and the Council of Economic Advisers. The Vice President, in effect, would replace the White House chief-of-staff.

The Ford team immediately brought the memo to Ford, who, according to Barrett, called it a "reasonable effort" but still expressed doubt about the feasibility of the plan. Greenspan, who was actually in Detroit as an economic adviser to Reagan, recalls that it became clear they were trying in a day's time to settle some of the most difficult organizational problems of the US government.

Ford met briefly with Reagan at 5:15 p.m. at Ford's request. He mentioned Kissinger and Greenspan as the kind of people he would like to see in the cabinet as Secretary of State and chief economic adviser. According to *Time,* Reagan responded: "Jerry, I know all of Kissinger's strong points, and there's no question that he should play a role . . . but not as Secretary of State. I couldn't accept that."

The turning point, in retrospect, came at 7 p.m., when Ford kept his previously scheduled interview with Walter Cronkite over the CBS television network. Suddenly, millions of viewers, plus the delegates to the Republican convention, learned that the former President was seriously considering the Vice Presidency. At last, Cronkite asked Ford a fatal question: "It's got to be something like a co-Presidency?" Ford did not reject the phrase or the idea, replying, "That's something Governor Reagan really ought to consider."

Watching in his hotel, Reagan was furious. He had kept the negotiations strictly confidential, and there was Ford discussing them at length with Walter Cronkite of CBS and, a few minutes later, with Barbara Walters of ABC. "Can you believe it?" he demanded of aides.

Both the former President and Mrs. Ford did not help matters by mentioning their strong support of ERA—a stand at direct variance with Reagan and the 1980 GOP platform.

At the Plaza Hotel, the two teams struggled to break the impasse, which grew with each passing hour. As Reagan's men saw it, the

Ford team was hinting that an "enhanced" Vice President would be able to name cabinet members, subject to the President's veto, and have a veto over some of the President's appointments. Ford's men deny any such intention.

At 9:15 p.m., Reagan called Ford to tell him that a decision had to be made that night, that rumors on the convention floor were getting out of hand. Ford responded, "My gut instinct is that I shouldn't do it," but refused to give a flat no.

The two teams continued to wrestle with language but to no avail. Kissinger suggested that a decision be put off until the next day, but there was little enthusiasm for any prolongation of the agony. Suddenly, at 10:30 p.m., Ford turned to his wife Betty and said, "I'm going down to tell him that I'm not going to do it." At 11 p.m., he made the short walk to Reagan's suite. The two men talked for only ten minutes, but reflected none of the tension and bitterness some of their aides felt over the collapse of a "dream ticket."

At 11:37 p.m., Reagan telephoned a surprised George Bush, who believed, along with most of America, that the ticket was going to be Reagan and Ford. Said Reagan: "I plan to go over to the convention and tell them you are my first choice for the nomination." An elated Bush responded, "I can campaign enthusiastically for your election and the platform."

A few minutes later, from the podium at Joe Louis Arena, Ronald Reagan announced: "We have gone over this and over this and over this and (President Ford) believes deeply that he can be of more value as the former President campaigning his heart out, which he has pledged to do, and not as a member of the ticket . . . I am recommending to this convention that tomorrow when the session reconvenes that George Bush be nominated." The delegates, who earlier that night had nominated Reagan with 1,939 votes to Anderson's 37 and Bush's 13, roared their approval.

Newsweek later opined that a Reagan-Ford ticket would have been a "political morass and a constitutional nightmare." Columnists Germond and Witcover referred to "a shotgun marriage." *Washington Star* reporter James Dickenson brought up the problems of joint press conferences "in which one man is addressed as 'Mr. President' and the other as 'Governor.' " Conservative James J. Kilpatrick called it "magnificent folly." *New York Times* columnist Anthony Lewis described the Reagan-Ford ticket as "a constitutional coup."

But many of the same commentators agreed with *Washington*

Star editor Edwin Yoder, who asked "whether the modern presidency is really a one-man job?" It may not have been the right time or the right place, but Ronald Reagan once again demonstrated his willingness to consider creative new solutions to the most vexing of old problems.

He also demonstrated with his moving acceptance address on Thursday night his consummate command of political rhetoric. *Time* called it "the most important—and very likely the best—speech of his career." *Washington Post* reporter David Broder, the most respected political journalist in Washington, termed it "masterful . . . well-conceived, well-written and well-delivered." By virtue of his nomination drive and acceptance speech, Ronald Reagan made it clear that, in the words of *Newsweek,* "he is one of the most formidable politicans of his time."

The polls quickly corroborated this. A Lou Harris poll released on July 23 had Reagan leading Carter by 61 to 33 percent—a twenty-eight point margin. An earlier AP-NBC poll put Reagan at 55 percent and Carter at 24 percent—a thirty-one point lead.

Reagan announced that he would conduct a "coast-to-coast, border-to-border campaign," with special emphasis on winning the blue-collar vote in the eight northern states of Connecticut, New York, New Jersey, Pennsylvania, Ohio, Michigan, Indiana and Illinois, which have a total of 178 of the 270 electoral votes needed for election.

On the last day of July, the Harris Survey reported that the American public's approval of President Carter had dropped to an all-time low for any sitting President in the last twenty years. Only 22 percent of the likely voters polled approved of Carter's performance in office, compared with 77 percent who expressed disapproval. The 22 percent figure compared with Richard Nixon's low of 25 percent just before he resigned as President in July 1974.

Ronald Reagan, however, was under no illusions. He knew that Jimmy Carter's ratings would rise sharply following the Democratic national convention in August and that it would be a very close race in the fall. A key factor, perhaps the most important one of all, would be the nationally televised debates. Reagan was very aware that Carter was a tough determined campaigner who would make full use of the Presidency and take full advantage of any mistake Reagan made. Reagan aides were especially concerned about the governor's fondness for ad libs that sometimes boomeranged.

But in the last analysis, Reagan was confident he would win if the race remained focused not on him the challenger but on the inept

performance of the incumbent. It was really very simple, he argued:
"We can't afford four more years of what we've had."

Chapter Twenty-One

Winning the Presidency

On Labor Day, September 1, 1980, President Jimmy Carter and Republican challenger Ronald Reagan formally began their efforts to convince the American public that each was the better man to lead the nation. Most of the national polls had them running about even, usually giving Reagan a statistically meaningless 2 percent advantage.

Carter returned to his political roots, attending an annual Labor Day picnic in Tuscumbia, Alabama, where he appealed to southerners to back one of their own. "You people here," he said, "have the same background, the same families, the same upbringing that I have." Carter's choice of the northwest Alabama town near the Mississippi and Tennessee borders was deliberate: his southern support had eroded after forty-five months in the White House and he was confronted by a conservative Republican with great appeal to southerners. He had to retain his southern base or face certain defeat on Election Day.

Carter also used the Tuscumbia event to break his official silence on the Polish labor strikes, saying that the U.S. was "inspired and gratified" by the success of the Polish workers. It was a comment aimed at the traditional anti-communist sentiment of the South.

The President then flew back to Washington, D.C., for the annual Labor Day picnic on the White House lawn, where he was joined by leaders of organized labor and their families, including Lane Kirkland, president of the AFL-CIO. He promised to work with them to win a national health insurance program and secure passage of labor law reform, a measure favored by the AFL-CIO and other unions but rejected by Congress in 1978. Here again,

Carter was appealing to a voting bloc which he urgently needed for reelection and which was being ardently wooed by Ronald Reagan.

On his very first day of campaigning, then, Jimmy Carter established a political pattern that he was to follow scrupulously for the next two months: appeal to traditional Democratic groups (southerners, blacks, organized labor) . . . be presidential (use the White House and other instruments of presidential power) . . . stress foreign affairs and play on the doubts about Reagan's expertise in the critical area of war and peace.

Carter showed how far he would go to highlight the differences between himself and Reagan in Independence, Missouri the following day:

"I believe in peace," he said, "I believe in arms controls, I believe in controlling nuclear weapons, I believe in the rights of working people in this country, I believe in looking forward and not backward, I don't believe the nation ought to be divided one region from another. In all these respects Governor Reagan is different from me."

Carter had engaged in similarly harsh political hyperbole against Sen. Edward Kennedy in the Democratic primaries and gotten away with it. This time his remarks were over-shadowed by a one-line ad-lib by Reagan about the Ku Klux Klan. Consequently, the President received no reproof from his staff, the public or the news media, which naturally encouraged him to use such overreaching rhetoric again.

As former Governor of California, Ronald Reagan might have been expected to launch his campaign inside the friendly boundaries of our most populous state. But Reagan once again did the unconventional, traveling to Jersey City, New Jersey, where, with the Statue of Liberty as a backdrop, he accused the Carter administration of "betraying" the aspirations of American workers. Insisting that the US was in a depression instead of a recession, as Carter maintained, Reagan told a flag-waving "ethnic picnic" of several thousand:

"Let it show on the record that when the American people cried out for economic help, Jimmy Carter took refuge behind a dictionary. Well, if it's a definition he wants I'll give him one. A recession is when your neighbor loses his job. A depression is when you lose yours. Recovery is when Jimmy Carter loses his."

Reagan contrasted Carter's lack of leadership with that of Lech Walesa, the Polish labor leader, whose father, Stanislaw Walesa, joined the Republican nominee at his rally in Hudson County (which

Carter carried in 1976 against Gerald Ford, but Reagan felt he could recapture in 1980).

He then flew to another Democratic stronghold, Detroit, where at the Michigan State Fair, he lambasted Carter's economic policies and promised that if elected, he would help the nation return to the spiritual and moral values held by American working men and women.

Reagan's first day on the hustings revealed his campaign plan: Go after the blue-collar, ethnic, Catholic vote . . . concentrate on Carter's sorry economic record . . . be conservative but not *too* conservative . . . demonstrate by doing that he was vigorous enough and smart enough to be President.

The first day also revealed some flaws. It was in Detroit, in the middle of a strong critique of the economy, that Reagan ad-libbed the following about his opponent: "I am happy to be here where you are dealing at first hand with economic policies that have been committed, and he's opening his campaign down in the city that gave birth to and is the parent body of the Ku Klux Klan."

There were several things wrong with the statement. First, Tuscumbia, Alabama is not the birthplace of the KKK—Pulaski, Tennessee is most frequently cited as having that dubious honor. Second, Tuscumbia is the headquarters of only one of several competing branches of the Klan—the Knights of the Ku Klux Klan. Third, Carter himself had denounced the Klan during his Tuscumbia speech and had, in fact, been picketed by KKK members. Fourth, it was a clumsy, *ad hominem* comment which drew everyone's attention away from the central theme of Reagan's speech—the persistently high inflation and unemployment caused by Carter's outdated liberal economics.

President Carter quickly took advantage of his opponent's verbal blunder. He blasted Reagan for "slurs and innuendos" against the entire South. "This is not the time," he charged, "for a candidate, trying to get some political advantage, to try to divide one region of the country from another." No fewer than seven southern governors (all Democrats who had endorsed Carter) denounced Reagan's comments as a "callous and opportunistic slap at the South."

Ronald Reagan beat a hasty retreat, telephoning his regrets to Gov. Fob James of Alabama and Tuscumbia's mayor and issuing a public apology. His remarks, he protested, had been "misinterpreted." He tried to take the offensive by calling on President Carter to disavow the comments of Democrats Andrew Young and Patricia Harris, who had earlier linked Reagan to the Klan and racism.

But the news media were more interested in using the Klan remark to discuss, once again, Reagan's penchant for verbal glitches and gaffes. In the last half of August, for example, the governor described the Vietnam war as "a noble cause," called for "official" US relations with the Republic of China on Taiwan while his running mate, George Bush, was visiting Peking, and agreed that the Biblical theory of creation as well as the Darwinian theory should be taught in schools.

Columnists Jack Germond and Jules Witcover of the *Washington Star* reflected the opinion of most political observers when they wrote: "What Reagan needs now more than almost anything else is always to sound as if he knows what he is talking about—without having to fall back on cheap shots."

Recovering quickly, Reagan did just that during the rest of his first week of campaigning. In Washington, D.C., he told a B'nai B'rith forum that America has an "ironclad (moral) bond" with Israel while also stressing a mutual self-interest based on US economic and military strength. Reagan charged that Jimmy Carter had endangered Israel because his policies had weakened the US economy and national defense.

In Jacksonville, Florida and New Oreleans (both located in winnable states in the eyes of Reagan strategists), Reagan stepped up his attack on President Carter, accusing him of deliberately compromising national security to win reelection. On August 22, at a nationally televised news conference, Secretary of Defense Harold Brown and Pentagon research director William J. Perry revealed previously secret details about the "Stealth" aircraft project. Reagan declared that the disclosure gave the Soviets a ten-year head start in developing counter-measures.

The Republican nominee received corroboration for his charges from Democratic members of the House Armed Services Committee, former Secretary of State Henry Kissinger and Gen. Richard H. Ellis, commander of the Strategic Air Command, who said the Pentagon should have stuck with "no comment" about "Stealth" even after the secret had been publicly revealed.

"Stealth" enabled Reagan to regain the initiative and to put his clumsy coupling of Jimmy Carter and the Klan where he wanted it—at the bottom rather than the top of news stories. More importantly, the Reagan campaign took an all-important step to forestall any more gaffes—they put Stuart Spencer, the veteran political consultant, on the campaign plane, permanently.

During his opening Labor Day trip, incredibly enough, Reagan was not accompanied by any Senator or Congressman, or his wife Nancy, or his longtime chief-of-staff, Edwin Meese. Every candidate needs someone he can talk to and someone who can talk to him—candidly and forcefully if necessary. Blunt-speaking Stu Spencer, who managed Reagan's first gubernatorial campaign in 1966 and Ford's presidential campaign in 1976, was just such an adviser. It is a fact that once Spencer was on board and providing political briefings at every stop, Ronald Reagan reemerged, in the words of *Washington Post* reporter Lou Cannon, as "the smooth effective campaigner who won the Republican nomination in a walk."

Meanwhile, the third man in the race, Independent John Anderson, was getting some much needed good news. By a vote of five to one, the Federal Election Commission ruled that Anderson's candidacy, although not party-affiliated, was eligible for post-election federal subsidies if he got more than 5 percent of the vote. That looked to be a very attainable goal at the time with Anderson receiving 15 percent in most national polls.

The FEC decision came at a time of increasing financial difficulty for the Anderson campaign. As of September 1, Anderson had raised only $6 million but needed at least $15 million to wage a serious national campaign. The qualifying 5 percent would net only about $3 million, but the potential would hopefully make borrowing for things like TV spots easier.

As candidates of the two established parties, Carter and Reagan each received $29.4 million in federal funds.

The next two weeks of the campaign were dominated by two things: the nationally televised presidential debate between Ronald Reagan and John Anderson and Jimmy Carter's charge that Reagan was practicing the politics of racism and hate.

On Tuesday, September 9, the League of Woman Voters formally invited Anderson to take part in its first presidential debate, based upon his 15 percent standing in major polls. Carter immediately pulled out. Reagan said he would show up in Baltimore on September 21 whether Carter did or not, commenting, "The ladies have decided that Anderson is a viable candidate, and I've always said if he was, he certainly should be included" in the debates.

Carter's campaign manager, Robert S. Strauss, explained that the President was "respectfully" declining the invitation because he wanted to debate Reagan one-on-one before he faced Anderson and Reagan together. But everyone knew the real reason: Carter did not want to elevate Anderson in any way that would enable him to take votes from Carter in November. The Carter campaign gambled they would be hurt less by refusing to debate than by appearing and thereby making Anderson a more legitimate candidate.

There was plenty of evidence that Anderson did indeed hurt the President more than his opponent. A Lou Harris survey showed that in eight large northern states, Carter led Reagan 47-45 percent without Anderson in the race but trailed Reagan 35-37 percent with Anderson in the running. Nationally, the Harris poll had Reagan leading Carter 41-37 percent, with Anderson receiving 17 percent. Without Anderson, Reagan's lead over Carter was reduced to just 48-46 percent.

The independent candidate described Carter's withdrawal from the debate as "running away from the American people . . . running away from the great issues that are framed and ready for debate." The Carter people hunkered down and hoped the storm of protest would blow away.

In the meantime, Ronald Reagan did not go away but continued to hammer at the Carter domestic record while carefully assuring key voting blocs that he was not the right-wing ogre suggested by the opposition.

In Philadelphia, the conservative Republican told a senior citizen's rally that he would defend the integrity of the social security system. In Chicago, he outlined a five-year program of income tax and government spending cuts to spur economic growth and sharply limit the growth of the federal government. "We must," he said, "balance the budget, reduce tax rates and restore our defenses. . . . I am asked: Can we do it all at once? My answer is: We must." While in Chicago, Reagan walked through a Lithuanian neighborhood and later had dinner with Polish-American leaders.

In Buffalo, the former California governor proposed a national maritime policy which would, not so incidentally, help that economically troubled port. "Buffalo and its people," he charged, "are victims of the Carter economy, of high taxes, high inflation and high unemployment." In Cleveland the day before, Reagan wooed Eastern European ethnic voters, attacked Carter's energy policy and appealed for black support.

The advertising campaign over television began in earnest. The first series of Reagan ads about inflation and foreign policy were low-key and politically moderate in tone, clearly appealing to Democrats and independents. They were also designed to emphasize Reagan's positive qualities. "We hope," said Peter H. Dailey, the advertising executive in charge of the Reagan media effort, "that people come away from these commercials with a feeling for the man, a feeling that here is a man who is confident, at peace with himself, responsible.'' Dailey asserted that the TV camera was "the microscope of the soul" and revealed Ronald Reagan as not "a threat" but a man whose ideas "are simply the common sense solutions to the problems that exist today.''

The basis for this advertising approach and indeed the entire Reagan campaign was a remarkable document, the Black Book, a 176-page strategy statement authored by Dr. Richard Wirthlin, the governor's longtime pollster and president of Decision Making Information (DMI), and his associates, Vincent J. Breglio, executive vice president of DMI, and Richard S. Beal, a DMI consultant on leave from Brigham Young University. The Black Book, finished in June, listed the following Democratic target groups for the fall campaign: (1) southern white Protestants: (2) blue-collar workers in industrial states: (3) urban ethnics: (4) rural voters, especially in upstate New York, Ohio and Pennsylvania.

Immediately after the Detroit convention, key Reagan advisers met with the governor to read and approve the Black Book recommendations. "They went through it page by page," Breglio recalled, "with Governor Reagan attending.'' Present were Ed Meese, William J. Casey, William Timmons, Peter Dailey, comptroller Vernon Orr, and Wirthlin. Stu Spencer later joined this strategy group.

"The Black Book pertained to strategy only," Wirthlin told *Advertising Age* after the election, "and it was up to the deputy directors to devise tactics; if the Black Book had tried to dictate tactics, the campaign would have failed."

The first anti-Reagan commercial produced by the Carter campaign ran the same week as the President's scathing attack on the former governor as a practitioner of racism and hate. The Carter commercial showed the Oval Office in the White House with no one in it while an announcer said:

"When you come right down to it, what kind of person should occupy the Oval Office? Should it be a person who, like Ronald Reagan, has a fractured view of America? Who speaks disdainfully about millions of us as he attacks the minimum wage and calls unemployment insurance a 'prepaid vacation'? Or should another kind of man sit here, an experienced man who knows how to be responsive to all Americans, all 240 million of us? Figure it out for yourself.''

This was a love letter compared with what Jimmy Carter himself said about Ronald Reagan at the Ebenezer Baptist Church in Atlanta while flanked by a number of black leaders, including former UN ambassador Andrew Young and Coretta Scott King, widow of Martin Luther King, Jr.

Carter declared that Reagan had injected hatred and racism into the campaign by using "code words like 'states' rights.' " He said that if the Republican were elected, there would probably never be a national holiday in memory of King. He warned the black leaders that the candidacy of Reagan threatened to undo all they fought so hard to win the last two decades. He grinned and shook the hand of Congressman Parren Mitchell (D-Md.), after Mitchell said of Reagan:

"I'm going to talk about a man who has embraced a platform that some men known as the Ku Klux Klan said couldn't be better if they'd written it themselves . . . who seeks the presidency of the United States with the endorsement of the Ku Klux Klan."

It did not matter to Mitchell that Reagan had immediately repudiated the Klan's endorsement. The Congressman was out to scare blacks about Reagan, and President Carter clearly approved of his tactics.

There was immediate and widespread condemnation of Carter's charges against Reagan. Columnists Germond and Witcover said the President had brought the 1980 campaign "down to a new level" and that accusations of racism and hatred had no "pertinence" to the politics of 1980. The *Washington Star* editorialized: "This squalid exercise in Dr. King's church should be the president's last indulgence of the sort in this campaign." In an editorial entitled, "Running Mean," the *Washington Post* said: "Jimmy Carter . . . seems to have few limits beyond which he will not go in the abuse of opponents and reconstruction of history."

Reagan himself said that Carter's attack was "shameful, because whether we're on the opposite sides or not, we ought to be trying to pull the country together."

In the days remaining before his debate with John Anderson, Reagan constantly challenged Carter to join them. He charged the President with trying to "hide his record and his performance from the American people." The former governor said he would like to debate Carter head to head, but added it would be "dishonorable" to drop Anderson from the debate.

At his first news conference in six weeks, just prior to the Reagan-Anderson debate, President Carter spent most of his time denying he had accused Reagan of injecting hatred and racism into the presidential campaign. With a straight face, he insisted: "I do not indulge in attacking personally the integrity of my opponents." Pressed again and again by an openly hostile press corps, Carter finally said that despite his remarks to black leaders in Atlanta, he didn't consider Reagan a "racist in any degree." He complained that "the press appeared to be obsessed" with the race issue.

But as the *Washington Star* reporter Lisa Myers pointed out, "There were no similar complaints, however, when the media was hammering away at Reagan . . . after the Republican incorrectly stated that Carter launched his re-election drive in the Alabama city which gave birth to the Klan. Then, Carter and his lieutenants labored to keep the issue alive."

The Carter campaign showed its true colors only one day later when the Carter-Mondale Re-Election Committee launched a nationwide advertising campaign in black newspapers claiming that Republicans were out to beat Carter because he appointed thirty-seven blacks to judgeships and cracked down on job discrimination.

Carter's emotional attacks on Reagan were undoubtedly prompted by his continuing second place finish in all the polls. A survey of Republican leaders and politicians in all fifty states, for example, showed Reagan leading Carter in states having a total of 320 electoral votes—50 more than the majority of 270 needed for election.

Carter's anti-Reagan rhetoric rejected the advice of one-time Democratic activist Mark Shields, now an editor and columnist for the *Washington Post,* who publicly counseled Carter: "No overkill on Reagan—voters will not believe he's a demon. Don't waste your time."

Few of the 55 million American who watched the Reagan-Anderson debate on Sunday evening, September 21, thought it was a waste of their time. For sixty minutes, the two Republicans exhibited "both confidence and clarity," in the words of political reporter David Broder, as they answered questions from a panel of six journalists chosen by the League of Women Voters. Their answers pointed up the sharp differences between them, with Reagan hewing to his traditional conservative philosophy of less government and Anderson proposing government solutions for the problems of energy and the inner city. Reagan repeated his call for a 10 percent tax cut for each of the next three years, noting, "It has been called inflationary by my opponent, by the man who isn't here tonight."

As columnists Germond and Witcover wrote, Reagan again and again displayed his unique ability to simplify the most complex of issues. He said that the problem with inflation is that "government is spending more than it takes in.'' On attracting more people into the volunteer army with more money: "The answer lies with just recognizing human nature." On federal programs for the cities and whether the money should come from local sources or Washington: "Wouldn't it make a lot more sense if the government let them keep the money in the first place?" On abortion: "I've noticed that everybody who is for abortion has already been born."

The veteran journalists summed up: "If Reagan is a candidate susceptible to the errant phrase, he didn't show it in what was supposed to be a high-pressure situation. On the contrary, he gave the impression at least of a remarkable command of his own of facts and figures."

Who won the debate? Reagan's pollster, Richard Wirthlin, showed an upswing for his man in the following week. Anderson got his answer when he arrived in Philadelphia the very next morning for a rally at the convention center adjacent to the mammoth campus of the University of Pennsylvania. Only 600 of the hall's 2,500 seats were filled, less than twenty-four hours after an exuberant Anderson told a post-debate reception in Baltimore: "We are on the way—I can feel it in my bones."

An immediate ABC-Lou Harris poll reported viewers believed that Anderson "outplayed" Reagan 36-60 percent, with 17 percent calling it a tie, 6 percent saying neither did well and 11 percent saying they weren't sure. But other national polls showed that in fact Anderson had been hurt by his performance and Reagan helped by his.

A Gallup poll published in *Newsweek* showed Reagan now beating Carter 39-35 percent with Anderson a weak third at only 14 percent—the same level of support the Illinois Congressman had been receiving since early August. The survey found more people had turned against Anderson as a result of watching him while more viewers said they were likely to vote for Reagan than before the debate.

According to a *New York Times*/CBS poll, Ronald Reagan was the only significant beneficiary of the first presidential debate. The survey showed that an increase number of people believed that Reagan understood the complicated problems facing a President, had a clear position on the issues, offered a clear vision of where he wanted to lead the country and would exercise good judgment under pressure. The overall standings, according to the poll, now stood at Reagan 40 percent, Carter 35 percent, and Anderson 9 percent.

President Carter's reaction to such ominous polls was consistent with his entire 1980 campaign. Earlier, he had called Reagan a racist. Now he said that his conservative opponent was a warmonger.

Campaigning in California, he told a town hall meeting in Torrance that the November election "will help decide whether we have war or peace." The same day, in remarks to state union leaders in Los Angeles, he put it even more bluntly: "Six weeks from now, the American people will make a very profound choice . . . that will determine what kind of life you and your families will have, whether this nation will make progress or go backward, and whether we have peace or war." In an interview over a Los Angeles TV station, Carter kept it up. "I don't know what he would do if he were in the Oval Office," he responded when asked if he considered Reagan a threat to peace. "But if you judge by his past highly rhetorical calls for the use of American military force in these altercations, it is disturbing."

Even Carter's staff realized their man had gone too far. Press secretary Jody Powell called his boss' "war or peace" assertion "an overstatement." He then offered several examples of Reagan's alleged fondness for military force:

● In response to the Soviet invasion of Afghanistan, the former governor said on January 29, 1980: "One option might well be that we surround the island of Cuba and stop all traffic in and out." In view of the fact that the Soviet invasion was the first time it had ever violated the sovereign territory of a contiguous nation since the post-World War II era, Reagan's suggestion of a blockade did not seem excessive to many foreign policy experts—including Richard Allen, his national security adviser, who proposed it in the first place.

● Asked whether the US should establish a military presence in the Sinai to counter the Russians, Reagan said on January 13, 1980: "I think that this might be a very, very good time for the United States to show a presence in the Middle East. I don't think it would be provocative and I don't think it looks like anyone bullying." To call this statement "disturbing" and a "threat to peace" was to reveal how committed Jimmy Carter and his advisers were to the notion of, "Let's not be beastly to the Russians."

● In response to the North Korean seizure of the *USS Pueblo*, Reagan said in January 1968: "I cannot for the life of me understand why someone in the United States Government, particularly the President, has not said: That ship had better come out of that harbor in 24 hours or we are coming in after it." That the Carter campaign would single out this quote, after the Carter administration's signal failure for one year to negotiate the release of the American hostages in Iran, reveals starkly why President Carter was trailing in all the polls and why Americans were responding to Ronald Reagan's call to make America great again.

In his response to Carter's warmonger charges, Reagan calmly took the high road, saying "I think it is inconceivable that anyone and particularly a President of the United States, would imply that any person in this country would want war, and that's what he's charging and I think it's unforgivable."

Independent John Anderson accused the President of "scare tactics," adding, "The choice is not peace or war" but which candidate's foreign policy will best serve U.S. interests.

Commented Lyn Nofziger, Reagan's press secretary, "We're not going to get down in the gutter with him. . . . It's like the things he's done in past campaigns. There's a sense that this will catch up with him."

There was also a growing sense among political observers that Jimmy Carter was not going to catch up with Ronald Reagan, that he was too far behind in too many states and that only an eleventh-hour event, like the release of the American hostages, could pull it out for the most unpopular President since Harry Truman.

On September 26, *New York Times* columnist Tom Wicker quoted Washington political consultant Horace Busby (a former close associate of Lyndon Johnson) as saying that Reagan had a lock on 90 percent of the West's electoral votes—more than half of the 270 needed to win. He rated Reagan as leading in six key non-western states—Illinois, Indiana, Connecticut, Wisconsin, Ohio and Pennsylvania. Busby concluded that Carter ought to be concentrating on the East. But as Wicker pointed out, economic problems, the disaffection of Jews, the presence of John Anderson on the ballot, and the lackluster support of organized labor all combined to make Jimmy Carter's race for the East "an uphill climb."

Meanwhile, Ronald Reagan was campaigning smoothly and shrewdly, often presenting specialized messages to key constituencies in the communities he visited. According to *Washington Post* reporter Lou Cannon, a Reagan aide called it "coupling," the technique of inserting an important local issue into the basic campaign speech.

In Miami, for example, Reagan won the cheers of the city's influential Cuban constituency by denouncing Fidel Castro and asserting that the US should be a refuge for people fleeing tyranny.

In Springfield, Missouri, he criticized Carter for a delay in declaring the state a disaster area when it needed help because of a drought. In Tyler, Texas, Reagan charged the President was afraid to debate energy policy with him. In Grand Junction, Colorado he said that westerners know how to manage their water resources better than the federal bureaucracy does.

As one observer noted, the content of Reagan's speeches remained conservative and Republican, but his style was Democratic as he skillfully worked to broaden his conservative base. His endorsement of basic American values like family, neighborhood, work, peace and freedom appealed to conservatives in both the Democratic and Republican parties.

In late September, in a reversal of its earlier position, the League of Women Voters invited Carter and Reagan to participate in a two-man debate in October, omitting independent John Anderson. Carter promptly accepted the invitation, which conformed to the position taken by his aides throughout the debate negotiations. Reagan rejected the invitation, explaining: "I cannot in good faith agree to . . . a series of presidential debates that would preclude John Anderson from debating President Carter in the same or a similar way that I debated Mr. Anderson." And that seemed to be that, although James Baker, a senior campaign aide, said that Reagan might be willing to debate Carter alone later in the campaign, "depending on the political circumstances."

For the next two weeks, the campaign settled into a predictable pattern, with Jimmy Carter warning what a dangerous President Ronald Reagan would make and Ronald Reagan pointing out what an inept President Jimmy Carter had been. Rarely before in American politics had there been such a reversal of roles with the President campaigning like the challenger and the challenger campaigning like the President.

A series of Carter TV commercials attacked Reagan through street-corner interviews in which Californians denounced his "ill-informed, shoot-from-the-hip politics" and said, "I think he would have gotten us into a war by now."

In Philadelphia, Carter himself accused Reagan of advocating a "radical departure" from the nation's "commitment to peace." Nor did he spare his other opponent. Asked about anti-Anderson TV commercials condemning the Congressman's "Jesus Christ

Amendment''* fifteen years before, he replied coolly: "I have never heard of the TV spot that you refer to about John Anderson and the Jesus Christ Amendment."

As columnists Rowland Evans and Robert Novak pointed out, the President was technically right—it was a *radio* commercial played extensively in Democratic areas. "The President's answer reflected his campaign style," Evans and Novak wrote. "The campaign is intended to eat up Reagan's lead, but in fact it [is] arousing hostility from . . . voters who expected something better."

What the voters got, instead, was even more hysterical rhetoric. Not content with the epithets of "racist" and "warmonger," President Carter declared that if elected Ronald Reagan would divide the nation. Incredibly, on October 6, Carter warned a Chicago audience that the voters will "determine whether or not this America will be unified or, if I lose the election, whether Americans might be separated, black from white, Jew from Christian, North from South, rural from urban."

Herblock, the liberal Pulitzer Prize winning editorial cartoonist for the *Washington Post,* summed up the feelings of most citizens with his cartoon, "The Shrinking Incredible Man." In it, the US public watched with dismay as a shrinking Jimmy Carter stamped through a dirty gutter carrying a dripping brush and a bucket of mud labeled, "Carter Statements."

White House press secretary Jody Powell tried to defend the smear by saying that Carter was deeply offended by Reagan's failure to condemn the Rev. Jerry Falwell, founder of the Moral Majority, for preaching that God hears only the prayers of "redeemed" Christians. Reagan had made it clear in a visit to Falwell on October 2 that he disagreed with that philosophy but did not specifically denounce it.

However, as *Washington Post* reporter Edward Walsh wrote, Powell's "explanation fell flat on its face because the President made exactly the same reference to the alienation of 'Christian from Jew' in a speech to a Democratic fund-raising dinner in Washington Sept. 30, three days before Reagan's visit" to Falwell.

Responded Reagan: "I can't be angry. I'm saddened that anyone . . . who has had that position (of President) could intimate such a thing. I'm not asking for an apology from him. I know who

---

* Early in his career, Congressman Anderson several times introduced a constitutional amendment to make the United States, officially, a "Christian" nation. He later disavowed the legislation.

I have to account to for my actions. But I think he owes the country an apology.''

Two days later, in a nationally televised interview with Barbara Walters of ABC News, President Carter admitted he had erred in personally attacking his opponent and promised he would "do my best" to engage in no more name-calling. But old habits die hard, and before the week was out, Carter declared in Florida that Ronald Reagan was not "a good man to trust with the affairs of this nation in the future"—"It would be a bad thing for our country if Governor Reagan were elected"—and, "I don't know what he would do in the White House."

Reacted liberal columnist Mary McGrory: "The campaign is nasty because the survivor in the White House has concluded that the only way Reagan can be beaten is to scare the country into voting for Carter."

Stated the *Washington Post:* "Jimmy Carter is campaigning like a politician gone haywire" with "frantic overstated, boomeranging attacks."

Wrote conservative columnist James J. Kilpatrick: "The Carter campaign has developed the sour taste of an acid stomach. Instead of defending the Carter record, the President has set out simply to demolish his Republican opponent by half-truths, whole lies and plain slander."

A front page article in the *Washington Star* on October 13 was headlined: "Tight Polls May Be Hiding Electoral Vote Landslide."

Richard Wirthlin, Reagan's pollster, obligingly explained why: Carter's negative approach had backfired. "The rock of Carter's image," he said, "is that he's a nice man, an honest man, who won't mislead on political matters." But the shrill attacks on Reagan changed the public's perception of the President.

For Carter, said Wirthlin, "it was like getting caught in the crosscurrents when you go out in the ocean. He came out as mean-spirited. Our image is very much intact and in attempting to shatter it, theirs developed a few cracks of its own."

With three weeks left in the campaign, Ronald Reagan still held a narrow lead in the popular vote and a comfortable margin in the electoral vote. Republicans were organized and united as rarely before. There was plenty of money for a final advertising blitz. The candidate was physically and mentally ready for intensive campaigning in key states like Pennsylvania, Michigan and Ohio.

But Reagan and his advisers were worried about the one thing over which they had no control: the American hostages in Iran.

Washington was alive with rumors about their imminent release. If they were freed at the last moment through the efforts of President Carter, what would be the public reaction? Would the American people be caught up in the euphoria of the moment and out of misguided gratitude reelect Jimmy Carter? Or would they remember that it was the Carter administration which had laid the groundwork for the seizure of the hostages through its inept foreign policy? Or would they dismiss the release as "October surprise" politics and vote their pocketbooks? The Reagan team concluded they could not afford to sit on a safe but slim lead and played their final trump card—they agreed to debate Jimmy Carter.

There were other factors that influenced their decision. One, Carter's personal attacks and commercials had raised some doubts about Reagan's ability to keep the nation out of war. A nationally televised debate would enable the governor to reassure the public directly about where he stood on war and peace. Two, the announcement of a debate would "freeze" the campaign where it presently stood, with Reagan ahead. Three, Reagan and his advisers were confident that he would top Carter. He had won every debate in his political career, starting with 1966 and Gov. Edmund (Pat) Brown right up to George Brush and John Anderson in 1980. Carter might have more facts and figures at his command, but television was Ronald Reagan's medium and he had just the message for the 100 million-plus Americans who would be watching him and the President—"Had enough?"* The debate was set for the evening of Tuesday, October 28, in Cleveland. It would be ninety minutes long and would cover both domestic and foreign policy.

In the interim, Reagan spent $150,000 for half an hour of prime time on CBS-TV on Sunday, October 19, to remind the nation that when he accepted the Republican presidential nomination in July, he asserted: "Of all the objectives we seek, first and foremost is the establishment of lasting world peace." He promised a bipartisan foreign policy, saying, "The cause of peace knows no party. The cause of peace transcends personal ambition. The cause of peace demands appeals for unity, not appeals to divisiveness. These are truisms which Mr. Carter has forgotten or chosen to ignore."

Declaring that the nation "must build peace through strength,"

---

* Their confidence was reinforced by what happened at the prestigious Al Smith dinner at the Waldorf Astoria Hotel in New York City on Thursday, October 16. Ignoring the unwritten rule against serious politics and speaking after Reagan's deft remarks, Carter tried to take advantage of his opponent so blatantly that the largely Democratic audience gave him, literally, a Bronx cheer.

Reagan proposed the following: (1) a "realistic" strategic arms limitation policy; (2) a "determined effort" to improve the quality of American armed forces; (3) a strengthening of relations with allies; (4) a "consistent" policy toward the Soviet Union in which the US seeks "neither confrontation nor conflict" but will "remain strong and determined to protect our interests." He said that as President he would "immediately open negotiations on a SALT III treaty" but in such a way "as to protect fully the critical security requirements of our nation."

Reagan and Carter exchanged sharp words over the hostages. The Republican challenger said the long imprisonment of the Americans in Iran was "a humiliation and a disgrace" to the US. Carter immediately accused his opponent of making a "political football" of the hostages and regretted that he had "broken his pledge" not to inject the issue in to the campaign. And then, once again, Carter went too far. Speaking in Waco, Texas, he described Reagan's campaign as so much "horse manure" and ridiculed what he called the Republican's "secret plan" to bring home the hostages.

It did not matter to the President that Reagan had made no mention of a "secret plan" but had responded, when asked, that he had "some ideas" on how to deal with the hostage question but would not discuss them in the campaign.

As the *Washington Star* editorialized, if it's a Republican habit to spread around manure right before an election, "the President's comments on the Reagan 'secret plan' suggest that the habit is contagious and that Mr. Carter has caught it."

In these closing days of the campaign, it became more and more clear that the Carter campaign was banking almost totally on the hostages to gain them victory. As columnists Evans and Novak wrote on October 24, eleven days before Election Day: "They are looking for Iran's release of the hostages to blot out poor organization, inadequate dedication and nearly four years of resentment." But many Democrats questioned the strategy. "I think it's a two-edged sword," said Ed Campbell, the Democratic state chairman in Iowa. "And my gut feeling is that it cuts against (Carter)." Simply put, there was the fear that the hostage issue looked too manipulative. Democrats feared that undecided independents and John Anderson supporters would see the possibility of the hostages being freed as just another Carter gimmick.

As the two men got ready for the most important ninety minutes of the campaign, a *New York Times*/CBS poll showed Carter and Reagan in a virtual tie, 39 percent for the President, 38 percent for the challenger, Anderson at 9 percent and 14 percent undecided. But in five of seven key states, Reagan led—in California, Ohio, Pennsylvania, Illinois and New Jersey—while Carter was ahead in only New York and Texas. The margins were two points or less in four states—Ohio, Texas, Pennsylvania, and Illinois. It appeared that Reagan had a lock on California and New Jersey while Carter was comfortably ahead in New York.

Two days before Debate Day, Dave Broder, the most respected political reporter in Washington, wrote: "The risk for Carter in the debate he so ardently sought is that if Reagan looks cool, confident and collected—as 40 years of professional training before the cameras have disciplined him to do—then to millions of viewers, he will probably look presidential. And if he looks presidential, he likely will be president."

The same day, the *New York Times* reported that the four reasons why people weren't buying Reagan were: (1) he says too many things carelessly; (2) he changes positions to get elected; (3) he does not understand the complicated problems of the Presidency; and (4) he would get us into a war.

As Reagan prepared for the debate, and how best to handle the above concerns, at his rented estate, Wexford, in northern Virginia, his private polls showed him pulling ahead of Carter in key industrial states. They gave him a 6 percent popular vote margin and 320 electoral votes. The only thing that seemed to stand in his way was the possible effect of a last-minute release of the hostages by the unpredictable rulers of Iran. The President might be reelected in a surge of national relief. At the same time, there could be a strong negative reaction if hopes were raised high and then dashed if none or only some of the Americans were released. If so, the October Surprise could quickly become the November Backlash.

American citizens got some bad news the weekend before the debate. In the last inflation report before Election Day, the Labor Department reported that consumer prices rose one percent in September and were 12.7 percent higher than in September 1979. Reagan immediately cited the depressing statistics as proving "the utter failure" of the Carter administration's economic policies. Carter's lame response was the increase showed that inflation was too serious to risk trying Reagan's tax-cut proposals.

By now, most of the nation's major newspapers had published their endorsements with the great majority choosing challenger Reagan over incumbent Carter. As of late October, 443 supported Reagan while 126 backed Carter. The *Chicago Tribune* said it preferred a Reagan administration rather than "four more years of pretty words, vacillation and national drift." The *Detroit News* called the conservative Republican "a decent man with some different and reasonable ideas about reducing unemployment and inflation while letting the world know—quietly—what the nation's foreign policy is."

The day of the debate, three national polls released conflicting data. Gallup said Carter had moved into a 3 percent lead. ABC-Harris said that Reagan was leading by 3 percent. AP-NBC declared Reagan was ahead by 6 percent. Reagan's private polls were in line with AP-NBC.

On Tuesday evening, October 28, in prime television time, Jimmy Carter and Ronald Reagan stood behind specially-constructed rostrums on the stage of Cleveland's Music Hall for their first and only debate of the 1980 presidential campaign. Their audience was an estimated 105 million Americans—half the nation. Both men wore dark suits and muted ties. The similarities ended there.

Carter was grim-lipped and gray-colored from his neck up. He stood rigidly and rarely looked at his opponent. In the words of the *New York Times,* he was "pinched, acidulous, aggressive." He went on the attack and stayed on the attack throughout the ninety minutes. He debated by the numbers: seven mentions of his being a Democratic President; seven mentions of lonely, life-and-death decisions; ten mentions of the Oval Office; and no less than fourteen mentions of his running against a challenger whose ideas were dangerous, disturbing, radical and ridiculous.

Reagan was calm, cool and presidential. He gestured with his hands and tilted his body to emphasize a point. He smiled often. He seemed to be enjoying himself. He spent much of his time patiently explaining where Carter had misquoted him, much like a professor pointing out the errors of an over-zealous student. As pollster Mervin Field put it, "Their roles were reversed. Reagan was the benign incumbent, gently but firmly fending off the challenger."

They disagreed on almost every issue. Reagan said the inflation rate was 12.7 percent (which it was over the last twelve months) and there were 8 million unemployed. Carter said inflation was 7 percent (which it was over the last three months) and employment was up 9 million jobs.

Carter blamed his Republican predecessors fot the decline in military spending, but Reagan charged the Carter administration with cutting former President Ford's budget by 38 percent.

Carter asserted that his opponent had displayed "a disturbing pattern" and "an extremely dangerous" attitude toward arms control. Reagan responded that he objected only to the SALT II treaty negotiated by Carter (as did several prominent Democrats) and wanted to pursue real arms control with the Russians.

Under the most incredible pressure, with everything they had worked for and believed in at stake, neither man made any fatal error. (Carter committed the most serious verbal gaffe when he said he had "had a discussion with my daughter Amy" about nuclear arms control.) But in the end, Ronald Reagan won the debate because the image which Jimmy Carter had labored night and day to create of his opponent was proven to be false. Over 100 million Americans could see with their own eyes that Reagan was not a dangerous mad bomber but, rather, a thoughtful conservative with an appealing vision of a better America.

The real climax of the debate came when Jimmy Carter once again misrepresented a Reagan position, this time on national health insurance. That familiar crooked grin appeared on Reagan's face and with a rueful shake of his head, he began his answer with, "There you go again." As columnist William Safire wrote, "with body English and a familiar phrase, he portrayed the President as an incorrigible distorter-of-the-facts, an inherently unfair person." The Carter campaign of fear of Reagan collapsed before the eyes of every viewer.

Reagan sealed Carter's fate with his closing remarks when he looked straight into the camera and quietly asked the viewer, "Are you better off than you were four years ago? Is it easier for you to go and buy things in the stores than it was four years ago?" There was only one possible answer to that question, and it was given in the voting booths on November 4.

An hour and a half after the debate ended, ABC announced the results of its random telephone poll: by 67 to 33 percent, viewers said Reagan had gained the most from the confrontation. An AP poll of 1,062 persons who watched the debate found 46 percent saying the Republican did the better job and 34 percent saying Carter won. A CBS poll revealed Reagan the winner over Carter by 44-36 percent, with 20 percent rating it a tie or not knowing. Even Carter's own pollster, Pat Caddell, admitted grudgingly, "On the question of who won, I think it is basically a wash, with perhaps Reagan having a slight advantage."

Many political analysts complained that nothing "new" emerged from the debate—that they had heard it all before. And so they wrote in the major newspapers and said on the TV networks that the debate had been inconclusive. What they failed to perceive was that for millions of Americans it was their first opportunity to see and appraise the two candidates. The bored reaction of the "professionals" to the presidential debate offers a clue as to why the national pollsters did not realize that a landslide was in the making.

Reagan himself had no doubts about his performance. He told a GOP rally later that night, "I feel great. It was wonderful finally to be able . . . to respond to some of the false accusations and charges." Were you nervous? one reporter asked. He smiled, and shaking his head, replied, "No, I've been on the stage with John Wayne."

The following night in Texas, he told an enthusiastic crowd of ten thousand in Houston's Tranquillity Park: "When I look at what he has done in the last four years, you can see why he spent so little time last night in the debate talking about his record. He has grown fond of referring to Franklin Roosevelt, Harry Truman and John Kennedy. There's one Democratic president he doesn't talk about, and that's Jimmy Carter."

It seemed, then, as though there was little more either candidate could do in the final six days of the campaign but exhort his supporters to make a last extra effort to get out the vote. Reagan, usually wary of overconfidence, campaigned exuberantly like a man who knew he was going to win. An exhausted Carter acknowledged to reporters that the election was "very much in doubt." The *Washington Post's* David Broder reported that Reagan "was in the driver's seat" and the electoral map clearly worked against Carter.

And then on Sunday, November 2, barely forty-eight hours before Election Day, the Iranian parliament voted its terms for freeing the fifty-two American hostages. The President melodramatically flew home at dawn to confer with his top advisers in the White House. He went on national television Sunday afternoon to say that the conditions "appear to offer a positive basis" for an acceptable settlement. But he refused to predict when the hostages might come home. And he pledged that "my decisions on this crucial matter will not be affected by the calendar."

A quick reading of the Iranian message by foreign policy experts explained the President's caution: the conditions were unacceptable. As the *Washington Post* pointed out in an editorial on Monday, November 3, they were presented by "international terrorists who are holding a whole embassy for ransom." The first condition of agreeing not to interfere in Iran's internal affairs presented no problem. But the other three—unfreezing Iranian assets, dropping financial claims against Iran and helping return the wealth of the late Shah—were impossible demands. "Clearly," the *Post* editorialized, "the Iranians are trying to exploit the American people's presumed impatience and Mr. Carter's presumed electoral vulnerability."

The October Surprise on which the Carter campaign had been heavily depending turned out to be a November Insult. Secretary of State Edmund Muskie admitted that Iran had set "harsh conditions" that would require negotiations. A senior Reagan aide commented: "It's not the triumphal return of the hostages. . . . It'll be too inconclusive to have a major impact on the election."

The White House seemed to agree. President Carter, who had played politics so often with the hostages, resumed campaigning but made no mention of the Iranian demands. He chose instead to make a desperate eleventh-hour appeal to Anderson supporters. "Obviously," he said again and again in a series of fast-paced airport rallies across the nation, "there are some differences between us, but on many of the key issues our views are very close." In a brutal last week, he logged fifteen thousand miles in the air, visiting twenty-six cities in fifteen states.

Anderson himself, with his national standing sagging to less than 10 percent, still insisted his election was "not just an impossible dream." But it was and everyone, including the independent candidate, knew it. Curiously, in the face of devastating rejection, Anderson revealed a sharp sense of humor. He told students in Minneapolis that he understood why "Amazing Grace" was Jimmy Carter's favorite hymn. "It would take," he said, "amazing grace on the part of the American people to forgive him for what he's done to the country."

The final national polls predicted Reagan would win but by so narrow a margin as to make the race, in their eyes, a toss-up. Gallup reported Reagan 47 percent, Carter 44 percent, Anderson 8 percent, undecided 1 percent, *CBS-New York Times* reported Reagan 44 percent, Carter 43 percent, Anderson 8 percent, undecided 5 percent. ABC/Harris came closer, reporting Reagan 45 percent, Carter 40 percent, Anderson 10 percent undecided 5 percent. Most of the state polls, including the usually accurate New York *Daily News* survey in New York, the Field Poll in California and the *Des Moines Register* poll in Iowa, were off by wide margins. The *Daily News,* for example, found that Carter would narrowly carry New York; he lost it to Reagan 47-44 percent. But the Reagan campaign didn't care what Gallup and Harris said—they had their own results, which were so encouraging that Richard Wirthlin locked them in a drawer.

On Monday night, November 3, almost sounding like he was already President, Ronald Reagan delivered his final message of the 1980 campaign over national television: "Together, tonight, let us say what so many long to hear: That America is still united, still strong, still compassionate, still clinging fast to the dream of peace and freedom, still willing to stand by those who are persecuted or alone." Of his opponent, he said, simply: "Are you happier today than when Mr. Carter became the President of the United States?"

The electorate's resounding answer produced a Reagan landslide on November 4. The end came with astonishing swiftness. NBC News formally projected Ronald Reagan the winner at 8:15 p.m., hours before the polls had closed in many states. ABC News followed at 9:52 p.m., minutes before President Carter's concession appearance. CBS News officially determined Reagan the winner at 10:32 p.m., almost forty minutes after Carter conceded.

When all the counting was over, Ronald Wilson Reagan, dismissed by many political analysts at the beginning of the year as too old, too conservative and too dumb, carried forty-four states (including Massachusetts) for a total of 489 electoral votes. Carter won only six states* and the District of Columbia for a total of 49 electoral votes. John Anderson failed to carry a single state.

Reagan received 51 percent of the popular vote to Carter's 41 percent while Anderson collected a meager 7 percent. Official returns gave Reagan 43,899,248; Carter 35,481,435; Anderson 5,719,437. As *U.S. News & World Report* said, it was "an impressive achievement" for the conservative Republican in a three-man race.

The magnitude of Reagan's win can be measured when you add *all* of Anderson's votes to those of Carter. The independent's vote did exceed the difference between Reagan and Carter in fifteen states with a combined total of 167 electoral votes. But even if Carter had carried every one of those states, his electoral count would still have been only 216—far short of the 270 needed to win. And ABC News found in polling exiting voters that ballots for Anderson would have been divided nearly equally between Reagan and Carter in a two-man race.   Ronald Reagan's astounding victory was across the board and across the country. He carried 54 percent of the male

* His home state of Georgia, Walter Mondale's Minnesota, plus West Virginia, Maryland, Rhode Island and Hawaii.

vote . . . 52 percent of the independents . . . 62 percent of the Protestants . . . 51 percent of the Catholics (despite their heavily Democratic orientation) . . . 55 percent of whites . . . 41 percent of the
union vote . . . all regions of the country—northeast, midwest,
south and border, and west. He received 22 percent of the liberals,
39 percent of the Jewish vote, 14 percent of the black vote and 36
percent of the Hispanic vote—all higher margins than analysts had
predicted.

The historic dimensions of his victory were reflected in the
amazing Republican gains in the Congress and the state houses. The
GOP picked up twelve seats in the US Senate, giving it majority
control for the first time in a quarter of a century. Without exception,
those Democrats who were defeated were liberals. The new line-up
would be fifty-three Republicans, forty-six Democrats and one independent (Harry Byrd of Virginia). In the House, Republicans
registered a net gain of thirty-three seats and defeated several leading
Democrats. The new line-up was 243 Democrats, 192 Republicans.
And Republicans won four new governorships; the new line-up was
twenty-seven Democrats and twenty-three Republicans.

To give Ronald Reagan's victory another perspective, his 43.9
million votes were the second-largest on record, behind only Richard
Nixon's 47.2 million in 1972. His electoral margin of 489-49 was
the third-widest in this century. His plurality of some 8.4 million
was five times Jimmy Carter's 1.7 million in 1976. While it is true
that only 54 percent of the voting-age population turned out, the
highest turnout since World War II was in 1960 when 62.8 percent
voted. The turnout in 1948 was only 51.1 percent—in 1972 just
55.5 percent.

Why did Reagan win? There are as many answers as there are
political analysts in Washington, D.C.

Pat Caddell, Carter's pollster, called his boss' loss "a protest
vote," intensified by last-minute frustration over the hostages in
Iran.

Pollsters Daniel Yankelovich described the returns as first and
foremost a personal repudiation of Carter.

Columnist Jack Germond said it was Carter's failure as a politician which led to his "brutal rejection."

The *New York Times'* Adam Clymer concluded that the old
Democratic coalition deserted Carter.

Time Magazine's Hugh Sidey: "Inflation up, income and Social
Security taxes rising, spendable earnings down, paper work swell-

ing, regulations tougher, future uncertain, Jimmy Carter out, Ronald Reagan in."

Just-defeated Sen. George McGovern declared that the voters abandoned American liberalism.

Columnist R. Emmett Tyrell, Jr.: "What now goes by the name of American liberalism . . . abandoned the voters."

Columnist James J. Kilpatrick: "A personal triumph" for Ronald Reagan.

Columnist/commentator Patrick Buchanan: "Both a national referendum on Carter and a mandate for Reagan to change things."

Reagan pollster/strategist Richard Wirthlin pointed to three pivotal decisions in the campaign—the commitment to run a six-week series of advertisements on Reagan's record as governor; the decision to have Reagan avoid personal criticism of Carter at a time when the President was sharply attacking Reagan; and the decision to debate Carter.

The *Washington Post's* Lou Cannon: "After all the strategizing and all the name-calling, it was Reagan's election. This time, it was the Gipper who won one for himself."

A *Washington Post* editorial titled, "Tidal Wave": "Nothing of that size and force and sweep could have been created over a weekend or even a week or two by the assorted mullahs and miseries of our times."

Hale Champion, former aide to Gov. Pat Brown of California, praised Reagan for "being what my mother used to call kitchen smart about what matters to voters and what doesn't."

Political reporter David Broder: "What defeated Jimmy Carter and the Democrats was the failure to control the costs of necessities and to demonstrate an ability to protect American lives and interests abroad."

Pollster Lou Harris: "Ronald Reagan won his stunning victory . . . not because the country as a whole went conservative, but because the conservatives—particularly the white moral majority —gave him such massive support."

Human Events: Reagan "rode to power on a national conservative tidal wave."

I'd like to add a few suggestions of my own, considering the five key elements of every political campaign.

Organization. The Republican Party was united behind and for its ticket. Former President Ford campaigned widely and effectively for Reagan. Even Betty Ford, no great fan of either Ron or Nancy, signed a letter which was mailed to 1.2 million women in six key states endorsing Reagan. The GOP's grassroots drive, Commitment '80, mobilized thousands of Republicans to canvass their neighborhoods and get out the vote on Election Day.

The Democrats, still divided after a bitter primary fight between Carter and Ted Kennedy, mounted no such organizational effort. They depended as usual on organized labor, and in 1980 the unions, although they tried, could not deliver the votes of union members as they did in the presidential campaigns of 1960 and 1968.

Money. Under federal law, both candidates were restricted to spending the $29.4 million provided by the federal treasury. But Reagan was helped by two other sources. The first was the Republican Party, which spent $7.5 million in 1980 on a nation-wide TV campaign with the theme, "Vote Republican. For a Change." Their ads—like the one featuring a Tip O'Neill look-alike, another about the incredibly shrinking dollar bill—were among the most effective TV advertising of the campaign. The second source was the independent campaign committees, which spent more than $6 million on both pro-Reagan and anti-Carter TV and radio advertising. Most of the ads were run in targeted states where the race was close and the shift of a few thousand votes made all the difference.

Carter had no similar financial help from the Democratic Party or independent campaign committees. He did benefit from the multi-million dollar expenditures of organized labor on in-kind services like literature, phone banks and Election Day activities. And he did use the perks of the Presidency, spending the taxpayer's money with an exquisite regard for its favorable political impact. It was no accident that a half billion dollar ship repair contract went to Philadelphia which he had to carry rather than Norfolk, Virginia, a city and state he knew he would lose.

Issues. There were two major ones in 1980—Jimmy Carter's record and Ronald Reagan's ability to govern. Once the focus shifted from the latter to the former, as it did following the October 28 debate, Carter was doomed.

Candidates. Carter was probably the poorest public speaker of any President in the twentieth century. His best strategy, therefore, was to avoid situations in which he would be directly compared with one of the most effective communicators in modern American politics—Ronald Reagan. But instead Carter challenged Reagan to meet him in free and open debate on national television. It was like Leslie Howard daring Clark Cable to step into the ring.

The news media. Most members of the press just didn't like Jimmy Carter and it often showed in their reporting. In contrast, they found Ronald Reagan to be personally charming, sincere and genuine although they didn't care much for his politics. As a result, Reagan got a much fairer break in news coverage than any conservative Republican could have expected.

But in the final analysis, I think Ronald Reagan won because he was a man with an idea whose time had come. As political historian Theodore White wrote during the campaign: "The simpler the ideas the more explosive they can be. Roosevelt's ideas were that government must see that people have jobs and then that the war should be fought and won. . . . Eisenhower's idea was that there was a time for war and a time for peace—and his was a time for peace. Kennedy's idea was that the society should be opened against prejudice—and he enlisted the best and the brightest to release us from the past."

Ronald Reagan's idea was that government had grown too big and should be reduced and America's military might had grown too weak and ought to be strengthened.

The American people liked his ideas and they elected him their fortieth President.

Chapter Twenty-Two

President Reagan

What kind of President will Ronald Reagan make? As he did as Governor of California, President Ronald Reagan will begin immediately to deliver on the promises he made to the American electorate in the fall campaign. As he told *U.S. News & World Report:* "I would start being President in the first 24 hours and not spend my first term, as many Presidents do, merely preparing to run for the second term."

Specifically, President Reagan will:

● Immediately freeze all federal hiring by executive order.

● Send a tax package to Capitol Hill, cutting personal income taxes by 30 percent over three years, eliminating taxes on estates and interest, and reducing taxes on business.

● Start developing a manned bomber, either the B-1 or a new plane.

● Deploy the neutron warhead in Europe (as our European allies agreed to do until Jimmy Carter changed his mind at the last moment).

● Ask for more money for defense in the fiscal year 1980 budget.

● Call for the dismantling of the Departments of Education and Energy.

● Propose legislation transferring federal welfare programs and their funding to the states.

It will be what *Fortune* writer Donald H. Holt called, "a thunderbolt beginning." Other early measures by President Reagan will include:

● An end to Jimmy Carter's embargo on grain shipments to the Soviet Union. Reagan argues that the move failed to pressure the

Russians into withdrawing from Afghanistan and has hurt American farmers.

● A move from conservation to production to solve the energy crisis. He will lower depreciation taxes, ease environmental controls, encourage more mining of coal and wider use of nuclear power "within strict safety codes."

● Reduce and consolidate federal rules and regulations which cost American business and consumers an estimated $120 billion every year.

● Propose either a law or a constitutional amendment limiting annual federal outlays to no more than 19 percent of the gross national product. The current rate of federal spending is about 22 percent of the GNP. Provisions will be made for additional spending for war or any national emergency.

● Increase military pay and fringe benefits to make our volunteer armed forces a more effective and efficient fighting force.

● Strengthen the Central Intelligence Agency, the National Security Agency and the Defense Intelligence Agency—all vital components of our now weakened intelligence network.

● Declare his willingness to negotiate arms control and reduction with the Soviets, but on a truly bilateral basis.

● Maintain diplomatic relations with the People's Republic of China, but strengthen our ties with Taiwan as provided under the 1979 Taiwan Relations Act.

● Reaffirm US support of Israel as "the last stable democracy" in the Middle East and as "a deterrent to further Soviet moves in that area."

What kind of President will Ronald Reagan make? He will combine the rhetorical skills of Franklin D. Roosevelt with the management approach of Dwight David Eisenhower and frugality of Calvin Coolidge.

(1) He will appoint sound experienced people as his aides and as the heads and subheads of the various federal departments and agencies—as he did as Governor of California. He will look for and pick the best man or woman, regardless of party or political loyalty. He has told his top campaign aides not to expect jobs in the White House.

Reagan told David Broder: "The Cabinet would be my inner circle of advisers . . . almost like a board of directors. (In Sacramento) we met three or four times a week . . . Every issue that came before us was roundtabled at the Cabinet, and the other Cabinet officers didn't sit back and let the one whose province was being discussed carry the ball. I wouldn't stand for that. . . . But we never took a vote. When decision time came, I knew I had to make the decision.''

Some of the cabinet possibilities are: Caspar Weinberger, Reagan's finance director in California and Secretary of Health, Education and Welfare under Nixon; William Simon, former Secretary of Treasury; Alan Greenspan, chief of the Council of Economic Advisers under Ford.

Also: Alexander Haig, former NATO commander; Donald Rumsfeld, former Secretary of Defense; Sen. Sam Nunn, a Georgia Democrat; Sen. Henry Jackson of Washington, another Democrat.

A black is almost certain to be selected for the cabinet. Among the leading possibilities are economist Thomas Sowell of UCLA; economist Walter Williams of Temple University; and New York lawyer Gloria Toote.

High on the list of potential female appointees is Anne Armstrong, former Ambassador to Great Britain, who was on Reagan's list of vice presidential possibilities in Detroit.

"One of my basic requirements," Reagan has often insisted about his appointees, "is I want people that will have to step down to take a position in government . . . people whose achievement is out in their own line in the world"—and people who would have to take a salary cut.

Reagan adviser Richard Whalen has written that Reagan has ideas for reorganizing and revitalizing outmoded parts of the executive branch. Cabinet members will not be captives *of* their bureaucracies but will present the President's policies *to* their departments, demanding concrete responses to new policies. It has been suggested that each cabinet member be given an office in or near the White House to facilitate the constant communication needed for such a different approach to governing.

(2) Reagan will work closely with both parties in both houses of Congress as he did in California. He is no stranger to the art of compromise. He had a Democratic legislature in six of the eight years he was governor, including the period when he put through his historic welfare reform program.

As he puts it: "If I found when I was governor that I could not get 100 percent of what I asked for, I took 80 percent."

(3) He will conduct our foreign policy with firmness and restraint. Although personally more experienced in domestic than foreign affairs, Reagan has carefully studied US foreign policy, concluding: We need to mend fences with our allies and to convince

them that we intend to act once again as the leader of the free world. And, he firmly believes, we must let the Soviet Union know that we will no longer settle for being number two in military strength. As President, Ronald Reagan could be expected to follow Theodore Roosevelt's maxim to talk softly but carry a big stick.

(4) He will communicate to the American people the urgent need for sacrifice, hard work and mutual assistance and toleration. Here, perhaps, more than anywhere else, Reagan has demonstrated a unique ability which is so urgently needed in our nation today.

His approach is a simple one, based upon an almost mystic belief that Americans will respond if they understand they must: "A President has got to take the truth to the people . . . tell the people what he is trying to accomplish, what's standing in the way, and then depend on the people to act."

It's what he did so brilliantly in California. He likes to tell the story of Jesse Unruh, once the powerful Democratic speaker of the assembly, who resisted many Creative Society proposals. But one day, after a series of televised Reagan reports to the people, Unruh said about a proposal: "Well, you won't have any trouble with me on that. I can count."

To keep the people of California involved, Gov. Reagan produced a series of two-minute TV briefings on current state issues. He later instituted a weekly "Governor and Students" television series with high school students. He held a weekly news conference (409 in eight years as governor) and granted more than 150 in-depth interviews. He will be no less accessible as President.

Regardless of what the news media have said or not said about him, Ronald Reagan has always made himself available to them. He has never refused to answer questions or hidden from the media.

In the words of *Washington Post* reporter Lou Cannon, who has been covering Reagan since he was governor: "He has . . . been unfailingly courteous and responsive to his media critics, never whining about the treatment he has been given or suggesting that the liberties of the press should be curtailed. The word one might have used in a pre-feminist age to describe Reagan is 'manly.' "

As President, Ronald Reagan will attract Democrats and independents with his own unique blend of social conservatism and economic activism. He is, in the words of Richard Whalen, "an instinctive coalition-builder." He will work to bring about a new political alignment, a lasting bipartisan coalition of moderate conservatives.

President Reagan will deal skillfully with the three million civilians in the federal bureaucracy, using a carrot and sometimes a stick to convince them that they should join rather than fight his crusade for better government. He told me about the initial reaction of the California civil service:

"When we started with our civilian task forces, there was a rebellious element in the bureaucracy that looked at them with a chip on their shoulder. But you'd be surprised how many government employees, once they found out someone really wanted to do something, came forward with suggestions that our task forces could never have found without them. And I think the same thing would be true at the federal level."

President Reagan will have an opportunity, as every chief executive does, to appoint qualified men to the federal judiciary, including the Suprème Court. Several of the justices, like William Brennan and Thurgood Marshall, are not well and very close to retirement. Their successors will have a profound effect on our legal system for decades to come. As a strict interpreter of the Constitution, Reagan will name jurists with similar respect for that great document."

President Reagan will be prepared for the inevitable test of will that the Russians subject every new American President to. The Soviet leaders will not be able to bluff or bully him as they did John F. Kennedy in early 1961 in Vienna. As a long-time student of communism, Reagan knows that the Soviets respect strength, and he will act firmly but not belligerently in any test of our national will and purpose around the world.

In summary, President Reagan will do what he did as Governor Reagan: Reduce and contain the role of government in the lives of Americans whenever and wherever possible.

During his presidential campaign, Ronald Reagan often quoted one of the early American colonists who landed on the rocky Massachusetts shore, telling the small band of men and women that the eyes of all mankind were on them and that they could be as "a shining city on a hill." Reagan asserted that the eyes of all mankind were still upon America, wondering if its people would keep their rendezvous with destiny and give hope to all who yearned for freedom and cherished human dignity.

Above all else, this is what he wants to do as President—to help America fulfill her destiny, to put her people once again on the freedom road to achieving the American dream.

Chapter Twenty-Three

The Shooting of the President

On the misty morning of Monday, March 30, as he began the seventieth day of his presidency, Ronald Reagan had good reason to feel satisfied. His cabinet-style government was working well—although Al Haig had created an embarrassing flap the previous week by resisting the formation of a "crisis management" team with George Bush and not himself as its head. The budget cuts in his economic recovery program had withstood the rhetorical challenge of Teddy Kennedy and other liberal senators. The Democratic House would produce tougher going, but he was prepared to step up his personal salesmanship on television and across the country. Dave Stockman was doing an incredible job—this young OMB director never seemed to sleep. The news media continued to act as though the honeymoon were still on—even Nancy was receiving more friendly treatment after an initial spate of carping stories. Conservatives had apparently been mollified by the many conservative appointments and were now calculating how best to help pass the budget cuts. Of course, there were problems, small hand-shaped clouds in the sky. His approval rating had leveled off at 59 percent—less than Jimmy Carter or Richard Nixon at a similar point in their presidencies. Soviet Russia continued to apply pressure on Poland, steadily and inexorably. Central America remained a tinderbox. Inflation had dipped only slightly, and unemployment was above 7 percent.

Still, during the campaign, he had promised a new beginning, and no one could deny that Washington, D.C. was a far different city today than it had been last November 4th. Some people called what had happened, "The Reagan Revolution."

It began with the selection of the cabinet. Reagan wanted a

group of men and women who were experienced in public affairs and government, committed to conservatism and to him, and, above all, team players. After an intense search and screening process (which eliminated such prominent Republicans as John Connally, William Simon and Anne Armstrong), the following were nominated and confirmed by the US Senate:

• Secretary of State Alexander M. Haig. The fifty-six-year-old former general had been deputy to Henry Kissinger on the National Security Council, Army vice chief of staff, Nixon's chief of staff during Watergate and NATO Commander. In testimony before the Senate Foreign Relations Committee, Haig declared his intention to assemble a group of experts who would deal with the fundamental tasks facing the United States: "The management of Soviet power, the reestablishment of an orderly international economic climate, the economic and political maturation of developing nations to the benefit of their peoples and the achievement of a reasonable standard of international civility." In plainer language, Haig believed it was time to get tough with the Soviets.

• Secretary of Defense Caspar W. Weinberger. A longtime Reagan colleague, the sixty-three-year-old Weinberger had headed Nixon's budget office where his zeal for cutting programs earned him the nickname, "Cap the Knife." He was Secretary of Health, Education and Welfare from 1973-1975 and an executive of the Bechtel Group since leaving government. Before the Senate Armed Services Committee, Weinberger pledged to redress the imbalance between US and Soviet forces, put existing troops and weaponry in better fighting condition and improve "the strategic balance," tilted dangerously in favor of Moscow.

• Secretary of Treasury Donald T. Regan. The sixty-two-year-old Regan had been chairman of Merrill Lynch and Company, one of the world's largest investment firms. He told the Senate Finance Committee that "we should see gradual improvement in the second half of this year and major improvement, if this program is enacted, within (about) fifteen months." The program he was referring to was, of course, President Reagan's economic recovery program of cutting taxes, reducing spending, restricting the regulatory agencies and tightening monetary control.

• Attorney General William French Smith. The sixty-three-year-old Smith had been the President's personal lawyer since the mid-sixties and the senior partner of a Los Angeles law firm. Before the Senate Judiciary Committee, Smith said, "I see my number one problem as a balancing of the right of government to govern and the rights of the individual.'' He took command of 4,200 federal attorneys who were stepping up a campaign against organized crime, drug smuggling and white collar crime.

● Secretary of Health and Human Services Richard S. Schweiker. The fifty-four-year-old Schweiker served four terms as a US Congressman and two terms as US Senator from Pennsylvania before retiring in 1980. He was Reagan's running mate in his 1976 bid for the GOP presidential nomination. In confirmation hearings, Schweiker emphasized that ''we're going to serve the needy people of this country.'' But he also made it clear that fraud and abuse would be eliminated from the health and social programs worth 220 billion dollars.

● Secretary of Agriculture John Block. The forty-six-year-old Block was head of a family-owned agribusiness enterprise worth 10 million dollars and had been director of the Illinois Department of Agriculture since 1977. Block told the Senate Agriculture Committee that he would aggressively promote sales of American farm goods abroad. He believed that high prices for farm goods—not price supports—were the best guarantees of high farm income.

● Secretary of Interior James G. Watt. The forty-two-year-old Watt had served previously in the Interior Department and had been director of the Bureau of Outdoor Recreation and federal power commissioner. Recently, he had headed a Denver public interest law firm opposing environmental groups. A prominent spokesman for the Sagebrush rebellion, Watt pledged sound management of government-owned resources for the good of the consumer, not just the environmentalist.

● Secretary of Energy James B. Edwards. The fifty-three-year-old Edwards, an oral surgeon, was South Carolina's first GOP governor from 1975-1979, and a strong backer of Reagan's presidential try in 1976. A proponent of nuclear power, he told the Senate Energy Committee that the energy industry should be deregulated and the marketplace allowed to determine oil and gas prices. He pledged to dismantle his department as Reagan promised in his campaign.

● Secretary of Labor Ray Donovan. The fifty-year-old Donovan was executive vice president of a New Jersey construction firm and its chief labor negotiator. The first labor secretary ever to support the Right to Work, Donovan also staked out conservative positions on common situs picketing (against it), minimum wage (for a lower minimum for teenagers) and jobs (for a shift from federal job-training programs to initiatives for business expansion).

● Secretary of Housing and Urban Development Samuel R. Pierce, Jr. The fifty-eight-year-old Pierce, Reagan's first black cabinet member, had served as an assistant US attorney in Manhattan, a Labor Department official in Washington and as New York state judge. He was a senior partner in a New York law firm specializing in labor issues. Pierce told the Senate Banking Committee that efforts to reduce federal spending and double-digit inflation took precedence over housing and urban issues. "I agree," he said, "with those who say we have to improve our economy before we can get the kind of results we want for housing."

● Secretary of Transportation Andrew L. (Drew) Lewis, Jr. The forty-nine-year-old Lewis was a management consultant and active Republican in Pennsylvania where he headed Reagan's presidential campaign in 1980. Before the Senate Commerce, Science and Transportation Committee, he said that the problems of the auto industry are the most important to his department. He supported continued deregulation of the airlines, trucks and railroads as well as state control of speed limits.

● Secretary of Commerce Malcolm Baldridge. The fifty-eight-year-old Baldridge was chairman of a small appliance manufacturer and head of Connecticut's Bush for President Committee in 1980. At his confirmation hearings, he told Senators that deregulation and lower interest rates should be top priorities. "We should deregulate from top to bottom," he said, including regulations hurting the auto industry.

● Secretary of Education Terrel H. Bell. The fifty-nine-year-old Bell was a former high school teacher, superintendent, state school head and federal Commissioner of Education from 1974-1976. Although he once argued for the creation of the Department of Education, Bell agreed to carry out Reagan's plan to disband the department. Bell told Senators that he favored tuition tax credits for private schools and opposed mandatory school busing for desegregation purposes.

● United Nations Ambassador Jeane J. Kirkpatrick. The fifty-four-year-old Kirkpatrick had been a political science professor at Georgetown University since 1967 and a resident scholar at the conservative American Enterprise Institute since 1977. A Democrat, Dr. Kirkpatrick came to Reagan's attention through an article in *Commentary* in which she outlined the difference between totalitarian regimes like Soviet Russia and Communist China and authoritarian governments like Chile and South Korea. She told the Senate Foreign Relations Committee that she would strive to curb

UN agencies from engaging in "mischievous ideological struggles" against American principles and global interests.

● Central Intelligence Director William J. Casey. The sixty-seven-year-old Casey served in the Office of Strategic Services (OSS), the predecessor of the CIA, during World War II. A highly successful New York lawyer, he was a past chairman of the Securities and Exchange Commission (1971-1972) and the Export-Import Bank (1973) before serving as Ronald Reagan's general campaign manager in 1980. At his confirmation hearings, he told the Senate Select Committee on Intelligence that he was opposed to any sweeping reorganization of the CIA and planned to concentrate on reversing its current "institutional self-doubt."

● Office of US Trade Representative William E. Brock. The fifty-year-old Brock had been chairman of the Republican National Committee and largely responsible for its significant grassroots gains in the late 1970's. A former US Senator from Tennessee, Brock expressed his eagerness to become involved in such critical trade issues as Japanese auto imports, wheat and their grain sales, and advanced technology exchange.

● Office of Management and Budget Director David A. Stockman. The thirty-four-year-old Stockman quickly emerged as the *wunderkind* of the Reagan administration. As the point man for the President's economic recovery program, Stockman was constantly on Capitol Hill, national television, and the firing line explaining where and why the budget cuts had to be made. A two-term Congressman from Michigan, Stockman tirelessly preached a gospel long articulated by Reagan: less government is better government.

While the cabinet selection process went on during November and December, the President-elect prepared himself and his administration for Inaugural Day and what he called "a running start."

Less than two weeks after Election Day, Reagan was in Washington and on Capitol Hill, wooing Members of Congress. Both Democrats and Republicans responded warmly, led by House Speaker Tip O'Neill of Massachusetts, who commented: "I liked him very much. I got along with his staff better than I did with the Carter staff at my first meeting." O'Neill was joined by Democrats Robert Byrd of West Virginia, (shortly to move from majority to minority leader in the Senate), Sen. Edward Kennedy, and even D.C. Mayor Marion Barry. After conferring with legislative leaders, Reagan again called for early enactment of the Kemp-Roth tax cut, reducing income tax rates by 30 percent over a three-year period.

The President-elect was clearly paying attention to documents like the "economic Dunkirk" memo of Dave Stockman (then still a Congressman) and Rep. Jack Kemp of New York. The young legislators pointed to such serious problems as sluggish output, skyrocketing inflation, zooming interest rates and regulatory over-kill. They urged immediate drastic action—"an economic blitz-krieg"—to stop "the present hemorrhage."

In an exclusive interview on December 20 with *Human Events*, Reagan's favorite weekly newspaper, Stockman called for a com-prehensive economic program "based on a sense of national emer-gency." He urged the President-elect to:

— "Act in a way that creates credibility in the financial markets and among the public at large."

— "Not equivocate at all on the tax program that he successfully advocated and ran on during the campaign."

— "Package almost all the fiscal and spending conrol pro-grams . . . in a series of measures to be acted upon by the Congress in the first five to six months of the ninety-seventh Congress."

Reagan determined to do all of this starting January 20, 1981. His new beginning received a priceless assist when the fifty-two Americans who had been held hostage in Iran were finally and reluctantly released at almost the precise moment he was sworn in as our fortieth President.

As *Newsweek* said, "Day 444 and Day One came together in rare historic symmetry—the end of the long ordeal of the hostages in Iran and the beginning of what Reagan promised would be 'an era of national renewal.' "

As is his custom on important speeches (and this was the most important speech of his life), Reagan personally drafted his inaugural address, on nine sheets from a yellow legal pad. During the drafting, he consulted with several aides, primarily speechwriter Ken Khach-igian.

For the first time, the inaugural stage was on the West Front of the Capitol. The others had been on the East Front looking out over the Capitol Plaza toward the Supreme Court and the Library of Congress. The change was striking. Now, the inaugural party had a sweeping view of the city and its most famous memorials. Reagan took note of the new location in his speech:

"Standing here, we face a magnificent vista, opening up on this city's special beauty and history. At the end of this open mall are those shrines to the giants on whose shoulders we stand."

The new President delivered his address beneath huge American flags and giant red-white-and-blue bunting that billowed gently in the wind. The sky was blue and the temperature in the unseasonable fifties. His message was neither dramatic nor filled with rhetorical tricks but a quiet reaffirmation of his basic conservative creed—reduce the cost and growth of government so that individual enterprise can flourish. "In this present crisis," he said, "government is not the solution to our problem. Government *is* the problem."

He appealed without apology to the basic patriotism of the nation and its basic optimism. "Let us renew our determination," he said, "our courage and our strength. And let us renew our faith and hope. We have every right to dream heroic dreams." As Lou Cannon of the *Washington Post* wrote, "It is in everyday American life, not in the government in Washington, where Reagan sees the strength of the nation."

He spoke of making America "the exemplar of freedom and a beacon of hope" for the rest of the world. He proclaimed his devotion to peace based on "sufficient" military strength. He closed with a moving eulogy to Martin Treptow, a World War I soldier killed in France. He quoted from Treptow's diary in which the young American had written his mother that he vowed to fight, save and sacrifice as if "the whole struggle depends on me alone."

We need, the President said, "to believe in ourselves and in our capacity to perform great deeds. To believe that, together and with God's help, we can and will resolve the problems which confront us. And, after all, why shouldn't we believe that? We are Americans."

It was a moving end to Ronald Reagan's poetic sermon on the Hill.

Less than thirty minutes later, he received word that the two planes carrying the American hostages were not only airborne but had cleared Iranian airspace and were on their way to Algiers. Commented Reagan: "It makes the whole day perfect."

The same afternoon and in the days following, the President took steps to show he meant business. He imposed a federal hiring freeze and asked for the resignation of more than one-thousand top policymakers—all Carter holdovers. He cut spending by limiting government travel and office refurbishing. He attached federal red tape by naming a task force under Vice President Bush to study how to eliminate regulations on business and others.

His first two foreign visitors were carefully selected—Jamaican Prime Minister Edward Seaga on January 28 and South Korean President Chun Doo Hwan on February 2. A disciple of free enterprise, Seaga had just defeated a pro-Castro Marxist in national elections while anti-Communist Hwan promised to institute a more democratic style of government.

A tell-tale signal was sent to Moscow when Soviet Ambassador Anatoli Dobrynin was denied access to a private entrance and elevator at the State Department, a privilege he alone had enjoyed for years. Dobrynin was told to use the front door like every other ambassador.

At his first news conference on January 29, President Reagan bluntly denounced the Soviet leadership as still dedicated to "world revolution and a one-world Socialist-Communist state," removed price controls on oil and gasoline and repeated his intention to abolish the Departments of Energy and Education. The *New York Times* did not care for his anti-communist rhetoric but said he was "right" to end oil decontrol "eight months ahead of schedule." The American people, though, liked their new President's tough talk. A Harris poll reported 76 percent of the public felt a major reason the Iranians freed the American hostages was "they were worried that Ronald Reagan as President would be tougher to deal with than President Carter."

As he had throughout his public career, the President lost no time in going directly to the people, giving a "fireside chat" from the Oval Office on February 5. Over national television, Reagan asserted that Americans must accept cuts in nearly every government program if the nation were to avoid an "economic calamity." He also pledged an income tax cut of 30 percent over the next three years—the Kemp-Roth proposal. And he promised to speed up depreciation tax breaks for business as a means of encouraging investment and creating jobs.

As usual, he used simple language and held up first a dollar bill and then a quarter, a dime and a penny to show how the dollar had declined in value to only 36 cents over the past two decades. But, he stressed, the spending cuts "will not be at the expense of the truly needy. We can, with compassion, continue to meet our responsibility to those who through no fault of their own need our help."

A week later, the White House confirmed the administration's intention not to hurt the truly needy (and removed one of the opposition's main arguments) by listing seven social programs that would *not* be cut: Social Security retirement benefits, Medicare, the Supplemental Security Income program, disabled veterans benefits, Head Start program for low-income pre-schoolers, summer youth jobs programs, and meals for low-income schoolchildren. Conservatives complained that Reagan was giving in to political expediency, which was accurate. The President knew he could not get through the budget cuts he wanted if he took on such powerful voting groups as senior citizens and veterans. The situation called for compromise and he accepted it.

On February 18, President Reagan delivered his economic message to the Congress and the people via national television. The revolutionary size and scope of the Reagan revolution was explicitly revealed to all.

He recommended spending reductions of 41.4 billion dollars from Jimmy Carter's fiscal 1982 request and tax cuts for individuals and businesses of 53.9 billion. He warned that the nation was facing a "day of reckoning" and urged immediate approval of his sweeping economic proposals. He described his program as "evenhanded" and promised to retain a "social safety net" of programs for the truly needy. He declared that "if we don't do this, inflation and a growing tax burden will put an end to everything we believe in and to our dreams for the future."

In fact, the Reagan economic message signaled an end to the old liberal dream of government solving all our problems. *Newsweek* called it a "second New Deal potentially as profound in its import as the first was a half century ago."

In one sense, the President was gambling his own future, his party's and to some extent the nation's on his belief in free market economics. Whatever their doubts, Congress gave Ronald Reagan a standing ovation such as rarely has been accorded any President. They seemed to be saying, "All right, let's give your old-fashioned conservative ideas a try—after all, they did make America great. Maybe they can make her great again."

The game plan was to start in the GOP-dominated Senate, using it to apply political pressure on the uncertain Democratic House. Hopefully, Senate Majority Leader Howard Baker would push the spending cuts through the budget committee within a couple of weeks and then request the other committees to shape their money requests accordingly. The political heat would shift to the House with Baker, in his own words, "standing in the Rotunda waiting for Tip O'Neill" to deliver. If he didn't, said Baker, "the people will decide who is right: the Republican Senate or the Democratic House . . . and if we don't pass this package, I think the country will rise up in a rage of indignation."

On March 10, Reagan provided Congress with the details of his budget for fiscal 1982, along with a blunt warning to adopt his spending and tax cuts or risk angering voters who told Washington the preceding November to put "America's economic house in order." The President declared that his plan to reduce spending by nearly 49 billion dollars and cut taxes by almost 54 billion would help move America "back toward economic sanity."

However, his "cuts" were not as radical as they were pictured by liberal opponents. They were, in fact, not cuts at all but rather a reduction in the growth of federal spending. Reagan's proposed budget of 695.3 billion dollars reduced the growth rate in the fiscal year of 1982 to 6.2 percent as contrasted with Jimmy Carter's proposed budget of 739.3 billion and a growth rate of 11.6 percent.

The only exception, and a major one, to the spending cuts was national defense. The 1981 and 1982 defense budgets were increased by 32.6 billion dollars with the largest share going to the navy. The 1982 plan amounted to a 15 percent increase over Carter's defense budget. Defense Secretary Weinberger said the increase would "significantly and quickly strengthen our ability to respond to the Soviet threat at all levels of conflict and in all areas of the world vital to our national interest." Hedrick Smith of the *New York Times* correctly terms the Reagan administration's military budget "a reversal of national priorities as basic and significant as the Great Society programs of President Johnson in the mid-1960's." In brief, Ronald Reagan was determined that the US should again achieve military superiority over the Soviet Union.

Ronald Reagan and his administration settled into a steady rhythm. In the White House itself, counselor Edwin Meese III, chief of staff James Baker III and deputy chief of staff Michael Deaver shared responsibility and authority, with no single adviser controlling all the levers of power. The Cabinet met at least once a week to discuss and agree on policy because that is what the President wanted. To the amazement of many observers, Reagan's concept of government by consensus seemed to be working.

Dedicated able conservatives were nominated or appointed to serve at all levels of government. People like James L. Buckley as Under Secretary of State for Security Assistance, Science and Technology; Melvin L. Bradley, Senior Policy Adviser for Urban Affairs: Robert B. Carleson, Special Assistant to the President for Policy Development; Donald J. Devine, Director of the Office of Personnel Management; Paul Craig Roberts, Assistant Secretary of Treasury for Economic Policy; Norman B. Ture, Treasury Under Secretary for Tax Policy; John F. Lehman, Jr., Secretary of Navy; Thomas W. Pauken, Director of Action; Richard S. Williamson, Special

Assistant to the President for Intergovernmental Affairs; Angela (Bay) Buchanan, Treasurer of the United States; Anne McGill Gorsuch, director of the Environmental Protection Agency; Gerald P. Carmen, Administrator of General Services; Morton C. Blackwell, Special Assistant to the President for Public Liaison; Roger W. Fontaine, Senior Staff Member, National Security Council; C. Everett Koop, Deputy Assistant Secretary, Department of Health and Human Services; Vincent E. Reed, Assistant Secretary for Secondary and Elementary Education, Department of Education; James C. Roberts, Director of the White House Fellows; Verne Orr, Secretary of the Air Force, and Murray L. Weidenbaum, Chairman of the Council of Economic Advisers.

There were problems. The State Department and the White House jockeyed for position in the area of foreign policy with the National Security Council, under Richard Allen, scrambling not to get caught in the middle. It was obvious that Secretary of State Haig was pushing a little too hard, encroaching on the authority of the White House. The news media, who did not like Haig because of his military background and his close association with Richard Nixon, were delighted to make the most of the struggle.

Reagan decided to create a "crisis management team" with Vice President Bush as the head. Secretary Haig publicly admitted his "lack of enthusiasm" over the idea. But management was certainly needed. There had been considerable confusion over El Salvador with Haig and the White House disagreeing over how to publicize the communist-backed insurrection there. Haig wanted to emphasize the El Salvador crisis while Reagan aides wanted to concentrate on the budget debate. Also, the White House was unhappy with the State Department's uneven planning of Reagan's trip to Canada in mid-March. Reagan would have preferred to work out the differences privately, but once Haig went public and broke the rules of government by consensus, the White House had to act.

The same day, March 24, that Secretary Haig openly expressed his "lack of enthusiasm" about a crisis management team headed by George Bush, news secretary James S. Brady announced that the Vice President had indeed been named to coordinate and control governmental action in time of international or domestic crisis. There was widespread talk of Haig resigning. The unofficial White House reaction was, "That's up to him." A suddenly prudent Haig decided he could live with the Bush management team. A White House official admitted there was need for "more close coordination" and "more communication" between Haig and the White

House. The next day, at the White House, Reagan personally reassured Haig that he remained the President's principal foreign policy adviser.

As Lou Cannon of the *Washington Post* wrote, "Secretary of
State Alexander M. Haig, Jr. may be learning the hard way what
other strong men have learned before him . . . it is dangerous to
preempt the prerogatives of Ronald Reagan." For all his easy-going
ways, the President never tolerated, for long, subordinates who
patronized him or made light of his abilities. Haig had really created
his own difficulties, beginning on Inauguration Day when he presented Meese and Baker with a proposed executive order that would
have made the State Department the lead agency in all inter-agency
working groups. It was a Kissinger-like bid for power, and it was
firmly rejected by the White House.

On March 27, President Reagan was interviewed by the *Washington Post*, using the occasion to evaluate the first two months of
his presidency. First came the statistics—a favorite Reagan device:
personal visits with more than four-hundred members of Congress,
some of them more than once . . . fourteen Cabinet meetings . . . ten
meetings with governors, mayors, state legislators . . . seven National Security Council meetings . . . meetings with seven heads
of state and six foreign ministers.

The main accomplishment: "Our economic program which calls
for the greatest attempt of savings in the history of the nation plus
a complete tax program." He expressed confidence that Congress
would approve it.

The main target: Inflation. "I don't think that inflation is something that has come upon us like a change in climate and that there
isn't anything we can do about it. Mankind created it. Mankind can
eliminate it. We had about 130 years with no inflation in this country
to speak of."

The main enemy: The Soviet Union. The President reiterated
his willingness to talk with the Soviets. "We're not slamming a
door on them; we're just going to be realistic about them."

He projected the serene self-confidence of a man who enjoyed
what he was doing and believed he was doing it well. The previous
weekend, in an address to the Conservative Political Action Conference at the Mayflower Hotel, he sounded a familiar theme:

"Fellow citizens, fellow conservatives—our time is now, our
moment has arrived. . . . Because ours is a consistent philosophy
of government, we can be very clear: we do not have a separate
social agenda, a separate economic agenda, and a separate foreign

agenda. We have one agenda. Just as surely as we seek to put our financial house in order and rebuild our nation's defenses, so too we seek to protect the unborn, to end the manipulation of school children by utopian planners, and permit the acknowledgement of a supreme being in our classrooms.''

He ended: "If we carry the day and turn the tide we can hope that as long as men speak of freedom and those who have protected it they will remember us and they will say, 'Here were the brave and here their place of honor.' ''

Reflecting on that last weekend in March, the President knew full well that turning the tide would be far from easy, but he took comfort in signs like the Harris poll showing that 70 percent of the American people believed his economic program was both "fair and equitable." He was not overly worried about the Haig flap nor the growing Democratic resistance to his budget and tax cuts. He was eager to take his campaign for economic recovery to the grass-roots, where his basic strength lay. He was scheduled to address the Illinois State Legislature Wednesday, April 1. And tomorrow Monday, March 30, he would talk to more than 3,500 AFL-CIO delegates at the Washington Hilton Hotel. He spent a quiet Sunday evening with Nancy in the family quarters of the White House. The same day, John W. Hinckley, Jr. checked into the Park Central Hotel on 18th Street, N.W., two blocks from the White House and less than one block from Secret Service headquarters.

*Monday, March 30, 1981**

Approximately 7 a.m.; President Reagan woke up, showered and put on a blue suit. At a breakfast with 140 sub-Cabinet-level officials of his administration in the East Room, he gave a pep talk, quoting Thomas Paine: "We have it in our power to begin the world over again."

8:45 a.m.: The President entered the Oval Office for the day's first briefing with his top aides—Ed Meese, Jim Baker and Mike Deaver. Richard Allen, his national security adviser, discussed the morning cables from overseas. Max Friedersdorf, his Congressional liaison head, went over the day's business on Capitol Hill.

(Two blocks away, John Hinckley got up early, dressed and left the hotel. He had a cup of coffee at the Lunchbox Carryout Shop, a few doors from the hotel, at 7:30 a.m. An hour later, he ordered

---

*The author is endebted to *Time*, *Newsweek*, the *Washington Post* and the *New York Times* upon whom he relied for most of the following narrative.

breakfast at Kay's Sandwich Shoppe, down the street from the Old Executive Office Building. He sat alone at the counter.)

Mid-morning: Reagan greeted over twenty Hispanic leaders in the Cabinet Room and met with them privately after pictures were taken. Aides Lyn Nofziger and Elizabeth Dole sat in on the meeting. A major topic: The President's efforts to place Hispanics in his administration.

(Hinckley was out of his room at 10 a.m. when a maid checked it. She noticed a two-suiter suitcase, a small travel alarm clock, a copy of *TV Guide* and a newspaper clipping about the President's schedule that day. It reported that Reagan would leave the White House at 1:45 p.m. to address a session of the AFL-CIO's Building and Construction Trades Department at the Washington Hilton.)

Approximately 12 noon: The President lunched in the family quarters of the White House. He ate an avocado and chicken salad, sliced red beets and an apple tart. He worked on his Hilton speech and then stretched out for a brief rest.

(At 12:45 p.m., Hinckley sat in his hotel room and began to write a five-paragraph letter on lined note paper. It began: "Dear Jodie, There is a definite possibility that I will be killed in my attempt to get Reagan." It ended: "This letter is being written an hour before I leave for the Hilton Hotel. Jodie, I'm asking you to please look into your heart and at least give me the chance with this historical deed to gain your respect and love. I love you forever." It was signed, "John Hinckley." Hinckley sealed but did not mail the letter to actress Jodie Foster, 18 years old, a freshman at Yale University whom he had never met.)

1:45 p.m.: The President climbed into his armor-plated black Lincoln limousine for the seven-minute drive to the Hilton. With him were Michael Deaver, his closest personal aide, Labor Secretary Ray Donovan and two Secret Service agents: Drew Unrue, who drove, and Jerry Parr, chief of the presidential protection detail, who sat next to Unrue. Reagan and Donovan reminisced about the New Jersey primary in which Donovan had played a crucial part. The President's car parked outside the Hotel's VIP entrance and Reagan walked in. He spent a few minutes shaking hands in a reception line, then huddled with Donovan, Deaver and Presidential News Secretary James Brady in a VIP waiting room.

(Rechecking rooms at 1:15, the maid found Hinckley still in his forty-two-dollar-a-night room. She hung up some fresh towels and left. Shortly afterward, Hinckley left for the Hilton, about one mile away. Upon arrival at the hotel, he stood in front of the curving stone wall near the VIP entrance. John M. Dodson was watching the entrance from the seventh floor across the street. He noticed a young man in a tan raincoat. "He looked fidgety, agitated," Dodson later recalled.)

2:20 p.m. A group of TV and still photographers waited for the President's exit. Other reporters were there, some with microphones and tape recorders. There were also curious onlookers, union members, women with Kodaks and children. Inside, the President was finishing up an eighteen-minute speech with only one sentence that would later be remembered: "Violent crime has surged 10 percent, making neighborhood streets unsafe and families fearful in their homes."

(Outside, standing close to the wall, Hinckley complained about the press, which had been complaining about onlookers getting in their way. AP Radio reporter Walter Rogers pushed his way along the wall, extending his fishpole mike, when he heard a young man say about reporters: "They ought to get here on time. They think they can do anything they want." The press and the young man jockeyed for position behind a rope, about 25 feet from the doors through which the President would exit.)

2:24 p.m.: President Reagan stepped out on the sidewalk and headed toward his car, parked fifteen feet from the exit and ten feet from the press rope. He raised his right hand high, waving to people standing across the driveway. Parr was at the President's right side. Deaver was on his left, between the President and the press. Secret Service Agent Timothy McCarthy waited at the limousine, standing behind the open rear door. Washington Patrolman Thomas Delahanty stood near the press rope. Reagan, just a few feet from his car, turned to his left and waved toward the reporters.

"Mr. President, Mr. President," called Michael Putzel, an AP reporter, hoping to ask Reagan a quick question. Brady stepped ahead of Deaver to handle the question. Still smiling, Reagan looked past McCarthy, Deaver, Brady and Delahanty at the group behind the rope.

2:25 p.m.: Hinckley quickly took out his gun, a .22-cal handgun loaded with six Devastator bullets designed to explode on impact. He dropped to a crouch, assumed a policeman's double-hand grip and opened fire. He shot twice, paused, then fired off four more rounds—all in a fleeting two seconds. The shots made a deceptively innocent popping sound.)

2:25 p.m.: At the first shot, Parr reached forward and grabbed the frozen President. Doubling Reagan over to reduce his target size, the agent hunched over him as a human shield and pushed him hard through the open back door and onto the floor of the limousine. Despite Parr's quick reaction, and without either man realizing it, one of Hinckley's shots ricocheted off the rear panel of the limousine, tore a hole in Reagan's suit, pierced his body below his left arm, bounced off a rib, punctured his left lung and came to a stop one inch from his heart. "Take off!" shouted Parr to the driver. "Just take off!" The limousine squealed out of the driveway, turned left on Connecticut Avenue and headed for the White House.

Behind them, news secretary James Brady lay on the sidewalk, blood seeping from his head. Agent McCarthy had been trained to try to block any shots at the President with his own body. When the shooting began, he instinctively turned toward the assassin and caught a bullet in the stomach that could well have hit the President. Patrolman Delahanty was hit in the neck and lay moaning in pain near the rope.

Along the wall, agents, police officers and a union official from Cleveland jumped on Hinckley, who struggled furiously for twenty seconds. At last, officers handcuffed Hinckley and drew a jacket up over his head as a makeshift straitjacket. He was hustled into a police car (after the rear door of another car was found locked) and sped off to Washington police headquarters, about three miles away. Within five minutes, three ambulances arrived and hauled away Brady, McCarthy and Delahanty.

2:26 p.m.: In the President's Lincoln, Reagan was having trouble breathing. He thought he had hurt his ribs. Parr said later: "I ran my hands over his body, under his arms, his back," detecting no wound. The President began to cough up red blood, and Parr recognized it as oxygenated blood from the lungs. He immediately directed the driver to change destination. Grabbing the car radio, Parr told the White House that they were going to George Washington Hospital and to notify the hospital.

2:35 p.m.: The presidential car pulled up at the hospital's emergency entrance, about twelve blocks from the Hilton. Incredibly, there was no stretcher, not even a wheel chair, waiting. Along with two other agents from a following car, Parr helped Reagan walk about forty-five feet toward the entrance when the President suddenly sagged. A paramedic took Reagan by the feet while the agents lifted him under the arms and carried him, faint but still conscious, to the "code room," a ten-by-twenty foot space where critical emergency cases are treated. It was not until they had lifted Reagan onto the table and cut off his coat and shirt that they finally realized the President had been shot.

The code room filled up with trauma team members and Secret Service agents. It was so noisy that a nurse taking Reagan's blood pressure could not hear through the stethoscope and ended up taking it by feeling the pulse in Reagan's arm. It was only about seventy-five—low enough to suggest the President was in danger of shock. His pulse was recorded at eighty-eight—slightly increased.

Quickly doctors inserted an intravenous tube and began running fluid into the President's veins. They took blood samples to measure the blood oxygen content and to match Reagan's blood for a transfusion. The President's blood type is O-positive.

Dr. Joseph M. Giardano, who headed the trauma team, saw Reagan within five minutes of his arrival. By then, the President's blood pressure had risen to normal, but he was coughing up blood, his breathing was fast, and surgeons had discovered the wound under his left arm. Concerned about a collapsed lung and the danger of internal bleeding, Dr. Giardano ordered a chest tube inserted.

2:36 p.m.: Nancy Reagan arrived at the hospital and asked to see her husband immediately. There was a delay. When she finally did see him, he greeted her with a line that has already become a classic: "Honey, I forgot to duck."

3:20 p.m.: The President was prepared for surgery. His bleeding had slowed and he had received a transfusion of five units of blood or 2½ quarts, about half his total blood volume. In all, through the operation, Reagan lost about 3.7 quarts of blood, some two-thirds of his blood volume. But because of constant transfusions, his blood loss was never life-threatening. As his bed was wheeled into the operating room, Reagan caught a glimpse of his three top aides, Meese, Deaver and Baker, standing in the hall. "Who's minding the store?" he asked with a wink. Inside, looking up at the surgeons, he quipped, "I hope you're all Republicans." One doctor responded: "Today, everyone's a Republican."

Meanwhile, the White House was adjusting to the attempted assassination after a somewhat shaky start. Vice President Bush, enroute from Dallas to Austin for a speech, was informed of the shooting shortly after 2:30 p.m., but was told erroneously, that the President was not hurt. A few minutes later, Dr. Daniel Ruge, Reagan's personal physician, delivered the bad news to the White House from the hospital: the President had been hit after all.

Treasury Secretary Donald Regan, Secretary of State Alexander Haig and others joined the top White House staffers in Jim Baker's office. It was decided that Meese, Baker and Deaver would set up a mini-command post at the hospital while Haig, Regan, Defense Secretary Caspar Weinberger and National Security Adviser Richard Allen moved to the Situation Room in the White House basement. CIA Director William Casey and Attorney General William French Smith soon joined the group.

Haig, an old hand at government crises, sent a wire by secure radio telecopier to Bush at approximately 2:45 p.m. It read: "Mr. Vice President, the President has been struck." Aboard the plane, Bush immediately gave the order to refuel in Austin and return to Washington. He wondered aloud: "How could anybody want to kill such a kindhearted man?"

3:18 p.m.: Some forty minutes after the Secret Service learned that Reagan had been shot, the White House finally informed the news media of the injury. Because of the delay and the many rumors circulating, the TV networks reported several errors, including that news secretary James Brady was dead. A CBS reporter stated that Reagan would undergo "open-heart" surgery when in fact it was open-chest surgery, a less dangerous operation.

4 p.m.: Deputy news secretary Larry Speakes gave a brief explanation of Reagan's presurgery treatment at the hospital. With TV cameras recording the exchange for millions of Americans, Speakes was asked: "If the President goes into surgery and goes under anesthesia, would Vice President Bush become the acting President at the moment or under what circumstances does he?" Replied an unprepared Speakes: "I cannot answer that question at this time." Speakes was then asked whether US military forces had been placed on alert. "Not that I'm aware," Speakes replied.

Reaction in the Situation Room was immediate. Fearful that the news media, the world and especially the Soviets might misinterpret the vague response, Haig snapped to Richard Allen: "Come on, come with me." Without telling anyone where they were going, Haig and Allen raced up a flight of stairs and strode into the White House press room. Haig's intention was to project an air of calm and assurance, but he was perspiring, his voice shook, and his hands trembled (from the run up the stairs, he later explained).

At 4:14 p.m.: Haig announced that the appropriate Cabinet officials were in the Situation Room, Vice President Bush knew what was going on, and no military alert had been ordered. When a reporter asked who was making the decisions, Haig misspoke: "Constitutionally, gentlemen, you have the President, the Vice President and the Secretary of State in that order, and should the

President decide he wants to transfer the helm to the Vice President, he will do so. I am in control here in the White House pending the return of the Vice President. If something came up, I would check with him, of course.''

In fact, the Speaker of the House (Democrat Tip O'Neill) and the President Pro Tempore (Sen. Strom Thurmond) follow the President and the Vice President in succession. And it is Weinberger, not Haig, who is in charge of emergency military commands. In fact, Weinberger had instructed Gen. David Jones, chairman of the Joint Chiefs of Staff, to order a low-level increase of readiness because no one knew whether the shooting of the President was an isolated incident or part of a conspiracy.

Haig meant well, but only partially succeeded in capping the crisis. It remained for Dr. Dennis S. O'Leary, dean of Clinical Affairs and spokesman for George Washington Hospital, to reassure the nation via TV at 7:30 p.m. that the President had ''sailed through'' surgery.

The operation began at approximately 3:30 p.m. The surgeon was Dr. Benjamin Aaron, director of chest and cardiovascular surgery at George Washington Hospital. It was quickly determined that the bullet had not penetrated the abdominal cavity, which would have seriously complicated the President's condition. The hole in Reagan's side was a slit wound, but the hole in his lung was round. Dr. Aaron concluded that the flattened bullet (which ricocheted before it hit) entered the chest like a disc, sideways, and then spun through the lung like a turning ball. ''When I found it,'' said the surgeon, ''it was about an inch from the heart and aorta, right against the heart's surface, almost. I think there was some kind of Divine Providence or something riding with that bullet. Because it still had a lot of zing and one can only conjecture how much worse things might have been.''

At first, Dr. Aaron couldn't find the bullet. He ordered X-rays and finally threaded a catheter down the bullet track to find it. And then he could not remove it. ''It was like trying to find a dime through a sponge. I came close to giving up and closing the chest a couple of times.'' But he did not and finally worked it to the lung's surface with his fingers. At about 5:30 p.m., two hours after surgery began, the bullet was removed. Dr. Aaron then took about one hour to remove some of the dead lung tissue, insert a drain into the bullet's track and close up the incisions.

Dr. O'Leary subsequently reported that the President ''was at no time in any serious danger. He has a clear head and should be able to make decisions by tomorrow." At about 7 p.m., with a breathing tube in his throat and still on a respirator, Reagan was taken to the recovery room.

7 p.m.: Vice President Bush arrived in the Situation Room in the White House. Richard Allen rattled off an agenda: the President's health, an update on the world intelligence situation, the status of US military forces, what the news media and the public had been told, the information given privately to members of Congress, the outlines of a statement for Bush, whether it was appropriate for Bush to visit Reagan at the hospital, information about Mrs. Reagan and the family, the cancellation of Bush's trip to Geneva and an update of next day's schedule which Bush would fill.

8:30 p.m.: Bush addressed the TV networks, reporting that the President "has emerged from this experience with flying colors and with most optimistic prospects for a complete recovery . . . I can reassure this nation and the watching world that the American government is functioning fully and effectively."

8:50 p.m.: The President, with the anesthesia having worn off, but with a tube still in his throat, scribbled a note to his doctors in the recovery room: "All in all, I'd rather be in Philadelphia." It was a famous movie line of comedian W.C. Fields. Everyone in the room laughed. When the message was relayed to the Situation Room, William French Smith, the President's personal lawyer for many years, said: "I know he's going to be all right."

The basic facts about John Warnock Hinckley, Jr. are beyond dispute. He was born on May 29, 1955, in Ardmore, Oklahoma, to Jo Ann and John Hinckley, Sr. His father was a petroleum engineer, a conservative Republican and a fundamentalist Protestant. Four years later, Hinckley Sr. moved to Dallas with his wife and three children, Scott, now 30; Diana, 28, and John. Never any problem as a child, John Jr. joined the YMCA's Indian Guides and excelled in elementary schoolsports. To all appearances, the Hinckleys were a happy, healthy, all-American family.

In 1966, they moved to Highland Park, *the* suburb of Dallas. Their house had a circular driveway, a private coke machine and a swimming pool. At first, John Jr. thrived, being elected president of his homeroom in the seventh and ninth grades and managing the baseball team one year. But in the fall of 1969, he entered Highland Park High School, one of the best and most competitive schools in Texas, where his sister, Diana, was a highly popular senior, candidate for homecoming queen, head cheerleader, Miss All-Everything. John was never elected president of anything again.

Academically, athletically, socially, he sank to the middle and stayed there. Most of his former classmates, following the assassination attempt, had to dig out their yearbooks to place Hinckley.

In the fall of 1973, he entered Texas Tech University in dusty Lubbock. Over the next seven years, he dropped out at least three times, majored in at least three subjects and lived in one cheap apartment after another. Hinckley was slightly above average as a student (he made the Dean's list one semester), but did not participate in Texas Tech's frequent drinking parties. After taking a wide variety of courses, he finally settled on English as a major by 1978. By then his attendance was sporadic. In *Newsweek*'s words, "he was turning into one of those familiar, pathetic campus figures who make their college careers last most of their twenties."

Hinckley began drifting, in space and time. In Lubbock, remembered a landlord, "he just sat there the whole time, staring at the TV." In 1976, he lived for a while in the seamy Selma Avenue district of Los Angeles—a haven for whores, drugs, homosexuals and other decadent diversions. In 1978, he allegedly joined the National Socialist Party of America, a pro-Nazi group, marching in one of their parades in St. Louis. (Law enforcement officials and the Anti-Defamation League have no record of Hinckley ever belonging to the party.) Michael Allen, the current party chief, claims he remembers that "after the rally (Hinckley) was like a different person. He was very agitated. He said we needed something more dramatic." Hinckley's militant attitude alarmed some of the Nazi leaders and his membership (or that of the young man thought to be Hinckley) was not renewed in November 1979. What is certain is that Hinckley took a course in Modern Germany at Texas Tech in the summer of 1978 and wrote a paper on Hitler's autobiography, *Mein Kampf*.

In September 1979, after a year's hiatus from Texas Tech, he registered for classes—and bought his first gun, a .38-cal. pistol, for eighty-six dollars. On September 26, he purchased two cheap .22-cal. handguns made by RG Industries of Miami. In February 1980, he sought help from a Lubbock physician, Dr. Baruch D. Rosen, who has refused to talk about his patient. Rosen treated him with the anti-depressant Surmontil and with 20 milligrams daily of Valium, a moderate dosage. At the end of 1980's second summer session at Texas Tech, Hinckley was dropped from the student rolls for nonpayment of fees.

In late September, Hinckley went to New Haven for the beginning of his fantasy courtship of actress Jodie Foster, best known for her role as a child prostitute in the film, *Taxi Driver*.

The film, according to a synopsis, concerns "a loner incapable of communicating," who "usually spends his off hours . . . eating junk food or sitting alone in a dingy room." When the protagonist is scorned by Foster's character, he mails her a letter and sets out to kill a presidential candidate. The coincidences are given credence by a letter that scriptwriter Paul Schrader got in the fall of 1980—from J. W. Hinckley.

A bartender at a New Haven hotel recalls a man he now thinks was Hinckley, drinking and bragging that Jodie Foster was his girlfriend and showing bartenders newspaper clippings about the young actress.

On October 9, John Hinckley, Jr. was arrested in the Nashville, Tennessee, airport for attempting to board a flight to New York carrying three handguns—two .22s and a .38—and a box of fifty hollow-point bullets. He was released after paying a fifty dollar cash bond and forfeiting his guns. Although President Carter was making a campaign appearance in Nashville the same day, the Secret Service was never informed of Hinckley's arrest. The FBI now suspects that Hinckley was stalking Carter and visited Washington, D.C. in late September and Chicago in early October when the President was campaigning there.

Four days after his arrest in Nashville, on October 13, 1980, John Hinckley bought two .22-cal. revolvers at Rocky's Pawn Shop in Dallas. They were inexpensive (forty-seven dollars each) blue-steel Rohn revolvers with checkered stocks, assembled in Miami from West German parts.

Hinckley's actions now became more erratic, more uncontrolled. He returned to his parents, now living in Evergreen, Colo., a wealthy suburb of Denver much like Highland Park. Here he received treatment from psychiatrist John Hopper. He applied for a job at Denver's two newspapers, giving references for jobs he never held. His parents were happy at his return, thinking he was at last settling down and planning to make something of himself. On January 21, he bought another gun, a .38-cal. Charter Arms Undercover revolver. He now had a trio of guns identical in caliber to the three he surrendered when he was arrested in Nashville.

In late February he traveled again to New Haven where he delivered more love letters to Jodie Foster. Two Yale students remember meeting Hinckley in a bakery where he showed them pictures of his "girlfriend"—Foster. Other students recall seeing him hanging around Jodie Foster's dorm in early March.

A week later, he was back in Denver where he stayed for sixteen days in a second-rate motel. He applied for a job at a record store and pawned his typewriter and guitar. On March 18, the suspicions of patrolman Chris Warsham were aroused by a man outside the Golden Hours Motel. "You see a man acting unusual, you just get a feeling." Warsham questioned the room clerk, ran a check on the man's car and went upstairs to his room. He knocked but there was no answer. To his surprise, he found himself drawing his gun—"something I rarely do." That evening, Warsham finally encountered John Hinckley, who politely identified himself. "I was going to ask him more questions," Warsham recalls, "but a call came over the radio. I never saw him again."

On March 25, Hinckley drove his white Plymouth Volare to his parents' house and then made his way to the Denver airport. He flew to Los Angeles by way of Salt Lake City, spending the night in L.A. On March 26, he headed back east by bus, changing in Cleveland and Pittsburgh on the long three-day ride to Washington, D.C.

Why did Hinckley do it? *Newsweek* called his attempted murder "the act of a loser—a twenty-five-year-old drifter who thought that shooting the President would make an impressive introduction to the teen-age actress he had never met." *Time* described the shooting as "the first openly extraordinary act of his life" and Hinckley himself as a "dangerous loner." *U.S. News & World Report* summed him as "one of society's losers," a "misfit who craved fame." The *Washington Post* pointed to his failure to graduate from college, to hold a job, to measure up to his brother and sister, to connect with his father, and, finally, to be recognized by actress Jodie Foster, for whom he developed an overwhelming obsession. The *New York Times* referred to a life that started with promise but took an increasingly "reclusive and aggressive path."

A prominent psychiatrist, Dr. Thomas Gutheil of the Massachusetts Mental Health Center, cautioned that no accurate explanation was apt to be simple: Hinckley's mind was a snake pit of emotions and delusions which all together led him to Washington. To this writer, John W. Hinckley, Jr. was a ticking time bomb waiting to go off.

He failed in his deadly mission because the man he shot at displayed rare, almost unbelievable courage, strength and grace. For several hours following the shooting, Ronald Reagan poured forth a stream of one-liners that reassured doctors, friends and the American people: the Gipper was going to pull through. In fact, the President had received a serious wound, but he refused to show it. A typical note (tubes in his throat kept him from talking) read: "As Winnie Churchill said, 'There is no more exhilerating feeling than being shot without result.' "

Columnist George Will declared that Reagan "was in a word, presidential . . . the president's imperishable example of grace under pressure gave the nation a tonic it needed." Columnist Hugh Sidey wrote that "the stuff of successful leadership is finally an accumulation of adversities bluntly confronted and firmly mastered. Nothing that Ronald Reagan has done so far has meant so much to his presidency as the stark but simple test (on March 30) that showed up something special behind the good guy smile."

James Reston of the *New York Times*: "Everybody knows that people seldom act at the margin between life and death with such light-hearted valor as they do in the movies. Yet Ronald Reagan did." Columnist James J. Kilpatrick: "To survive danger, to walk tall, to laugh in the face of death—this is the stuff of which legend is fashioned."

Columnist Charles Bartlett, a close personal friend of John F. Kennedy, expressed the hope that the nation would not plunge into a dark, breast-beating mood: "The developing mood of optimism should not be lost in a siege of hand-wringing. It is one thing to lament this ugly event, another to relapse into a morbid outlook full of doubts about the country's claim on good fortune. We need instead to continue in the revival to which Reagan has been pointing us, searching eagerly for reasons to be hopeful about the future."

The White House was flooded with messages of shock and sympathy for the wounded President from leaders around the world. British Prime Minister Margaret Thatcher, the first European leader to meet with Reagan after his inauguration, sent a message saying she prayed his injuries were not serious. West German Chancellor Helmut Schmidt, who had spoken by telephone to Reagan the morning of March 30, expressed his "deep horror." French President Valery Giscard d'Estaing cabled wishes for a complete recovery and "the pursuit of your activity in the leadership of the United States." President Anwar el-Sadat of Egypt said, "We pray to God Almighty to bestow on you quick recovery to continue leading your great nation." Israeli Prime Minister Menachem Begin expressed his shock and astonishment.

Soviet leader Leonid Brezhnev said: "We have learned with

indignation of the attempt on your life. We resolutely condemn this criminal act. In the name of the Soviet leadership and myself personally, I wish you, Mr. President, a full and speedy recovery." Chinese Premier Zhao Ziyang cabled: "Shocked to learn of your being wounded in an assassination attempt. I wish you a speedy recovery."

Typically, Ayatollah Ruhollah Khomeini said that Iranians would not be forced to express sympathy this time. Pars, the official press agency, said Khomeini recalled that when President John F. Kennedy was slain in 1963, Iranian students "were made to mourn the occasion" by officials of the government of Shah Mohammed Riza Pahlevi. No message was received from Fidel Castro of Cuba.

Here at home there was anger mixed with fear and prayer. In cities as different as Boston and Oklahoma, prayer services were announced for Reagan and the three other victims. The Texas Legislature unanimously adopted a resolution condemning the shooting. The Iowa House stood for a moment of prayer. The President's former colleagues in the movie industry postponed the Academy Award ceremonies for twenty-four hours. But NCAA officials decided not to cancel or postpone the scheduled championship basketball game between North Carolina and Indiana. Jimmy Carter's office in Atlanta issued a brief statement that the former president and Mrs. Carter joined "the entire nation in prayer for the well-being of all those wounded and for their families."

In a Senate speech, Sen. Edward Kennedy, recalled the murders of his brothers, President John F. Kennedy and Senator Robert F. Kennedy, saying:

"Violence and hatred are alien to everything that this country is about. It does not bring about a change in policy. It is alien to what is best in our nation. With our prayers for those who have been wounded today must go our resolution to rid our society of violence and to commit ourselves to do everything that we possibly can to eliminate hatred and the causes which contribute to hatred in our society."

Comedian Bob Hope recalled being with Reagan during the presidential campaign when the candidate showed his longtime friend a bullet-proof jacket that had been built into his raincoat. "I wish he'd been wearing that today," Hope said.

It also needs to be said that most Americans were not shocked. Angry, anxious, sad, even fearful, but not shocked. David Rosenbaum of the *New York Times* laid the widespread acceptance of the assassination attempt to three factors: (1) the wide availability of

handguns, (2) the glorification of the President, and (3) the open
Presidency. Because there are so many handguns (an estimated 56
million), there is no practical way to confiscate them or keep them
out of the hands of someone determined to get one. Because the
President is our leading celebrity, experts believe that to strike at
such a symbol is the ultimate goal of a psychopath seeking fame.
And despite all the risks, presidents prefer to ride in open cars and
attend outdoor rallies, rather than restrict themselves to indoor appearances and televised addresses.

There were inevitable questions about the protection of the President. Secret Service Director H. Stuart Knight later told a Senate
committee that "this is the sort of democratic society in which the
President wants to see the people and the people want to see
him . . . Sure there is a fool proof way of protecting him—keep
him locked up inside the White House."

The Secret Service has a 170 million dollar annual budget, sixty
field offices, a list of four-hundred people who are direct threats to
the President, another list of 25 thousand people who might be
dangerous and courageous agents like Timothy McCarthy, who
leaped between Hinckley and President Reagan.

But as FBI Director J. Edgar Hoover said after President Kennedy's assassination: "Absolute security is neither practical nor
possible. An approach to complete security would require the President to operate in some sort of vacuum, isolated from the general
public and behind impregnable barriers. His travel would be in
secret; his public appearances would be behind bullet proof glass."

That's a role Ronald Reagan will never play.

Twelve days after he was shot, Ronald Reagan went home. At
the hospital, he declined to ride a wheel chair and strolled out the
front door with Nancy holding his right arm and his daughter Patti
holding his left. He had lost some weight (about ten pounds) and
he walked a little stiffly. But he told reporters he felt "great" and
he grinned broadly as aides and friends cheered his arrival at the
White House.

Polls revealed widespread public admiration for Reagan's courage and humor during his grim ordeal. A *Washington Post*-ABC
survey found 73 percent approval of his performance as President
with only 16 percent disapproval. By 72 to 23 percent, the public
rejected the idea that the President should isolate himself for safety's
sake. Observers agreed that the increased popularity would make
it more difficult, but not impossible, for opponents to challenge his
economic recovery and other programs.

"Sympathy," cautioned Sen. Paul Laxalt, the President's closest friend in Congress, "is a short-term commodity on Capitol Hill."

"In the long term," suggested Senate Majority Leader Howard Baker, "the President is likely to be even more popular. . . . But I don't think it's likely to have any legislative impact."

"The sympathy and admiration attaches to the President," said House Democratic Whip Thomas Foley of Washington, "but it doesn't mean that every proposal is immune from respectful criticism or comment."

Congressman Morris Udall of Arizona, a liberal Democrat and former candidate for his party's presidential nomination, was more eloquent than many of his colleagues: "This is a long-term plus for Reagan. He has been through the fire and escaped. There is an aura there that wasn't there before."

Vice President Bush conducted himself with exceptional dignity and calm, strengthening his position within the Reagan administration as well as his potential as a future presidential candidate. After a shaky beginning, the President's top aides—Meese, Baker and Deaver—demonstrated they too could handle a crisis. Reagan's concept of cabinet government was tested in the extreme and found effective.

The President will certainly come under strong pressure to curtail or restrict his public appearances. But it is most unlikely that Ronald Reagan will agree to a carefully programmed presidency. He is a man who chafes at physical restrictions, who enjoys a casual outing with friends as well as a formal banquet with thousands. He will take his lead, I suspect, from Abraham Lincoln, who said shortly before he was assassinated: "If I am killed, I can die but once; but to live in constant dread of it is to die over and over again." It can be said with certainty that Reagan is not going to let any bullet, or the threat of one, prevent him from carrying out what he believes he was elected to do: Lead a conservative political reformation to redirect the role of government and transform the political landscape for the rest of this century.

And it is also certain that the American people, now more than ever before, will want to see, hear and touch Ronald Reagan, who in his seventy-first year and on the seventieth day of his presidency, after varying life roles as sportscaster, actor, union leader, corporate spokesman, governor, radio commentator and President, became in every sense of the word a true American hero.

APPENDIX I

Acceptance Speech
by
Governor Ronald Reagan
Republican National Convention

Detroit, Michigan
July 17, 1980

Mr. Chairman, delegates to this convention, my fellow citizens of this great nation:

With a deep awareness of the responsibility conferred by your trust, I accept your nomination for the Presidency of the United States. I do so with deep gratitude.

I am very proud of our party tonight. This convention has shown to all America a party united, with positive programs for solving the nation's problems; a party ready to build a new consensus with all those across the land who share a community of values embodied in these words: family, work, neighborhood, peace and freedom.

I know we have had a quarrel or two in our party, but only as to the method of attaining a goal. There was no argument about the goal. As President, I will establish a liaison with the 50 Governors to encourage them to eliminate, wherever it exists, discrimination against women. I will monitor Federal laws to insure their implementation and to add statutes if they are needed.

More than anything else, I want my candidacy to unify our country; to renew the American spirit and sense of purpose. I want to carry our message to every American, regardless of party affiliation, who is a member of this community of shared values.

Never before in our history have Americans been called upon to face three grave threats to our very existence, any one of which could destroy us. We face a disintegrating economy, a weakened defense and an energy policy based on the sharing of scarcity.

The major issue of this campaign is the direct political, personal, and moral responsibility of Democratic party leadership—in the White House and in Congress—for this unprecedented calamity which has befallen us. They tell us they have done the most that humanly could be done. They say that the United States has had its day in the sun; that our nation has passed its zenith. They expect you to tell your children that the American people no longer have the will to cope with their problems; that the future will be one of sacrifice and few opportunities.

My fellow citizens, I utterly reject that view. The American people, the most generous on earth, who created the highest standard of living, are not going to accept the notion that we can only make a better world for others by moving backwards ourselves. Those who believe we *can* have no business leading the nation.

I will not stand by and watch this great country destroy itself under mediocre leadership that drifts from one crisis to the next, eroding our national will and purpose. We have come together here because the American people deserve better from those to whom they entrust our nation's highest offices, and we stand united in our resolve to do something about it.

We need a rebirth of the American tradition of leadership at *every* level of government and in private life as well. The United States of America is unique in world history because it has a genius for leaders—many leaders—on many levels. But, back in 1976, Mr. Carter said, "Trust *me*." And a lot of people did. Now, many of those people are out of work. Many have seen their savings eaten away by inflation. Many others on fixed incomes, especially the elderly, have watched helplessly as the cruel tax of inflation wasted away their purchasing power. And, today, a great many who trusted Mr. Carter wonder if we can survive the Carter policies of national defense.

"Trust me" government asks that we concentrate our hopes and dreams on one man; that we trust him to do what's best for us. My view of government places trust not in one person or one party, but in those values that transcend persons and parties. The trust is where it belongs—in the people. The responsibility to live up to that trust is where *it* belongs, in their elected leaders. That kind of relationship, between the people and their elected leaders, is a special kind of *compact;* an agreement among themselves to build a community and abide by its laws.

Three-hundred-and-sixty years ago, in 1620, a group of families dared to cross a mighty ocean to build a future for themselves in a new world. When they arrived at Plymouth, Massachusetts, they formed what they called a "compact": an agreement among themselves to build a community and abide by its laws.

The single act—the voluntary binding together of free people to live under the law—set the pattern for what was to come.

A century-and-a-half later, the descendants of those people pledged their lives, their fortunes and their sacred honor to found this nation. Some forfeited their fortunes and their lives; none sacrificed honor.

Four score and seven years later, Abraham Lincoln called upon the people of all America to renew their dedication and their commitment to a government of, for and by the people.

Isn't it once again time to renew our compact of freedom; to pledge to each other all that is best in our lives; all that gives meaning to them—for the sake of this, our beloved and blessed land?

Together, let us make this a new beginning. Let us make a commitment to care for the needy; to each our children the values and the virtues handed down to us by our families; to have the courage to defend those values and the willingness to sacrifice for them.

Let us pledge to restore, in our time, the American spirit of voluntary service, of cooperation, of private and community initiative; a spirit that flows like a deep and mighty river through the history of our nation.

As your nominee, I pledge to restore to the federal government the capacity to do the people's work without dominating their lives. I pledge to you a government that will not only work well, but wisely; its ability to act tempered by prudence, and its willingness to do good balanced by the knowledge that government is never more dangerous than when our desire to have it help us blinds us to its great power to harm us.

The first Republican President once said, "While the people retain their virtue and their vigilance, no Administration by an extreme of wickedness or folly can seriously injure the government in the short space of four years."

If Mr. Lincoln could see what's happened in these last three-and-a-half years, he might hedge a little on that statement. But, with the virtues that are our legacy as a free people and with the vigilance that sustains liberty, we still have time to use our renewed compact to overcome the injuries that have been done to America these past three-and-a-half years.

First, we must overcome something the present Administration has cooked up: a new and altogether indigestible economic stew, one part inflation, one part high unemployment, one part recession, one part runaway taxes, one part deficit spending and seasoned by an energy crisis. It's an economic stew that has turned the national stomach. It is as if Mr. Carter had set out to prove, once and for all, that economics is indeed a "dismal science."

Ours are not problems of abstract economic theory. These are problems of flesh and blood; problems that cause pain and destroy the moral fiber of real people who should not suffer the further indignity of being told by the White House that it is all somehow their fault. We do not have inflation because—as Mr. Carter says—we have lived too well.

The head of a government which has utterly refused to live within *its* means and which has, in the last few days, told us that this year's deficit will be $60 billion, dares to point the finger of blame at business and labor, both of which have been engaged in a losing struggle just trying to stay even.

High taxes, we are told, are somehow good for us, as if, when government spends our money it isn't inflationary, but when we spend it, it is.

Those who preside over the worst energy shortage in our history tell us to use less, so that we will run out of oil, gasoline and natural gas a little more slowly. Conservation is desirable, of course, for we must not waste energy. But conservation is not the sole answer to our energy needs.

America must get to work producing more energy. The Republican program for solving economic problems is based on growth and productivity.

Large amounts of oil and natural gas lay beneath our land and off our shores, untouched because the present Administration seems to believe the American people would rather see more regulation, taxes and controls than more energy.

Coal offers great potential. So does nuclear energy produced under rigorous safety standards. It could supply electricity for thousands of industries and millions of jobs and homes. It must not be thwarted by a tiny minority opposed to economic growth which often finds friendly ears in regulatory agencies for its obstructionist campaigns.

Make no mistake. We will not permit the safety of our people or our environmental heritage to be jeopardized, but we are going to reaffirm that the economic *prosperity* of our people is a fundamental part of our environment.

Our problems are both acute and chronic, yet all we hear from those in positions of leadership are the same tired proposals for more government tinkering, more meddling and more control—all of which led us to this state in the first place.

Can anyone look at the record of this Administration and say, "Well done"? Can anyone compare the state of our economy when the Carter administration took office with where we are today and say, "Keep up the good work"? Can anyone look at our reduced standing in the world today and say, "Let's have four more years of this"?

I believe the American people are going to answer these questions the first week of November and their answer will be, "No—we've had enough." And, when the American people *have* spoken, it will be up to us—beginning next January 20th—to offer an Administration and Congressional leadership of competence and more than a little courage.

We must have the clarity of vision to see the difference between what is essential and what is merely desirable; and then the courage to use this insight to bring our government back under control and make it acceptable to the people.

We Republicans believe it is essential that we maintain both the forward momentum of economic growth and the strength of the safety net beneath those in society who need help. We also believe it is essential that the integrity of all aspects of Social Security be preserved.

Beyond these essentials, I believe it is clear our federal government is overgrown and overweight. Indeed, it is time for our government to go on a diet. Therefore, my first act as Chief Executive will be to impose an immediate and thorough freeze on federal hiring. Then, we are going to enlist the very best minds from business, labor and whatever quarter to conduct a detailed review of every department, bureau and agency that lives by federal appropriation. We are also going to enlist the help and ideas of many dedicated and hard-working government employees at all levels who want a more efficient government as much as the rest of us do. I know that many are demoralized by the confusion and waste they confront in their work as a result of failed and failing policies.

Our instructions to the groups we enlist will be simple and direct. We will remind them that government programs exist at the sufferance of the American taxpayer and are paid for with money earned by working men and women. Any programs that represents a waste of their money—a theft from their pocketbooks—must have that waste eliminated or the program must go—by Executive Order where possible; by Congressional action where necessary. Everything that can be run more effectively by state and local government we shall turn over to state and local government, along with the funding sources to pay for it. We are going to put an end to the money merry-go-round where our money becomes Washington's money, to be spent by the states and cities only if they spend it exactly the way the federal bureaucrats tell them to.

I will not accept the excuse that the federal government has grown so big and powerful that it is beyond the control of any President, any Administration or Congress. We are going to put an end to the notion that the American taxpayer exists to fund the federal government. The federal government exists to *serve* the American people and to be accountable to the American people. On January 20th, we are going to re-establish that truth.

Also on that date we are going to initiate action to get substantial relief for our taxpaying citizens and action to put people back to work. None of this will be based on any new form of monetary tinkering or fiscal sleight-of-hand. We will simply apply to government the common sense we all use in our daily lives.

Work and family are at the center of our lives; the foundation of our dignity as a free people. When we deprive people of what they have earned, or take away their jobs, we destroy their dignity and undermine their families. We cannot support our families unless there are jobs; and we cannot have jobs unless people have both money to invest and the faith to invest it.

These are concepts that stem from the foundation of an economic system that for more than two hundred years has helped us master a continent, create a previously undreamed-of-prosperity for our people and has fed millions of others around the globe. That system will continue to serve us in the future if our government will stop ignoring the basic values on which it was built and stop betraying the trust and good will of the American workers who keep it going.

The American people are carrying the heaviest peacetime tax burden in our nation's history—and it will grow even heavier, under present law, next January. This burden is crushing our ability and incentive to save, invest and produce. We are taxing ourselves into economic exhaustion and stagnation.

This must stop. We *must* halt this fiscal self-destruction and restore sanity to our economic system.

I have long advocated a 30 percent reduction in income tax rates over a period of three years. This phased tax reduction would begin with a 10 percent "down payment" tax cut in 1981, which the Republicans in Congress and I have already proposed.

A phased reduction of tax rates would go a long way toward easing the heavy burden on the American people. But, we should not stop here.

Within the context of economic conditions and appropriate budget priorities during each fiscal year of my Presidency, I would strive to go further. This would include improvement in business depreciation taxes so we can stimulate investment in order to get plants and equipment replaced, put more Americans back to work and put our nation back on the road to being competitive in world commerce. We will also work to reduce the cost of government as a percentage of our Gross National Product.

The first task of national leadership is to set honest and realistic priorities in our policies and our budget and I pledge that my Administration will do that.

When I talk of tax cuts, I am reminded that every major tax cut in this century has strengthened the economy, generated renewed productivity and ended up yielding new revenues for the government by creating new investment, new jobs and more commerce among our people.

The present Administration has been forced by us Republicans to play follow-the-leader with regard to a tax cut. But, we must take with the proverbial "grain of salt" any tax cut proposed by those who have given us the greatest tax *increase* in our history.

When those in leadership give us tax increases and tell us we must also do with less, have they thought about those who have always had less—especially the minorities? This is like telling them that just as they step on the first rung of the ladder of opportunity, the ladder is being pulled up. That may be the Democratic leadership's message to the minorities, but it won't be ours. Our message will be: we have to move ahead, but we're not going to leave *anyone* behind.

Thanks to the economic policies of the Democratic party, millions of Americans find themselves out of work. Millions more have never even had a fair chance to learn new skills, hold a decent job, seize the opportunity to climb the ladder and secure for themselves and their families a share in the prosperity of this nation.

It is time to put America back to work; to make our cities and town resound with the confident voices of men and women of all races, nationalities and faiths bringing home to their families a decent paycheck they can cash for honest money.

For those without skills, we'll find a way to help them get skills.

For those without job opportunities we'll stimulate new opportunities, particularly in the inner cities where they live.

For those who have abandoned hope, we'll restore hope and we'll welcome them into a great national crusade to make America great again!

When we move from domestic affairs and cast our eyes abroad, we see an equally sorry chapter in the record of the present Administration.

• A Soviet combat brigade trains in Cuba, just 90 miles from our shores.

• A Soviet army of invasion occupies Afghanistan, further threatening our vital interests in the Middle East.

• America's defense strength is at its lowest ebb in a generation, while the Soviet Union is vastly outspending us in both strategic and conventional arms.

• Our European allies, looking nervously at the growing menace from the East, turn to us for leadership and fail to find it.

• And, incredibly, more than 50 of our fellow Americans have been held captive for over eight months by a dictatorial foreign power that holds us up to ridicule before the world.

Adversaries large and small test our will and seek to confound our resolve, but the Carter Administration gives us weakness when we need strength; vacillation when the times demand firmness.

Why? Because the Carter Administration lives in the world of make-believe. Every day, it dreams up a response to that day's troubles, regardless of what happened yesterday and what will happen tomorrow. The Administration lives in a world where mistakes, even very big ones, have no consequence.

The rest of us, however, live in the real world. It is here that disasters are overtaking our nation without any real response from the White House.

I condemn the Administration's make-believe; its self-deceit and—above all—its transparent hypocrisy.

For example, Mr. Carter says he supports the volunteer army, but he lets military pay and benefits slip so low that many of our enlisted personnel are actually eligible for food stamps. Re-enlistment rates drop and, just recently, after he fought all week *against* a proposal to increase the pay of our men and women in uniform, he helicoptered out to our carrier the *U.S.S. Nimitz,* which was returning from long months of duty. He told the crew that he advocated better pay for them and their comrades! Where does he really stand, now that he's back on shore?

I'll tell you where *I* stand. I do *not* favor a peacetime draft or registration, but I do favor pay and benefit levels that will attract and keep highly motivated men and women in our volunteer forces and an active reserve trained and ready for an instant call in case of an emergency.

An Annapolis graduate may be at the helm of the ship of state, but the ship has no rudder. Critical decisions are made at times almost in Marx Brothers fashion, but who can laugh? Who was not embarrassed when the Administration handed a major propaganda victory in the United Nations to the enemies of Israel, our staunch Middle East ally for three decades and then claimed that the American vote was a "mistake," the result of a "failure of communication" between the President, his Secretary of State and his U.N. Ambassador?

Who does not feel a growing sense of unease as our allies, facing repeated instances of an amateurish and confused Administration, reluctantly conclude that America is unwilling or unable to fulfill its obligations as leader of the free world?

Who does not feel rising alarm when the question in any discussion of foreign policy is no longer, "Should we do something?", but "Do we have the capacity to do *anything?*"

The Administration which has brought us to this state is seeking your endorsement for four more years of weakness, indecision, mediocrity and incompetence. No American should vote until he or she has asked, is the United States stronger and more respected now than it was three-and-a-half years ago? Is the world today a safer place in which to live?

It is the responsibility of the President of the United States, in working for peace, to insure that the safety of our people cannot successfully be threatened by a hostile foreign power. As President, fulfilling that responsibility will be my Number One priority.

We are not a warlike people. Quite the opposite. We always seek to live in peace. We resort to force infrequently and with great reluctance—and only after we have determined that it is absolutely necessary. We are awed—and rightly go—by the forces of destruction at loose in the world in this nuclear era. But neither can we be naive or foolish. Four times in my lifetime America has gone to war, bleeding the lives of its young men into the sands of beach-heads, the fields of Europe and the jungles and rice paddies of Asia. We know only too well that war comes not when the forces of freedom are strong, but when they are weak. It is then that tyrants are tempted.

We simply cannot learn these lessons the hard way again without risking our destruction.

Of all the objectives we seek, first and foremost is the establishment of lasting world peace. We must always stand ready to negotiate in good faith, ready to pursue any reasonable avenue that holds forth the promise of lessening tensions and furthering the prospects of peace. But let our friends and those who may wish us ill take note: the United States has an obligation to its citizens and to the people of the world never to let those who would destroy freedom dictate the future course of human life on this planet. I would regard my election as proof that we have renewed our resolve to preserve world peace and freedom. This nation will once again be strong enough to do that.

This evening marks the last step—save one—of a campaign that has taken Nancy and me from one end of this great land to the other, over many months and thousands and thousands of miles. There are those who question the way we choose a President; who say that our process imposes difficult and exhausting burdens on those who seek the office. I have not found it so.

It is impossible to capture in words the splendor of this vast continent which God has granted as our portion of his creation. There are no words to express the extraordinary strength and character of this breed of people we call Americans.

Everywhere we have met thousands of Democrats, Independents and Republicans from all economic conditions and walks of life bound together in that community of shared values of family, work, neighborhood, peace and freedom. They are concerned yes, but they are not frightened. They are disturbed, but not dismayed. They are the kind of men and women Tom Paine had in mind when he wrote—during the darkest days of the American Revolution—"We have it in our power to begin the world over again."

Nearly one-hundred-and-fifty years after Tom Paine wrote those words, an American President told the generation of the Great Depression that it had a "rendezvous with destiny." I believe *this* generation of Americans today also has a rendezvous with destiny.

Tonight, let us dedicate ourselves to renewing the American Compact. I ask you not simply to "Trust *me*," but to trust your values—our values—and to hold me responsible for living up to them. I ask you to trust that American spirit which knows no ethnic, religious, social, political, regional or economic boundaries; the spirit that burned with zeal in the hearts of millions of immigrants from every corner of the earth who came here in search of freedom.

Some say that spirit no longer exists. But I have seen it—I have felt it—all across the land; in the big cities, the small towns and in rural America. The American spirit is still there, ready to blaze into life if you and I are willing to do what has to be done; the practical, down-to-earth things that will stimulate our economy, increase productivity and put America back to work.

The time is *now* to limit federal spending; to insist on a stable monetary reform and to free ourselves from imported oil.

The time is *now* to resolve that the basis of a firm and principled foreign policy is one that takes the world as it is and seeks to change it by leadership and example; not be lecture and harangue.

The time is *now* to say that while we shall seek new friendships and expand and improve others, we shall not do so by breaking our word or casting aside old friends and allies.

And, the time is *now* to redeem promises once made to the American people by another candidate, in another time and another place. He said,

". . . For three long years I have been going up and down this country preaching that government—federal, state and local—costs too much. I shall not stop that preaching. As an immediate program of action, we must abolish useless offices. We must eliminate unnecessary functions of government. . . .

". . . we must consolidate subdivisions of government and, like the private citizen, give up luxuries which we can no longer afford.

"I propose to you, my friends, and through you that government of all kinds, big and little be made solvent and that the example be set by the President of the United States and his cabinet."

So said Franklin Delano Roosevelt in his acceptance speech to the Democratic National Convention in July, 1932.

The time is *now*, my fellow Americans, to recapture our destiny, to take it into our own hands. But, to do this will take many of us, working together. I ask you tonight to volunteer your help in this cause so we can carry our message throughout the land.

Yes, isn't *now* the time that we, the people, carried out these unkept promises? Let us pledge to each other and to all America on *this* July day 48 years later, we intend to do *just that*.

At the end, Reagan departed from his prepared text:

I have thought of something that is not a part of my speech and I'm worried over whether I should do it.

Can we doubt that only a divine providence placed this land, this island of freedom, here as a refuge for all those people in the world who yearns to breath freely: Jews and Christians enduring persecution behind the Iron Curtain, the boat people of Southeast Asia, of Cuba and of Haiti, the victims of drought and famine in Africa, the freedom fighters of Afghanistan and our own countrymen held in savage captivity.

I'll confess that I've been a little afraid to suggest what I'm going to suggest. I'm more afraid not to. Can we begin our crusade joined together in a moment of silent prayer?

God bless America.

APPENDIX II

Inaugural Address of President Ronald Reagan

January 20, 1981

To a few of us here today this is a solemn and most momentous occasion. And, yet, in the history of our nation it is a commonplace occurrence.

The orderly transfer of authority as called for in the Constitution takes place as it has for almost two centuries and few of us stop to think how unique we really are. In the eyes of many in the world, this every-four-year ceremony we accept as normal is nothing less than a miracle.

Mr. President, I want our fellow citizens to know how much you did to carry on this tradition. By your gracious cooperation in the transition process you have shown a watching world that we are a united people pledged to maintaining a political system which guarantees individual liberty to a greater degree than any other. And I thank you and your people for all your help in maintaining the continuity which is the bulwark of our republic.

The business of our nation goes forward. These United States are confronted with an economic affliction of great proportions. We suffer from the longest and one of the worst sustained inflations in our national history. It distorts our economic decisions, penalizes thrift and crushes the struggling young and the fixed-income elderly alike. It threatens to shatter the lives of millions of our people.

Idle industries have cast workers into unemployment causing human misery and personal indignity. Those who do work are denied a fair return for their labor by a tax system which penalizes successful achievement and keeps us from maintaining full productivity.

But great as our tax burden is, it has not kept pace with public spending. For decades we have piled deficit upon deficit, mortgaging our future and our children's future for the temporary convenience of the present. To continue this long trend is to guarantee tremendous social, cultural, political and economic upheavals.

You and I, as individuals, can, by borrowing, live beyond our means but for only a limited period of time. Why should we think that collectively, as a nation, we are not bound by that same limitation?

We must act today in order to preserve tomorrow. And let there be no misunderstanding—we are going to begin to act beginning today.

The economic ills we suffer have come upon us over several decades. They will not go away in days, weeks, or months, but they will go away. They will go away because we as Americans have the capacity now, as we have had in the past, to do whatever needs to be done to preserve this last and greatest bastion of freedom.

In this present crisis, government is not the solution to our problem; government is the problem.

From time to time we have been tempted to believe that society has become too complex to be managed by self-rule, that government by an elite group is superior to government for, by and of the people. But, if no one among us is capable of governing himself, then who among us has the capacity to govern someone else?

All of us together—in and out of government—must bear the burden. The solutions we seek must be equitable with no one group singled out to pay a higher price.

We hear much of special interest groups. Our concern must be for a special interest group that has been too long neglected. It knows no section boundaries, crosses ethnic and racial divisions and political party lines.

It is made up of men and women who raise our food, patrol our streets, man our mines and factories, teach our children, keep our homes and heal us when we're sick. They are professionals, industrialists, shopkeepers, clerks, cabbies and truck drivers. They are, in short, "We, the people." This breed called Americans.

Our objective must be a healthy, vigorous, growing economy that provides equal opportunities for all Americans with no barriers born of bigotry or discrimination. Putting America back to work means putting all Americans back to work.

Ending inflation means freeing all Americans from the terror of runaway living costs. All must share in the productive work of this "new beginning," and all must share in the bounty of a revived economy. With the idealism and fair play which are the core of our system and our strength, we can have a strong, prosperous America at peace with itself and the world.

As we begin, let us take inventory. We are a nation that has a government—not the other way around. And this makes us special among the nations of the earth. Our government has no power except that granted it by the people. It is time to check and reverse the growth of government which shows signs of having grown beyond the consent of the governed.

It is my intention to curb the size and influence of the federal establishment and to demand recognition of the distinction between the powers granted to the federal government, those reserved to the states or to the people. All of us need to be reminded the federal government did not create the states; the states created the federal government.

Now so there will be no misunderstanding, it is not my intention to do away with government. It is rather to make it work—work with us, not over us; to stand by our side, not ride on our back. Government can and must provide opportunity, not smother it; foster productivity, not stifle it.

If we look to the answer as to why for so many years we achieved so much, prospered as no other people on earth, it was because here in this land we unleashed the energy and individual genius of man to a greater extent than had ever been done before.

Freedom and the dignity of the individual have been more available and assured here than in any other place on earth. The price for this freedom has at times been high, but we have never been unwilling to pay that price.

It is no coincidence that our present troubles parallel and are proportionate to the intervention and intrusion in our lives that have resulted from unnecessary and excessive growth of government.

We are too great a nation to limit ourselves to small dreams. We are not, as some would have us believe, doomed to an inevitable decline. I do not believe in a fate that will fall on us no matter what we do. I do believe in a fate that will fall on us if we do nothing.

So, with all the creative energy at our command, let us begin an era of national renewal. Let us renew our determination, our courage, and our strength. And let us renew our faith and our hope. We have every right to dream heroic dreams.

Those who say we are in a time when there are no heroes—they just don't know where to look. You can see heroes every day going in and out of factory gates. Others, a handful in number, produce enough food to feed all of us and much of the world beyond.

You meet heroes across a counter—they're on both sides of that counter. They are entrepreneurs with faith in themselves and faith in an idea who create new jobs, new wealth and opportunity. They are individuals and families whose taxes support the government and whose voluntary gifts support church, charity, culture, art, and education. Their patriotism is quiet but deep. Their values sustain our national life.

I have used the words "they" and "their" in speaking of these horoes. I could say "you" and "your" because I am addressing the heroes of whom I speak—you, the citizens of this blessed land. Your dreams, your hopes, your goals are going to be the dreams, the hopes and goals of this administration, so help me God.

We shall reflect the compassion that is so much a part of your makeup. How can we love our country and not love our countrymen? And loving them reach out a hand when they fall, heal them when they are sick and provide opportunity to make them self-sufficient so they will be equal in fact and not just in theory?

Can we solve the problems confronting us? The answer is an unequivocal and emphatic yes. To paraphrase Winston Churchill, I did not take the oath I have just taken with the intention of presiding over the dissolution of the world's strongest economy.

In the days ahead I will propose removing the roadblocks that have slowed our economy and reduced productivity. Steps will be taken aimed at restoring the balance between the various levels of government.

Progress may be slow—measured in inches and feet, not miles—but we will progress. It is time to reawaken this industrial giant, to get government back within its means, and to lighten our punitive tax burden. And these will be our first priorities, and on these principles, there will be no compromise.

On the eve of our struggle for independence a man who might have been the greatest among the Founding Fathers, Dr. Joseph Warren, president of the Massachusetts Congress, said to his fellow Americans, "Our country is in danger, but not to be despaired of. . . . On you depend the fortunes of America. You are to decide the important question upon which rest the happiness and liberty of millions yet unborn. Act worthy of yourselves."

I believe we the Americans of today are ready to act worthy of ourselves, ready to do what must be done to ensure happiness and liberty for ourselves, our children, and our children's children.

And as we renew ourselves here in our own land, we will be seen as having greater strength throughout the world. We will again be the exemplar of freedom and a beacon of hope for those who do not now have freedom.

To those neighbors and allies who share our freedom, we will strengthen our historic ties and assure them of our support and firm commitment. We will match loyalty with loyalty. We will strive for mutually beneficial relations. We will not use our friendship to impose on their sovereignty, for our own sovereignty is not for sale.

As for the enemies of freedom, to those who are potential adversaries, they will be reminded that peace is the highest aspiration of the American people. We will negotiate for it, sacrifice for it; we will not surrender for it—now or ever.

Our forbearance should never be misunderstood. Our reluctance for conflict should not be misjudged as a failure of will. When action is required to preserve our national security, we will act. We will maintain sufficient strength to prevail if need be, knowing that if we do so we have the best chance of never having to use that strength.

Above all we must realize no arsenal or no weapon in the arsenals of the world is so formidable as the will and moral courage of free men and women. It is a weapon our adversaries in today's world do not have. It is a weapon that we as Americans do have. Let that be understood by those who practice terrorism and prey upon their neighbors.

I am told that tens of thousands of prayer meetings are being held on this day, and for that I am deeply grateful. We are a nation under God, and I believe God intended for us to be free. It would be fitting and good, I think, if each Inaugural Day in the future should be declared a day of prayer.

This is the first time in our history that this ceremony has been held on the West Front of the Capitol building. Standing here, we face a magnificent vista, opening up on this city's special beauty and history. At the end of this open mall are those shrines to the giants on whose shoulders we stand.

Directly in front of me, the monument to a monumental man. George Washington, father of our country. A man of humility who came to greatness reluctantly. He led America out of revolutionary victory into infant nationhood.

Off to one side, the stately memorial to Thomas Jefferson. The Declaration of Independence flames with his eloquence.

And then beyond the Reflecting Pool, the dignified columns of the Lincoln Memorial. Whoever would understand in his heart the meaning of America will find it in the life of Abraham Lincoln.

Beyond these monuments to heroism is the Potomac River, and on the far shore the sloping hills of Arlington National Cemetery with its row upon row of simple white markers with crosses or Stars of David. They add up to only a tiny fraction of the price that has been paid for our freedom.

Each one of those markers is a monument to the kind of hero I spoke of earlier. Their lives ended in places called Belleau Wood, The Argonne, Omaha Beach, Salerno and halfway round the world on Guadalcanal, Tarawa, Pork Chop Hill, the Chosin Reservoir, and in a hundred rice paddies and jungles of a place called Vietnam.

Under one such marker lies a young man—Martin Treptow—who left his job in a smalltown barber shop in 1917 to go to France with the famed Rainbow Division. There, on the Western Front, he was killed trying to carry a message between battalions under heavy artillery fire.

We are told that on his body was found a diary. On the flyleaf under the heading, "My Pledge," he had written these words: "America must win this war. Therefore I will work, I will save, I will sacrifice, I will endure, I will fight cheerfully and do my utmost, as if the issue of the whole struggle depended on me alone."

The crisis we are facing today does not require the kind of sacrifice that Martin Treptow and so many thousands of others were called upon to make. It does, however, require our best effort, and our willingness to believe in ourselves and in our capacity to perform great deeds. To believe that, together and with God's help, we can and will resolve the problems which confront us.

And, after all, why shouldn't we believe that? We are Americans.

God bless you and thank you.

INDEX